British Labour Seeks a Foreign Policy,

1900-1940

British Labour Seeks a Foreign Policy, 1900-1940

1900-1940

Henry R. Winkler

Transaction Publishers
New Brunswick (U.S.A.) and London (U.K.)

Library of Congress Catalog Number: 2004058858
ISBN: 0-7658-0264-3
Printed in the United States of America

Library of Congress Cataloging-in-Publication Data

Winkler, Henry R. (Henry Ralph), 1916-
    British labour seeks a foreign policy, 1900-1940 / Henry R. Winkler.
        p. cm.
    Includes bibliographical references and index.
    ISBN 0-7658-0264-3 (alk. paper)
    1. Labour Party (Great Britain)—Platforms—History. 2. Great Britain—
Foreign relations—1901-1936. 3. Great Britain—Foreign relations—1936-
1945. 4. Great Britain—Politics and government—1901-1936. 5. Great
Britain—Politics and government—1936-1945. I. Title.

JN1129.L32W565   2004
327.41'009'041—dc22   2004058858

Once again, for Bea

.

Contents

Acknowledgements

As always, I owe a large debt of gratitude to the librarians and archivists of the repositories noted in the bibliography of this essay. In particular, I have been helped generously by my friends and colleagues, Sally Moffitt, Associate Librarian of the Langsam Library of the University of Cincinnati and Stephen Bird, Archivist of the Labour Party Archives, now housed in Manchester. My son, Allan M. Winkler, Distinguished Professor of American History at Miami Univertsity of Ohio, and my daughter, Karen J. Moulton, long-time staff member of the *Chronicle of Higher Education,* have consistently been my severest and thus my most useful critics. They went over the manuscript word for word, not only helping my avoid the inevitable verbal infelicities that inevitably seem to creep into a work in progress, but more importantly to sharpen my argument and give it the clarity I hope to have achieved. My wife Beatrice—Bea to everyone—worked along with me every step of the way. It is her book as much as it is mine.

Introduction

In the past half century, the British Labour Party has played a significant role in dealing with the complex issues of a troubled world. As one of the two major parties in the British system of government, Labour was central to the organization of the recovery of Europe after World War II. It shared leadership with the United States in shoring up the defenses of the Western world and in creating the North Atlantic Treaty Organization (NATO) to protect it during a difficult Cold War. Throughout this period, Labour governments acted responsibly and in accord with the views of a substantial majority of the British people. It was not always so.

The adoption of such a mainstream position marked just how far the Labour Party had moved from the attitudes and assumptions of the labour movement that gave it rise in the early twentieth century. Organized primarily to pursue a domestic political agenda, it focused first on industrial issues—wages, hours of work, safety in the workplace, and conditions of work in general. For the most part, its founders had little interest in foreign policy. Yet, over the years, gradually and haltingly, Labour came to confront the world as it existed and eventually to take its place as one of the shaping forces in modern international life.

Various aspects of Labour's approach to foreign policy have been well studied over the years. We have a series of exceptionally perceptive biographies, although there has, perhaps, been a tendency to emphasize dramatic figures like Ramsay MacDonald while not giving full consideration to other, less prominent, contributors to the foreign policy debate. We also have a number of investigations of particular parts of the story, ranging from studies of foreign policy positions during the First World War or in the 1920s and 1930s to evaluations of the first and second minority Labour governments. In addition, there are several useful accounts dealing with foreign policy issues. These, however, are either substantially theoretical in their thrust or offer little more than a compendium of Labour Party and Trades Union Congress resolutions, with little attention to the internal arguments that were at the heart of policy formation. There is still a need to explore how Labour's foreign policy, so important in the world today, gradually emerged.[1]

Labour's foreign policy in these formative years has been given relatively little attention primarily because the party had almost no experience in office during the period. When it did form a government, in 1924 and in the period from 1929 to 1931, it was a minority government and was in office only long enough to make a modest contribution in international affairs.[2] Day-to-day domestic concerns, dealing with bread-and-butter issues important to working people, were inevitably more important to party leaders—and to subsequent scholars as well. During the Second World War and after, however, Labour's leaders served first as key members of the coalition prosecuting the war and then as a government with a huge majority responsible for the conduct of British foreign policy in the immediate aftermath of the conflict. Not surprisingly, therefore, far more attention has been paid to the Labour Party's international policy in the postwar period, than to the formative years in which many of the principles of that policy were gradually fashioned.

The key to understanding the development of Labour's approach to international affairs in the first half of the twentieth century is to observe that it was characterized by a struggle between principles and practice, an attempt to relate socialist theory to the changing realities of the international scene.[3] The controversy over policy that took place within the party was complex, including, at different times and in different places, arguments against capitalism and imperialism, commitments to religious and secular pacifism, and efforts to promote broad-based rather than limited international organization—all within the context of changing relations with Europe, the United States, and then the Soviet Union.

Until the First World War, Labour demanded the rejection of "militarism" in the hands of capitalist and imperialist governments and argued that war itself could only be avoided by the cooperation of the working classes, that is, by socialist governments in much of the advanced world. Only a few working-class leaders gave much attention to foreign affairs beyond the reiteration of slogans and formulas that had little chance of being translated into reality.

Despite this rhetoric, the war itself came as a surprise to Labour. Far from acting as a unifying force, the conflict revealed the fissures that were to continue, in varying degrees, for years to come. Although pacifists and conscientious objectors, critics of prewar diplomacy, and advocates of a negotiated settlement with the enemy formed only a small minority within the labour movement when compared to those who supported the war more or less unquestioningly, the group of dissidents grew more substantial as the years of war dragged on. Despite the tensions, however, the war also fostered consideration of the kind of world Labour looked forward to at the end of the conflict. Although a number of important Liberals were prominent in developing plans for an international organization, the various Labour contributions to the idea of a League of Nations became by far the most far-reaching.

After the war, the path to a realistic foreign policy was not smooth. Hopes for a genuinely different international order, based on the surrender of some sovereignty to an international body, were dashed by the various bargains and settlements reached at the Paris Peace Conference. Virtual total disillusionment led many in the labour movement to reject the League entirely as a capitalist tool and to revert to the negativism of prewar days. Only gradually did a small group of less doctrinaire leaders persuade the rank-and-file to confront the world as it existed, using the League itself as a vehicle for making the desired changes. The move towards realism accelerated as the Labour Party took office for the first time in 1924, when its relative success in foreign affairs under the leadership of Ramsay MacDonald helped turn the party further away from emphasis on sterile criticism.

Meanwhile, a group of increasingly important leaders concentrated on what they called a League of Nations policy. They argued, for example, that collaboration with other nations in the development of instruments to substitute discussion and various forms of "arbitration" for armed conflict could be a prelude to the use of the international body for more constructive measures, such as international economic cooperation. But their view that the operation of the League system, in the final analysis, required the backing of force was anathema to substantial numbers of the labour movement, whether in its political or industrial sectors.

When Labour once again took office in 1929, it attempted, under Foreign Secretary Arthur Henderson, to implement a League of Nations policy, which briefly appeared promising, but quickly faltered in the face of the Great Depression and the emergence of challenges to the whole international order by the Nazi dictatorship in Germany, the Fascist regime in Italy, and the militarists of Japan in the Far East. The result was confusion and conflict within the Labour Party in the early 1930s, as it tried to relate its notions of a cooperative community to repeated assaults on the international status quo. As the international scene became darker, a number of League of Nations advocates concluded that the threat, from the German Nazis above all, was so great that British rearmament—long opposed by Labour—was necessary. Despite their suspicion of a National government accused of surrendering to the threat of force, if not of collusion itself with the dictators, these leaders held that a radical change in Labour policy was essential. By 1937, they had their way. As a result, the Labour Party was prepared to serve under Winston Churchill when his great wartime coalition was formed, and finally to mount a postwar foreign policy that had substantial support from most of the people of Britain. Not all the initiatives Labour subsequently pursued were necessarily wise, as the Cold War threw a pall over international relations. But the Labour Party had clearly come to assume the role, which it has retained to this day, of the normal alternative to the Tories in the conduct of the foreign policy of the British people.

1

Background

The Labour Party, in its earliest days, was not primarily concerned with foreign affairs. Formed in 1900 by 129 delegates who gathered in London's Memorial Hall, the Labour Representation Committee was essentially a party whose main purpose was to serve the domestic needs of working-class people. The weight of the trade unions ensured that external relations would take a secondary place to the bread-and-butter concerns that the unions were organized to address. International affairs never had a high priority in the years before the outbreak of the Great War. Just as important, the fact that Labour was an infant minority party meant that it was not in a position to have a significant impact on setting the foreign policy direction of a major power. As a result, most of its views on foreign policy were reactive, limited to criticizing the actions of Conservative and Liberal governments rather than tackling the more difficult task of working out a viable and constructive set of initiatives to be adopted.[1]

Despite that limitation, the traditional picture of a labour movement that neglected foreign affairs needs to be modified. Even in these early years, a few party leaders—Philip Snowden, Bruce Glasier, F. W. Jowett, and, above all, Keir Hardie and Ramsay MacDonald—each thought seriously about international issues and tried to instruct the labour movement about their importance.[2]

Long before his death in 1915, Hardie had become as legend in Labour circles. Seen on the left as an incorruptible idealist and the model of uncompromising socialism, he was often hailed as the antithesis to his less ideological successors as leaders of Labour. By Conservatives, he was damned as an impractical doctrinaire, attacking the royal family, demeaning Parliament by his flamboyant appearances, cultivating the legend of "the man in the cloth cap." In fact, he was a pragmatic and sometimes self- contradicting politician, far from being the advocate of a narrow and inflexible sect.[3] Deeply influenced by late nineteenth-century radicalism, he was, on balance, a supporter of a broad labour alliance of socialists and trade unionists.[4]

Hardie was clearly an internationalist, although his internationalism focused mainly on the collaboration of the working classes rather than on the international relations of the various sovereign states. From the beginning of his Parliamentary career, Hardie directed a barrage of criticism at the government's handling of external affairs. As a spokesman for the Independent Labour Party, he saw the Boer War as a foul crime through which the government seemed to operate simply to carry out the will of the mine owners of the Transvaal. Socialists, he declared, must be sympathetic to the Boers, who had a republican form of government and produced "for use" rather than "exploitation for profit." This caricature of Boer society was contrasted to the "cosmopolitan" interests castigated in the ILP's *Labour Leader* and *I.L.P. News,* often in anti-semitic terms. In Parliament Hardie expressed his outrage at the herding of Boer women and children into concentration camps and similar methods, a policy, he declared, of which no civilized nation should be guilty [5]

Like Hardie, Ramsay MacDonald opposed the South African War. Even as a young man, MacDonald never seemed comfortable with the working men and women whom he represented. As the years went by, his loneliness increased, perhaps accentuated by the early death of his wife in 1911. He had few friends among his Labour colleagues, preferring the acquaintance as he grew older of London society. His impatience with criticism and frequent self-pity alienated many of his colleagues, even when they regarded him as an indispensable leader. Unlike Hardie, he was seldom loved. Yet his courage was indisputable. When the Fabian Society Executive Committee refused by a narrow margin to condemn the Boer conflict, MacDonald resigned from the Society. He was not opposed to empire, but rather saw himself as a "constructive imperialist," advocating a program of trusteeship and the exercise of a moral responsibility towards colonized people. While not accepting George Bernard Shaw's unveiled contempt for "stray little states lying about in the way of great powers," MacDonald was perhaps closer to the views of the Radicals in the Liberal Party who were among the most extreme pro-Boers.[6] The Fabians who opposed denouncing the war feared splitting the Society by taking a position on a "non-socialist" matter of policy.

Robert Blatchford, too, denied that the war had any connection with socialism. Blatchford was the colorful editor of *Clarion*, which attracted a significant number of working-class readers by its astute mixture of politics with the sponsorship of country outings and bicycle excursions. An old soldier, he had opposed imperial expansion before the war, but rallied to the support of Britain as his socialism became increasingly more patriotic and national. Still, by the end of 1901, Blatchford, like many of those on the left who had supported the war, had become heartily sick of it and concentrated on exploring, with a variety of correspondents, possible terms of a settlement. For his own part, he suggested that the nation was ready to consider any peace proposals of a "clear, definite, and reasonable character."[7]

The newly formed Labour Representation Committee gave little attention to the issues of the South African War. The comment is perhaps correct that it was lucky the LRC was so new it did not have to agree on a policy, since the currents of disagreement within the labour movement might have been strong enough otherwise to threaten the fragile federation recently created.[8] The very weakness of the new organization tended to ensure that for its first decade or so potential differences on matters of external relations did not have a prominent place in party deliberations. Instead, almost to the eve of the First World War, the chief parochial opposition to Labour's stance came from the two figures who were increasingly on the margins of the new initiative. Blatchford and, to a lesser extent, H.N. Hyndman, the embattled leader of the Marxist Social Democratic Federation, combined their opposition to the emerging Labour Party with an anti-German and pro-"preparedness" propaganda, the rejection of which formed a substantial element in mainstream labour attitudes. Those attitudes, in turn, were largely shaped by the Independent Labour Party (ILP), which, until the Labour Party's adoption of a new constitution in 1918, was the base upon which socialist leaders like Hardie and MacDonald rested their influence.

When the LRC met in conference at Manchester on February 1,1901, it did adopt unanimously, but significantly without discussion, a resolution that attributed the South African war mainly to the corrupt agitation of the Transvaal mine owners who sought the acquisition of monopolies and a cheap supply of colored and European labor. Going on to protest against the destruction of the two Boer republics as contrary to the ideals of national political justice, it called upon the government to submit all matters in dispute between Britain and the two South African states to arbitration under the provisions of the Hague Convention. There was subsequently no exploration of ways to follow up the resolution.[9]

The conflicting reactions to the war in South Africa, both from pragmatic and ideological positions, did not deter the ILP, clearly the major Labour voice on the conflict, from taking its stand. Resolutions at the annual ILP conferences in 1900, 1901, and 1902 repeated what was to become a recurring mantra—opposition to imperialism, militarism, and conscription. Other resolutions condemned "atrocities" and "barbarities" and in 1902 the conference rejected by a large majority a motion to get on with socialist propaganda without "worrying about the war." Still, it has been argued that such evidence as the decline in the circulation of Keir Hardie's *Labour Leader* or the support for the jingoism of J. Havelock Wilson of the Seamen's Union suggests that working-class attitudes were less positively pro-Boer and antiwar than were those of the delegates to the conferences. On the other hand, there is some evidence of a considerable working-class dissent to the war. To be sure, disapproval of Britain's position was somewhat inchoate. But the absence of a charismatic, dominant figure in the various stop-the-war and conciliation committees ensured that there was no one who could have become the leader of a mass opposition. More important, programs proposed by middle-class Radicals, which stressed issues of morality rather than the consequences of imperialism for social reform, left many working-class people simply indifferent to the arguments of religious and other groups organized to oppose the war.[10]

In the years that followed the end of the Boer War, most of the discussion of international affairs continued to come at the initiative of the ILP. The *Labour Leader,* which was edited by Keir Hardie until 1904 and then by Bruce Glasier, carried an occasional article that anticipated positions that later became important. Even such positions—Fred Jowett's assessment of the perils of secrecy in foreign policy or Bruce Glasier's welcome to the idea of a United States of Europe—rested heavily on arguments that had been more fully aired by some of the Radicals in the Liberal Party over a number of years. [11]

At the annual conferences of the Labour Party, as the Labour Representation Committee had become in 1906, ILP members took the lead in offering international resolutions of a general character which were usually carried without discussion. Their flavor may be sampled in the resolution of 1907: "Recognising militarism to be a thing inherently evil in itself, an enemy of progress, and a potent means of maintaining ancient feuds and thereby keeping the workers of the world divided, this Conference protests against the manifold efforts now being made to popularise it by proposals for citizen armies, and to poison the minds of youth by means of School Rifle Clubs, Boys' Church Brigades, and the like, and declares in favour of arbitration being substituted for war as a preliminary to universal disarmament."[12]

These general statements, which invariably avoided the sanctions that the Labour Party intended to employ if the resolution should not be heeded, were augmented by participation in the broader collaboration of the heterogeneous group of societies that made up the peace movement.[13] When the Universal Peace Congress, a gatherings of those societies, was held in London in July, 1908, it was honored at Windsor by Edward VII, commended by the prime minister, and addressed by Lloyd George, while the ILP and the Trades Union Congress held a rally against war in Trafalgar Square at which Ramsay MacDonald spoke.[14] And when the National Peace Congress met in London in May of 1912, and adopted such usual resolutions as those on Anglo-German relations, military aviation, and nationalities and subject races, the Labour Party, the ILP and the Fabian Society were among the representatives present.[15] Such participation, however, often appeared to be routine and pro forma. Commenting on the 1908 international conference, for example, Ramsay MacDonald noted that eminent people had attended but that the conference was grossly mismanaged. While it was sitting, he remarked, the Executive of the Labour Party had passed one simple resolution regarding Anglo-German relations, which "one felt" did more for peace than all the deliberations of the

International Congress. He further insisted that when Labour members to the Congress proposed a mission of fraternity to Germany, the public, both in England and in Germany, sensed the authority that was behind the action. "International peace," he declared, "is in the hands of International Socialism."[16]

Aside from such resolutions and demonstrations, most Labour discussion was reactive. After the election of 1906, which brought the Liberals back into office and saw the seating of some twenty-nine Labour M.P.s, the foreign secretary, Sir Edward Grey, became the target of Labour criticism, both in the House of Commons and in the Labour press. To be sure, from time to time Labour even found reason to agree with Grey. When in 1908 he protested the Austrian coup in Bosnia-Herzegovina, Labour's leaders expressed satisfaction with his action, as they did a year later when it appeared evident that France and Germany had reached accord over their differences in Morocco, where conflict over economic access hardly concealed the power struggle between the two countries. Nevertheless, even in the case of Bosnia-Herzegovina, the *Labour Leader*, for example, found it preferable to condemn the "nefarious complicity" of Russia and Germany and the hypocrisy of the Concert of Europe. Perhaps more to the point, there was more concern about unemployment at home than about a quarrel in an obscure corner of the Balkans.[17]

Germany and Russia increasingly became the focus of Labour's assessment of the Liberal government's foreign policy. Growing tension between Britain and Imperial Germany, marked by the beginning of a naval building competition and by mutual recriminations in the press of the two countries, aroused the concern of both the Labour Party and the ILP, while the rapprochement with Tsarist Russia elicited widespread and fervent criticism. In the case of Germany, Robert Blatchford played the role of the devil's advocate. Alienated from the mainstream of Labour after his unsuccessful resistance to the formation of the Labour Representation Committee, he still maintained a substantial following through the pages of *Clarion*, which was livelier and indeed more frequently interesting than its rival *Labour Leader*. Early in the century he had raised the question whether England could be invaded, concluding that the Germans not only thought so, but said so, and were openly and steadily preparing to make the attempt.[18] From about 1908 he stepped up his campaign to alert his readers to the danger of German militarism and the threat it posed for Britain. In addition, he opened the pages of *Clarion* to H.N. Hyndman, who like Blatchford was bitterly opposed to the Labour Party and obsessed by a coming German war. "There is not the slightest doubt," Hyndman wrote on July 31, 1908, "that Germany, under the leadership of Prussia, is steadily making ready at heavy cost, which the German Empire at present can ill afford, for a crucial naval engagement in the North Sea, followed by an invasion of this country." The danger, he argued, was far greater than any faced in the time of Napoleon. As for the notion that the German people had no quarrel with the people of Britain, he commented that the German people quite clearly had no control over their government. Prussia in foreign affairs dominated Germany and Prussia was, and always had been, a predatory power.[19]

But it was Blatchford in the *Clarion* who most forcefully made the case that was vehemently challenged by both the Labour Party and the ILP. Charged with being led astray by alarmist articles in the British and German press, Blatchford insisted that it was acts, not mere words that had convinced him and those who agreed with him about the German danger. Germany had increased, and was increasing, her fleet. She had made, and was still making, the fullest preparations for the embarkation of an army. And against whom were these preparations directed? Germany was certainly not going to invade France by sea, nor was she going to attack Russia in that manner. All the evidence went to prove that Germany was preparing to make war upon Britain. "If Keir Hardie, Philip Snowden, or J. Ramsay MacDonald can dispute this assertion," Blatchford challenged, "let them speak. I for one shall be delighted to find that I have been mistaken."[20]

Much of Hyndman's and Blatchford's posture in 1908 reflected the fears of the war scare of that year. When it had died down, Ramsay MacDonald, whose monthly "Socialist Outlook" in the *Socialist Review* more or less reflected, at this time, the outlook of the leadership of both the ILP and the Labour Party, censured those socialists who fed the flames by accepting silly canards that were soon debunked. "So long as people believe in the stupid aphorism that the way to keep peace is to prepare for war," he maintained, "not only will those scares occur, but they will every now and again lead to actual conflict." [21] In another article he criticized not only Sir Edward Grey, but the British people themselves. "Perhaps no people in Europe give less intelligent thought to foreign policy than ourselves," he argued. Without even suspecting it, they had given Germany good reason for believing that Britain was determined to isolate her in Europe and reduce her influence to the vanishing point. And the foreign secretary, who had the opportunity to end the period of national jealousy and fear expressed in alliances, instead had only succeeded in shifting the balance of power and making Germany an enemy.[22]

When Blatchford's contrary view of the German threat appeared in a series of articles commissioned by the conservative *Daily Mail,* its tone was so extreme it disturbed the Liberal government and even concerned the king.[23] The Labour Party and the ILP continued to dissociate themselves from his position. The *Labour Leader*, where Bruce Glasier had already branded Blatchford's *Clarion* articles a "humiliating incident" which had disfigured the history of the labour movement, now denounced him for digging up the bogey of a German menace with the aid of a vivid imagination, a lucid literary style, and a soldier's ignorance of the facts. The timing of the *Daily Mail* articles meant that they would be used by every Tory paper against every Labour candidate in the general election already scheduled for early 1910.[24]

Concern for deteriorating relations with Germany was accompanied by sharp disapproval of the government's Russian policy. The 1905 revolution, which was viewed as having been precipitated as much by Russian tyranny and internal weakness as by defeat in the Russo-Japanese War, had been greeted with satisfaction and its failure with disappointment. Perhaps because they felt unable to prevent the forging of the British entente with the tsarist regime, no members of the Parliamentary Labour Party took part in the debate on the impending treaty with Russia.[25] Subsequently, however, Labour took the lead in denouncing the new relationship. In the summer of 1908, for example, the *Socialist Review* carried a trio of articles under the rubric "The King and the Tsar" shortly after it was announced that Edward VII would visit Nicholas II at Reval. Two of the three authors, Sir Charles Dilke and and H. W. Nevinson, were Liberals and H. N. Brailsford had only recently joined the ILP. Brailsford's affiliation was later replicated, during and immediately after the Great War, by a number of gifted Liberals who placed their own unmistakable stamp on the shaping of Labour's interwar foreign policy.

In his *Socialist Review* article, Nevinson expressed shock that the British king would honor a man whose name would go down in execration side by side with that of the "Red Sultan" of Turkey. Dilke and Brailsford, for their part, emphasized the danger that the Russian connection would be seen, dangerously, as a policy of isolating Germany. "The whole scheme," wrote the latter, "is an attempt to conclude, if not a Triple Alliance, at least a Triple *Entente*"—of course against Germany. Beyond that, Brailsford warned, the British *entente* would not differ in its effect from the earlier Russo-French alliance. "Tsarism has corrupted Paris," he declared. "Republicanism has not permeated the Russian Court."[26]

In Parliament, when Labour moved a reduction in the Foreign Office budget, Keir Hardie protested that for the king to pay an official visit to the tsar was to condone the atrocities for which the tsar's government, and the tsar personally, must be held responsible. Called to order for using the word "atrocities," Hardie finally withdrew the word, but commented that, despite the attempt to minimize conditions in Russia and to make it appear that the tsar and his advisers were not to be held responsible, he could prove that not only had they connived at what was done in Russia, but approved the official hangings and shootings that so troubled his party.[27]

To Grey his Labour critics were "extreme and violent men" and he easily survived the vote on supply. When the tsar proposed to visit Britain in 1909, defenders of the government tended to accept the legal fiction that he was a constitutional monarch and that to receive him would be to help the cause of liberalization in Russia. Labour rejected such an assessment. To the contrary, MacDonald wrote in *Socialist Review* of "judicial murders, blacker reaction, and more blackguardly methods of administration," while he insisted that the desire, in Russian governing circles, to abolish the fledgling Duma was becoming more evident. The revolution, for the time being, had been suppressed. Beyond all this there was a further issue. The most pressing problem of British policy was to establish friendly relations with Germany and to throw the weight of the British Empire behind liberal movements abroad. Instead, Sir Edward Grey had supported moves by Russia which were regarded as hostile by Germany and had sanctioned Russian intervention in Persia. Altogether, Grey's foreign policy disclosed "little but miscalculation, an indefiniteness of purpose, an incapacity to work intelligently for a given end, an amiable statement of general principles and intentions on the one hand and a failure to fulfil the expectations which these statements arouse."[28]

The fact that Labour, either in the House of Commons or the columns of its newspapers, proposed no new initiatives to solve the ills of the international situation or offered no "revolutionary panacea" needs to be considered in the context of the times.[29] A new party, still relatively weak in its political instruments, concentrating on judicial and other moves that threatened the future of its industrial associates, understandably devoted little time to working out a fully developed posture on foreign policy matters that might rest, in some persuasive fashion, upon the "socialist" view of the world that increasingly was the framework of the labour movement's rhetoric. In many cases, Labour representatives tended to parallel—if not to follow the lead of—the Radicals in Parliament and outside who were the most prominent critics of the policies of their own Liberal government.

A major theme during these years—and later as well—centered upon what Labour regarded as the government's excessive expenditure on armaments. Echoing the apprehensions of some of the leading Radicals, in 1910, for example, the ILP took the lead in organizing several hundred meetings throughout the country against the burden of the armament buildup. Labour spokesmen deplored the growth of militarism and charged the government with reckless disregard for the consequences of their actions. W. C. Anderson, chairman of the ILP, used the pages of the *Labour Leader* to promote "Labour's War against War," arguing that it was widely felt that an armed peace, as at present, with its panics and scares and crushing taxation, was a curse only second to that of war. Every increase in armaments, every advance in militarism, disturbed and embittered international relationships and paved the way for conscription. Similarly, Ramsay MacDonald used his column in the *Socialist Review* to insist that the army and navy estimates demonstrated the increasing firmness of the grip that militarism was gaining in the nation. The navy estimates in particular were "enough to make any sensible man gasp with amazement."[30]

In the House of Commons, Hardie argued that no member would disagree with the statement that, in proportion to its taxable capacity, the country was spending more upon its army and navy than was warranted. What was a large army for, he asked? "Is it to enable this country to depart from its island security and to become embroiled in Continental affairs?" Or "to enable us to take part in Continental wars, interfering in affairs with which we have no concern?" If so, he averred, it marked a complete change from the well-established policy of the country. As for the threat of the German navy, Hardie insisted that Germany was building its navy to protect its merchant fleet as it more and more encroached upon the trade that had hitherto been a British monopoly. The answer was not to build up big navies and armies, but to improve economic efficiency with a low tax, low armament system. Citing the conclusions of Norman Angell's recent book, *The Great Illusion,* that wars did not pay, Hardie contended that the notion that trade followed the flag had been discredited. Even Blatchford gave room in the *Clarion* for the argument that the government's proposed navy estimates in 1910 were a further step in what Campbell-Bannerman, the late prime minister, had called the rebarbarization of Europe, a gratuitous and wilful action by Britain which in Germany could only be translated as a threat that "we shall maintain the tyrannical power of sweeping off the seas any ship that does not bear the British flag."[31] In subsequent sessions of Parliament, Hardie was joined by Ramsay MacDonald in continuing the attack on the naval estimates, although it is interesting to note that the demand for greater information concerning foreign affairs, upon which budgetary decisions should rest, came mostly from members of the Liberal Party, both Radicals unhappy about policy, like Noel Buxton, and firmer supporters of Grey's policy, such as J. Swift MacNeill.[32]

Despite the efforts of Hardie and MacDonald, it is a telling fact that about half the Labour members of Parliament continued to be, at best, indifferent to the campaign against militarism. Indeed, Philip Snowden protested, in the pages of the *Labour Leader*, that there was nothing in the record of the Labour Party more regrettable than the fact that some of its members had always voted for every increase in the army and navy expenditures. It was no sufficient excuse, he declared, that these members represented dockyard and arsenal towns. "Socialist principles must not be abandoned in order to keep seats."[33]

No doubt some of what Snowden deplored reflected the absorption of Labour politicians in their posture towards the social reform initiatives of the Liberal government after 1906, to say nothing of the growing storm over the power of the House of Lords and its relation to the authority of the House of Commons. Throughout this period, opposition to the possibility of conscription, on the European model, in Great Britain formed another element in both Labour Party and ILP suspicions of the trend in foreign policy. While Blatchford, Hyndman, and a handful of others argued the necessity of drafting men into service, the Labour parties as well as the Trades Union Congress consistently voiced their refusal to accept conscription as a viable system of military recruitment. Shortly before the advent of the crisis of July, 1914, the ILP undertook a "no conscription" campaign, mounting a series of meetings to describe the corrupting effect of compulsion upon those called into service in other European countries and paralleling aversion to such an innovation with resistance to militarism and excessive armaments.[34]

Meanwhile, by early 1911, the question of whether the working class could go beyond toothless criticism of armaments, militarism, and a hypothetical conscription was raised at a special conference on disarmament and the international situation organized by the Executive of the Labour Party. The conference was held in Ramsay MacDonald's constituency of Leicester. MacDonald's introductory remarks as chairman were fairly colorless and he offered little in the way of concrete suggestions for action. The Executive's resolution, presented by J. R. Clynes, was so typical that it merits quotation in full:

> That this Conference, believing that Militarism and War are subversive of civilisation and national well-being, protests strongly against the heavy and growing burden of Armaments, which arrests social reform and endangers international solidarity, goodwill, and peace. It further affirms that Militarism, whilst profitable to certain financial interests, to the activities of which not a little of our scaremongering can be traced, imposes a needless tax on the lives and the wages of the workers, and threatens to inflict on Great Britain the evils of compulsory military service. The Conference, therefore, declares that disputes between nations should be settled, not by brute force, but by reason and arbitration, and urges the workers of this country to take organised action with their fellows in Germany and other lands in counteracting the influence of scares and in bringing about an understanding between all nations to secure international peace and to advance social justice.

After the resolution had been seconded and discussed and a "right to work" amendment defeated, Keir Hardie offered another amendment about which the rest of the conference proceedings centered. The amendment first proposed that a series of four propositions endorsed at a recent meeting of the International Labour and Socialist Congress, including the requirement that all treaties be subject to Parliamentary ratification before being signed, be adopted. To these customary demands Hardie added the request that the International Bureau of the Labour and Socialist International "take the opinion" of the organized working-class movement of the world on the utility of a general strike as a means of preventing war. To illustrate, he explained that the intention of the clause was that if war was going to come between Germany and Britain, or was threatened, an international congress would be held between the workers of the two countries and of France and they would pledge that the day war was declared they would stop producing until the war came to an end. Hardie pointed out that at the last Labour Party conference a resolution was passed instructing the Executive to take steps to form an international committee to bring about united action on the part of the workers of the world to stop war. What he was asking was that they endorse the opinion they gave the previous year, agree to the amendment, and have the subject considered by the International Bureau, so that it could then come up for final decision at the meeting of the International Congress in Vienna in two years' time.

After the amendment was seconded by Bruce Glasier and was discussed by several delegates, Arthur Henderson, who was secretary of the British Section of the International, rose to propose the deletion of the clause referring to the general strike. Speaking particularly for the unions who would have to organize any laying down of tools and pointing to the seriousness of the concept of a workers' strike, he argued that, while there might be a good deal to be said for such a policy under certain circumstances, it ought to be thoroughly discussed by the bodies they represented. Such discussion, so far as he was aware, had never taken place. He himself, with his present knowledge and information, was very averse to the principle of the general strike, particularly since it would divert attention from the use of Parliamentary action as the instrument of the social and economic salvation of the workers. Additionally, he emphasized the suffering of the women and children which must inevitably follow such a policy. They were not sufficiently informed to give a lead to the workers in favor of a general strike. Henderson's intervention, as spokesman for the Labour Party Executive, proved decisive. By a narrow vote of 125 to 119 the general strike clause was deleted from Hardie's amendment, which was then carried easily.[35]

The narrowness of the vote on the exploration of the strike weapon reflects the ambivalence of a number of the leaders of Labour on the issue. While Hardie, along with Edmund Vaillant, the French socialist, recommended its use to prevent war, it seems clear that neither of them had any illusion that the present International would be able to organize a strike against war. Rather they believed in the propaganda value of the idea. As one historian has put it, "They believed, that is, that it made sense to offer guidance to the people by threatening the ruling class, and that keeping the anti-war strike alive would help create the determined majorities against war which they knew did not yet exist." [36] That view was well illustrated by Ramsay MacDonald in his "Outlook" column in the pages of the *Socialist Review.* Regretting that the issue was not more fully debated at Leicester, he concluded that on the whole the weight of consideration was on the side of the strike. He understood that it might break down if it ever had to be adopted. There was an almost unanswerable force in the argument that if the masses of the people could not prevent war through their representatives in Parliament, an attempt to get them to paralyze hostilities would fail. But that was not the question. The mere declaration of a threat to strike in the event of war would at least make war more difficult: "It would certainly be a demonstration of solidarity which would have a considerable effect on the Foreign Offices of Europe."[37]

The concept of a general strike was quite clearly divisive in the Labour Party, but the ILP, most of whose members accepted a strategy that rested on the action of the international proletariat, continued to press for investigation of an international work stoppage. Late in 1911 the ILP's Head Office circulated several propositions drafted for submission to the next Labour Party Conference. The key resolution expressed hearty approval for the proposal to investigate whether and how far a stoppage of work, "either partial or general," in countries about to engage in war would be effective in preventing an outbreak of hostilities. It commended the whole subject to the consideration of every section of the labour movement and asked the Labour Party Executive to take action to secure a full report by the next year's conference.[38]

For the next several years, the general strike continued to be discussed in the Labour press and at various meetings. In a long editorial, for example, the *Labour Leader* made it clear that the ILP had never advocated the strike as a means of redressing social equality. That had to be achieved through the gradual capture of political power. But under certain circumstances it might be brought into action to end the possibility of a crime against civilization. Recognizing that a strike against war would require real sacrifice from the working class, the editorial retorted that sacrifice had always been a motive power of the world's progress. The wage earners who had braved long weeks of hunger rather than suffer unjust reductions in their wages were equal to the sacrifice necessary to establish the reign of universal peace. The ILP hoped, therefore, that the organized workers of Great Britain would show their readiness to make war on war.

While many in the Labour Party were considerably less sanguine about the general strike than were members of the ILP, leaders of the party continued to explore the question in various venues. Thus, William Walker attended the Seventh Annual Congress of the Peace Association where, in his words, "Theologians and Anti-Theologians, Socialists and evidently Anti-Socialists" mingled together for the purposes of the gathering. He claimed that when Keir Hardie moved an amendment in favor of a strike as a protest in the event of a war being declared it would, if pressed to a vote, have been carried. But the plea of many delegates that they had no instructions on the matter induced the withdrawal of the amendment—probably to be tested at the next annual Congress. Walker's report was almost certainly more positive than was warranted, but the issue of the general strike continued to be debated until the outbreak of war made it moot.[39]

The image of a somnolent society, blissfully unaware that the dogs of war were ready to be unleashed, hardly fits the leaders of the labour movement, even if the same cannot be said of the rank and file of their followers. In the few years before the outbreak of conflict, these leaders continued to criticize Sir Edward Grey's foreign policy. The idea of alliances and treaties, the game of secret intrigue, the high-sounding phrase "European Equilibrium," all seemed to Grey, wrote Ramsay MacDonald, the ideal of a great foreign minister, not forgetting the interests of the financiers and grabbers, of the adventurous concessionists, and of the emoluments of certain aristocratic families. Particularly deplorable, in MacDonald's view, was the drawing closer to Russia, even after the massacre of Jews, "arranged by the Tsar's friends with the support of his Government." Keir Hardie, too, saw British policy as being about the protection of profits and dividends. He censured Grey for having gone out of his way to create bad blood between England and Germany, in order to make a friend of Russia.[40]

Not only Grey, but other members of the Liberal government were the objects of Labour's criticism. Lloyd George's dramatic Mansion House speech, which appeared to signal his shift to support for a more aggressive foreign policy, was greeted with dismay and alarm, particularly since the little Welshman had so often been the ally of Labour in the past. Now, his threatening speech, if it meant anything at all, meant that Britain, under a Liberal administration, was ready to make war on Germany in the interests of the "commercialists" of France.[41]

At the same time, Labour spokesmen made it clear that they deplored the aggressiveness of the German government. Somewhat unrealistically, they gave considerable weight to the German Social Democrats' opposition to the belligerence of the kaiser's ministers. At the height of the Morocco crisis, triggered when Germany sent a gunboat to Morocco, MacDonald denounced German policy as the work of a court clique with the kaiser as chief adviser. He warned that while Labour in Parliament would continue its support for peace propaganda there should be no mistake about the fact that in the event of war, whatever the international movement might do, national unity would again assert itself. If anyone in Berlin was counting upon national divisions to help his nefarious designs he would be much mistaken. MacDonald hoped that negotiations under way would result in peace, but, in any case, there would be sections of the country that would strive, whether it was popular or not, to make it impossible for two professedly Christian countries to resort to armed conflict to settle a dispute that could easily be adjudicated by the Hague Court.[42]

In the years before the war Labour continued to emphasize the argument developed by Norman Angell in a series of articles and in his popular book, *The Great Illusion*. Angell had proved conclusively, wrote W.C. Anderson, that it did not pay to go to war. Victor and vanquished alike were both heavy losers. Only certain entrenched interests found war remunerative and that fact, in turn, had implications for the welfare of the working classes [43]. In the words of the *Labour Leader*, the outbreak of war could only be prevented by the organized workers breaking the governments which were responsible for the "diabolical game."[44] On the very eve of conflict, the journal professed to believe that if the organized workers would demonstrate with sufficient force, a European war could be made absolutely impossible. No nation which was divided against itself could be expected to wage war successfully. Many European conscripts were socialists and viewed their task with loathing and abhorrence. Victories could not be won with armies of that nature. In Britain, if the protest of the Labour and socialist movement was strong enough, the government would not be able to withstand its demand for peace.[45]

It is no doubt correct that Labour's concern with the possibility of war was especially centered about the fear of being dragged into a continental conflict as an ally of the tsar, but it seems too much to contend that the ILP was more inclined than any other Radical group to ignore international issues and to be preoccupied with domestic problems. [46] While rank and file members may have been indifferent to the international scene, Hardie, MacDonald, Snowden, Anderson, as leaders of the party, associated issues of foreign policy with the domestic needs of their followers and, far from neglecting international questions, stepped up their warnings of danger as the European world drew closer and closer to the arbitrament of war.[47]

Similarly, Labour Party leaders, whatever the indifference of the general membership, continued their criticism of governmental policy up to the outbreak of war. Excessive naval armaments were regularly condemned, as was the British insistence on the right to capture private property at sea in time of war.[48] The particular concern of the party, as international tensions grew, was reflected in a long resolution prepared by the National Executive and sent to the prime minister and foreign secretary by various organizations. The resolution contended that the provision by the German people of an ever-increasing proportion of their human and physical resources to the construction of gigantic armaments was an enormous waste as well as an enemy of international good will. Certainly, it went on, neither the interests of the workers nor of the commercial classes of both countries were bounded by national frontiers. Indeed, the outbreak of hostilities would not only be a crime against civilization, but would inflict lasting injury upon both British and German democracies and would retard the growing sentiment of international friendship throughout Europe. It was therefore desirable, the resolution concluded, that all disputes between the two countries should be subjected to arbitration, "thus securing that the spirit of emulation and rivalry at present expended in warlike, wasteful and destructive competition should be diverted into peaceful, permanent, and constructive purposes of science, commerce, and social progress." [49]

The weak political position of Labour needs to be taken into consideration when assessing the limitations of its approach to foreign policy. Especially after the second election of 1910, the forty-two Labour members of Parliament were hardly an effective cadre with which to mount an effective challenge to governmental foreign policy, particularly since constitutional and social issues loomed so high in the order of national priorities. Like the small group of Liberal Radicals who condemned the international positions of their own party leaders, Labour members had as yet developed no really constructive programs with which to challenge the conventional wisdom of Liberal—and indeed Conservative—leadership. Beyond a rhetorical reliance upon a Labour and Socialist International, the fragility of which was quickly to be demonstrated when war broke out, Labour's stance was essentially negative, reflecting an often compelling critique of British foreign policy, but offering little in the way of viable alternatives.

In the years before World War I, Labour had been made increasingly aware of the importance of foreign policy issues, even if they clearly took second place to the social and economic questions which were at the heart of the labour movement's concerns. [50] The years ahead were to witness the slow struggle to achieve some measure of agreement on international policy as Labour began, for the first time, to face the possibility that it might have to assume responsible political office.

2

The First World War

Before 1914 the various branches of the labour movement had pursued an ineffective campaign, emphasizing the horrors of war and its devastating consequences for the working classes, opposing expenditures on armaments at the expense of the social programs, denouncing initiatives that appeared to threaten a move towards conscription in the future. The "no-conscription" movement attracted trade union representatives of labour who otherwise displayed little interest in the foreign policy positions of the political arm of the movement. By way of contrast, it was frequently the middle-class element in the ILP and to a lesser extent the Labour Party that made such argument as was mounted against a system that, it was charged, benefited the rich and powerful at the expense of the vast majority of the population. [1]

Despite the antiwar rhetoric of the prewar years, the July crisis took the labour movement by surprise. Even as the first shots were fired between Austria and Serbia, Labour joined with others in the peace movement to try to persuade the British government to stay out of the conflict. As late as July 30, for example, W. C. Anderson, the chairman of the ILP, professed to be uncertain that even now the "Big Powers" of Europe and the financial interests behind them would allow the struggle to be carried very far. Yet the danger was there. What was to be done? "We have to make it clear to the Government and to Sir Edward Grey that the workers here have no intention of letting the country be dragged into war over some Hapsburg quarrel."

There should be a strong Labour pronouncement in Parliament and resolutions should be passed at all trade union, Labour and socialist meetings and then forwarded to the foreign secretary. No time was to be lost.[2] A few days later, after war was declared, the ILP's major journal devoted its front page to a manifesto. "Down with the War!" it declared. "The workers never benefit by war.… It is the war of the British Ruling Class, of the German Ruling Class, of the French Ruling Class, and of the Austrian Ruling Class." What to do? "Workers," the statement urged, "even now you can stop this terrible calamity if you will. No Government can continue to engage in war if its people say with sufficient strength: THERE MUST BE PEACE. SAY IT! Say it in your thousands. March through the streets and say it. Gather together in your squares and market places and say it. Say it everywhere. Say it, and go on saying it until the Government heeds." [3]

As late as the end of July there was hope that war might be averted. On July 30, the Parliamentary Labour Party (PLP) adopted a resolution expressing gratification that Sir Edward Grey had taken steps to secure mediation of the Austro-Serbian dispute. While regretting that neither power had accepted his proposal, the PLP hoped that on no account would Great Britain be dragged into the European conflict in which the prime minister himself had stated the country had no direct or indirect interest. The party called upon all Labour organizations in the country to watch events vigilantly so as to oppose any action which might involve Britain in war.[4]

When a protest meeting was held in Trafalgar Square many of the leaders of Labour spoke against the war. Keir Hardie, Arthur Henderson, Will Thorne, Mary Macarthur, Margaret Bondfield, and George Lansbury participated, but Ramsay MacDonald was conspicuously absent. It is overly simple, as some suggested at the time, to conclude that he did not want to commit himself to a public statement, particularly since he did give the complicated rationale for his position in the House of Commons on August 3. There as it became clear that war with Germany was imminent, he made the argument, agreed upon in a Parliamentary Labour Party meeting, criticizing the policy that had been pursued by Grey, denying that the foreign secretary had demonstrated that the country was in danger, that its honor required involvement on the continent of Europe, or that indeed French endangerment justified entering into a war. Above all, he raised the question of the implication of war for the power of Russia in Europe. The country, he concluded, ought to have remained neutral.[5]

Once war was declared, the fissures in the labour movement, often papered over in a minority faction with relatively little political influence, became apparent as the pressure for national conformity became ever more intense. Those differences were particularly evident in the first years of the conflict. The leaders of the Labour Party, along with those of the trade unions, rallied to the support of the war effort and took office in the coalition cabinet of Herbert Asquith. Most—though not all—of the ILP spokesmen continued to oppose the war, even as they gave their support to the men in the trenches. On the issue of conscription, which again came to the fore in 1915 and 1916, there was for a time more agreement. Before the war, the labour movement had feared the imposition of conscription, often viewing it as the first step towards the mobilization of labour for the benefit of the capitalists who governed the country. The same issues united the various sections of the labour movement for some time during the war, but, as the inadequacies of the Derby Scheme for voluntary recruitment became increasingly evident, the Labour Party and the unions for the most part reluctantly acquiesced in a military draft, so long as industrial compulsion was not involved. The ILP, on the other hand, continued to object, and indeed, a pacifist minority within the group was instrumental in creating the No-Conscription Fellowship of war resisters. And in the final years of the war, the ILP's attention, like that of the Labour Party, was increasingly directed to the postwar settlement. An international organization of some sort, it was more or less agreed, must emerge after the war, but there was wide disagreement on what should be its structure and its functions.[6]

Meanwhile, many of the ILP leaders were pacifists and took an all-out position of opposition to the war. The views of others were closer to those of MacDonald, deploring the policies that had led to British involvement, but accepting the necessity of preventing Germany from winning the struggle. Officially, the National Council of the ILP made clear its conviction that British policy had not been wholly white and German policy black. German workers, no less than those of France and Russia, remained brothers who were, like British workers, victims of the militarism that had precipitated the conflagration now enveloping Europe. Now the workers everywhere must press for diplomatic policies after the war, "controlled by themselves," that would bring an end to that militarism and—most incidentally—foster the establishment of a United States of Europe, "thereby advancing toward the world's peace."[7]

Keir Hardie was especially disillusioned. Having hoped against hope that the government would refuse to be drawn into the European conflict unless British interests were directly threatened, he was embittered by the "flimsy" reasons offered by Grey for the change in his attitude. In an article labeled "The Government's Crime," he deplored the hypocrisy of claiming to protect the independence and neutrality of a small nation—Belgium, while having gone hand in glove with Russia in destroying the liberties of another—Persia. Denouncing the propaganda that quickly began to demonize the German people, he noted the threat posed to Prussia by Russia's millions of trained soldiers and unlimited population and asked pointedly whether it was British policy to substitute tsarism for German militarism. But Hardie had no illusions: "Ten million Socialist and Labour votes in Europe, without a trace or vestige of power to prevent war! Our demonstrations and resolutions are all alike futile. We simply do not count."[8] Other ILP activists gave their own reasons for opposing Britain's decision for war. For Fred Jowett, who had made his way up from employment in a Bradford textile mill to prominence in the ILP and the Labour Party, war was due to the evils of capitalism and especially to the secret diplomacy that had made dangerous commitments, while Robert Smillie, the president of the Miners' Federation of Great Britain, emphasized the machinations of the "war lords, the financiers, and those who supplied the instruments of destruction." [9] Like his ILP associates, Bruce Glasier opposed the war with the only weapon he had, words, about which he had his doubts.[10]

Not all the ILP leaders accepted the antiwar stand adopted by the party. G. N. Barnes had been a pioneer in the movement towards independent parliamentary representation for Labour and was later to be a key figure in bringing into being the International Labour Organization. From the start of the war he agreed with many in the rank-and-file of the ILP in rejecting opposition to the war.[11] Like Barnes, J. R. Clynes, the soft-spoken party loyalist who served as vice chair of the Parliamentary Labour Party in 1910 and 1911 and was to be its deputy leader from 1923 to 1931, supported the war and all that was required for its prosecution. The ILP's Bruce Glasier could not persuade more than a handful of members of his local branch to attend a specially summoned meeting to endorse the position of the leadership, while Hardie himself was shouted down by a dissentient element at Manchester where a resolution in favor of the National Administrative Council antiwar policy was carried by a vote of only 88 to 56. In West Yorkshire, trade unions appear to have supported the war effort in the first two years, but their influence was in some measure offset by the membership of local trade unionists in the ILP. As the war dragged on, most of the trade unions accepted, with varying degrees of commitment, the peace movement of the ILP politicians.[12] Various commentators have also cautioned against exaggerating the breach between the ILP and the Labour Party during the war. They did indeed cooperate on a wide range of issues, most notably on the issue of conscription which was widely opposed until it had become a fait accompli. By the middle of 1916 Arthur Henderson and the official leaders of the Labour Party had become reconciled to the need for universal male suffrage and even limited female suffrage, more or less as a quid pro quo for the reluctant acceptance of conscription. On the other hand, they demanded certain concessions, such as the full enfranchisement of fighting soldiers, even eighteen-year-olds. [13] The deeper estrangement that developed later came about gradually. Nevertheless, there was significant division on the issue of the war, a division on matters of foreign policy that was to continue, in one form or another and with differing personalities, long after the ILP had left the Labour Party and well into the years after the Second World War.[14]

The uncertainties of the hectic early days of August are nowhere more apparent than in the actions of the Labour Party's representatives. On August 5, the National Executive Committee criticized Sir Edward Grey for making secret commitments to France, and called upon the labour movement to work for peace at the earliest possible moment on conditions that would restore amicable relations between the workers of Europe. By the time the decision was communicated to the movement, in a letter of August 7 from W. C. Anderson and Arthur Henderson, the NEC position had been superseded by the refusal of the Parliamentary Labour Party to accept Ramsay MacDonald's proposal that the party abstain from the war credits vote.[15] MacDonald's subsequent resignation as chairman of the Labour Party (he retained the office of treasurer) stemmed from his rejection of the sheer irrationality of the conflict.[16] There is little reason to doubt the sincerity of his horror of war and the courage with which he spoke out against it from the very outset. He opposed the war and his opposition drew him closer to the ILP, as well as to the antiwar Radicals in the Liberal Party with whom he had had much in common in the years before 1914. At the same time he found it unthinkable that Germany should win. Because of what has been called the "amorphousness" of his personality, his position was often misunderstood. For many, despite his support for the recruiting effort and a fight to the finish, he became a symbol of the pacifism and defeatism they decried.[17]

The critics, both of the decision for war and the purposes for which it was being fought, with whom MacDonald joined were a diverse group. They ranged from the left-wing pacifist, Fenner Brockway, to the Liberal Party Radical, E. D. Morel, who was subsequently to follow a number of his fellow Radicals into the Labour Party via membership in the ILP. Both Brockway, a life-long stalwart of the democratic left, and Morel, still a member of the Radical wing of the Liberal Party, spent time in prison during the war. The former was detained under the Military Service Act for refusing to support the war by doing noncombatant work, the latter on a technicality for sending a pamphlet, *Tsardom's Part in the War,* to the French pacifist Romain Rolland, then living in neutral Switzerland. Throughout the war, most of the national press paid scant attention to these dissenters, except to denounce them, often in unmeasured terms. *John Bull,* for example, labeled MacDonald and Hardie the two high priests of "damnable treason" and demanded that MacDonald be taken to the Tower and shot at dawn after a trial by court martial.[18] For the critics of the war or, as in the case of MacDonald, wartime policy, the best chance of being heard was through occasional pamphlets and manifestos, equally occasional meetings, and the very limited Labour press. *Clarion* was committed to the war (although Robert Blatchford denounced as a government plot the suggestion that conscription of men, but not of property, might be needed in the prosecution of the war). George Lansbury's *Herald* decried the war but was likewise supportive of the men who were doing the fighting. As a result, the ILP's *Labour Leader* was especially crucial as a platform for a significant spectrum of the most active opponents of the war.[19]

From early in the war, *Labour Leader* hammered away at a few themes. Brockway and MacDonald denied that the war was one of liberation, emphasizing how ridiculous that claim was when Britain was fighting as an ally of tsarist Russia. Morel attacked the secret diplomacy that he saw as the cause of the war and denounced the commitments to France that had made Britain's participation virtually inevitable. And the editors of the paper, in a series entitled "After the War—What?" argued that only when the means by which the community was supplied were held by the community itself would the war between capital and labour—between master and slave, as *Labour Leader* defined the relationship—would the warfare of industrialism be ended. On the international side, beyond the recurring condemnation of secret diplomacy, the journal opted in somewhat general terms for the "United States of Europe" it had advocated in an earlier issue. That should be set up by a free choice of the peoples instead of by unwilling submission to force. At this stage, the ILP organ ventured no further and indeed agreed that it was too early to discuss terms of peace.[20]

Within the year, however, the ILP had changed its tune. In its "Points for the Workers," the National Administrative Council in April 1915 distributed a manifesto calling upon the Labour and Socialist forces of all the belligerent countries to demand the terms of peace. Each country, it emphasized, believed itself to be fighting for "liberty," "freedom," and other terms, but the conflict, while it might determine which nation had the biggest guns or the deadliest shrapnel, would not solve on an equitable basis the questions of nationality, militarism, trade, and other matters which supposedly were involved in the struggle. Meanwhile a series of war pamphlets—*How the War Came; Belgium and the Scrap of Paper; Persia, Finland, and our Russian Alliance; The War and the Far East; Morocco and Armageddon*—continued to outline the ILP case against the war, although some difference of opinion about the pamphlet *How the War Came* led to the decision that future pamphlets should bear the name of the author.[21]

Probably more significant than the ILP's pamphlet material was the consideration of the postwar world in the pages of the *Labour Leader*. Edited now by Fenner Brockway, it undertook to explore the kind of international order that ought to be sought as an outcome of the war. Key contributors were a number of the Radicals in the Liberal Party who later found their way into the ranks of Labour. Thus Norman Angell, the author of the enormously popular book, *The Great Illusion*, which argued that war did not pay, called for a new statement of principles, decrying the idea of a balance of power as an illusion unlikely in any way to end the curse of militarism. Arthur Ponsonby, who had been born at Windsor Castle where his father was private secretary to Queen Victoria and who had served in the diplomatic corps, emphasized the need for popular control of foreign policy while making the case for a United Europe. His fellow Liberal, Sir Charles Trevelyan, another scion of a family of political and intellectual distinction, centered his analysis on ways to ensure the rights of nationalities. Other articles included Fred Jowett's case against secret diplomacy, Walton Newbold's argument for the nationalization of the armaments industry, Bruce Glasier 's case for real disarmament, and E. D. Morel's insistence that urgent social problems needed to be addressed if the sacrifices of patriotism were to have any meaning..[22]

Morel, Trevelyan, Angell, and Ponsonby had joined with Ramsay MacDonald on the morrow of the declaration of war to found the Union of Democratic Control which grew into a major source of dissent during the struggle. All but MacDonald were Liberals and all eventually became important members of the Labour Party. Central to the purpose of the UDC was the demand for open diplomacy and the "democratic control" of foreign policy. Sometimes pointing to the American Senate's Committee on Foreign Relations as a model, the group argued that Parliamentary ventilation of possible obligations before they were incurred would provide a check upon the kind of secrecy which had enabled Sir Edward Grey to make commitments that neither Parliament nor the nation knew anything about.[23] With the exception of MacDonald the leadership of the UDC was made up of Liberal dissidents from the foreign policy of Sir Edward Grey. Originally intended as a behind-the-scenes ginger group outlining the requirements for a proper peace, the UDC went public after its existence was revealed by the *Morning Post*.[24]

In short order the group's original members recruited not only other Liberals such as J. A. Hobson, Bertrand Russell, H. B. Lees Smith, R. D. Denman, but also ILPers F. W. Jowett, W. C. Anderson, H. N. Brailsford, Philip and Ethel Snowden, and Labour Party leaders Arthur Henderson, Robert Smillie, Ben Turner, and J. H. Thomas, who, like some of the ILP recruits, were trade unionists as well. It recruited not only individuals but also organizations, a large proportion of which came from the labour movement. In particular cooperation on issues of foreign policy between the UDC and the Independent Labour Party was crucial to the work of both groups. While most of the Liberal leaders of the UDC were hardly enamored of the socialism of the ILP, they shared platforms with the labour group, often, as has been noted, airing their views in its *Labour Leader* and *Socialist Review*, and in general playing down the real differences, such as the demand for a negotiated peace as against the immediate end of the war, however achieved, that separated the two organizations.

While it is difficult to agree that dissent meant the UDC, it is indeed the case that the UDC included some of the most vocal and cogent critics of the war.[25] This is not to say that criticism, even within the UDC, was all of one piece. Ramsay MacDonald made no bones of his opinion that a real peace largely depended upon Labour, Arthur Ponsonby disapproved of all war on moral grounds, Norman Angell saw it as economically irrational, E. D. Morel was more interested in the causes of war than its results, and some UDC members were supporters of the war, even to the extent of serving in the armed forces.[26] Morel, who assumed the secretaryship of the group early on, threw himself into its work with such energy that the organization soon took on the aspect of virtually a personal crusade.[27] As yet, like Trevelyan and others, he remained a Liberal. They were concerned that to take a definite step towards political change of allegiance—too early a move into the ILP, for example—would be, as Trevelyan wrote on an invitation to Morel, fatal to any progress with Liberals.[28]

The importance of the UDC was that so many of its most active leaders were "respectable" middle-class individuals, well connected, and not necessarily left-wing ideologues who might more easily be silenced by the authorities.[29]

The UDC, therefore, for its first two years remained predominantly an organization of dissident Liberals. The gap between many of the UDC leaders and those of the labour movement, however much they cooperated on the foreign policy front, became evident after the middle of 1915 when both military and industrial planners had to deal with vast and unanticipated requirements for manpower. As early as November 1914, a minority within the ILP, led by Fenner Brockway, had participated in the creation of the No-Conscription Fellowship (NCF) formed to oppose conscription and support conscientious objectors—and by implication to oppose the war. In its early stages the NCF looked with suspicion at the registration of manpower and regarded the Derby Scheme as a giant step on the slippery slope to compulsion. By the end of 1915, the organization had attracted a membership of about 5,000, including Christian and secular pacifists and a substantial cadre of socialists to whom the war was anathema.

To E. D. Morel, the activities of the NCF posed a threat. From early on, he had wanted the UDC to develop a connection to labour organizations and to seek the support of trade unions in order for its principles to take root among the working classes, but he clearly envisaged cooperation on his own terms. [30] Commenting on a proposed resolution which would commit the UDC and its branches "to oppose to the utmost any attempt to impose compulsory service either for military or industrial purposes as being unnecessary for the needs of the nation and inadvisable in its best interests," Morel saw the suggestion as a tremendously grave step indeed. If "to the utmost" meant anything more than rhetoric it indicated that the UDC must preach actual resistance to what might become the law of the land. It would bring the organization within measurable distance of prosecution for sedition and rebellion. "I don't want the U.D.C. to commit itself irrevocably," he wrote to Sir Charles Trevelyan, "without realising quite clearly the outcome of its act. The resolution, as drafted, constitutes an irrevocable step, by which the UDC must stand or fall, irrespective altogether of its main programme."[31]

Once conscription was adopted in January 1916, the NCF concentrated on giving support—information, representation, whatever appeared necessary— to those who claimed conscientious scruples against military or even, in many cases, non-combatant service. While the British provision for objectors was in some respects quite generous—it recognized non-religious objection to service—the tribunals set up to evaluate individual requests for exemption were varied in their application and generated a substantial need for the advice of the NCF. As time went on, of the various options available to conscientious objectors—absolute exemption, non-combatant military   service, alternative civilian service—emphasis came to be placed on support for those requesting alternative service rather than absolute exemption, although there were sharp differences over tactics between the "absolutists" and "accommodationists" in the NCF. What is strikingly different about the NCF from many of the dissident bodies during the First World War is the efficiency with which its work was conducted. A register of almost all conscientious objectors was kept and the organization was divided into departments of the press, literature, and campaigns along with a political section and those concerned directly with the support of conscientious objectors and their dependents. *Tribunal*, the weekly journal of the NCF, at one time reached a circulation of about 10,000 copies.[32]

The No-Conscription Fellowship touched a considerable vein of sympathy far broader than among socialist and/or pacifist war resisters. The Labour Party's 1916 conference heard its chairman warn that it was impossible to have forced military service without the risk of forced industrial service. Later a resolution of opposition to conscription passed by a 4 to 1 vote, while subsequently the Military Service Act was condemned by an even larger margin.[33] Once conscription was an accomplished fact, the Labour Party continued its criticism. At its Manchester conference in January 1917, R. C. Wallhead, an artist in copper and bronze who had become known as a most effective propagandist in Labour and socialist circles, introduced a resolution for the ILP which protested against governmental abuses of the wide powers conferred on the authorities under the Defence of the Realm Acts, particularly the use of these powers by local authorities to suppress freedom of speech and writing and to punish opinions to which they were opposed politically. The resolution then went on to reaffirm the opposition of the conference to conscription and to claim further that the Military Service Acts had been administered harshly and inequitably, both in the case of men unfit for service for a variety of reasons and in that of men with a deep conscientious objection to participation in war. To round off its charge, the resolution viewed with alarm and hostility alleged proposals of the new Lloyd George government in the direction of a system of industrial compulsion, which it deemed both unnecessary and a violation of official pledges. Such a resolution would almost certainly not have been accepted earlier as the Labour Party supported the war effort and the government in which its own Arthur Henderson and G. N. Barnes served. Now, however, even before Arthur Henderson's intention to attend a conference in Stockholm of socialist representatives from allied, enemy, and neutral countries precipitated his resignation from the government and freed the party's leadership to take a more independent position, anguish over the enormous human cost of the conflict and doubts about its outcome were reflected in the critique both of the war and of its conduct by the coalition governments. Seconded by a delegate from the Toolmakers' Union, the Wallhead resolution was adopted unanimously and without further discussion. [34]

During the first several years of the war neither the Labour Party nor the ILP paid much attention to the ideas for postwar organization that began to surface among critics of the existing order. Absorbed by the issues relating to the war and its conduct, they gave little consideration, especially, to the plans for some kind of League of Nations that eventually were to become a major element in Labour's prescription for international change. Like the initiative of the Union of Democratic Control, much of the early thinking about the structure of such an association was the work of dissident Liberals, both as individuals and through such bodies as the League of Nations Society and a group whose central figure was Lord Bryce, the distinguished former ambassador to the United States and astute observer of the American political scene.[35] Two major studies were significant exceptions. The one, by Leonard Woolf, greatly influenced the ideas of the leaders of the Labour Party, while H. N. Brailsford's design for the future was to be reflected, above all, in the proposals of the ILP.

Shortly after the outbreak of war, Beatrice Webb had written to Woolf, who had seen colonial service in Ceylon and was now married to Virginia Stephens. Beatrice and her husband, Sidney Webb, were well into the heart of their amazing collaboration in the field of the social sciences and social history. Already they had founded that lasting memorial to their partnership, the London School of Economics and Political Science, and had been extraordinarily productive in promoting specific reforms based on their scholarly investigations. Woolf, already a gifted publicist, had chatted with Sidney Webb about the possibility of international organization after the war. Following up on that conversation, Mrs. Webb asked him to take the lead in an enquiry by a small committee of the Fabian Research Bureau into "the whole arrangements of international control over Foreign Policy, Armaments and methods of warfare."[36]

The result was *International Government*, a thorough study that emphasized the predicament that made a new institution necessary and described the step-by-step internationalization of world activity that had already paved the way for the next steps. Aired in several articles in the *New Statesman*, then published as a book, the project was the basis for a detailed plan for international organization presented by the Fabian Society in the form of a draft treaty. The Fabian document was deliberately and severely limited, making no proposal for curtailment of national sovereignty, retaining the right of each state to go to war if it could not attain satisfaction in an international dispute, and bypassing the issue of disarmament in the hope that experience with an international body would promote disarmament in the normal course of events. Essentially, the Fabian plan mirrored various Liberal proposals in placing its major emphasis on the provision of machinery for the pacific settlement of international disputes. Detailed recommendations were made, on the one hand to protect the sovereignty of regional groupings, on the other to ensure that the major powers continued to have the authority to accompany their responsibility. The Fabian plan had little to say about economic issues, although in characteristic fashion it paid considerable attention to the practical need for an international secretariat to take care of the administrative tasks of the new organization. By the end of 1916, the society had published in *Fabian News* the rationale for its position. Aspirations for democratic control of foreign policy, universal free trade, reduction of armaments and government control of their manufacture might all be worthwhile, but the imperative first need was for machinery for the prevention of future wars. As the war dragged on, the *New Statesman* assumed the burden of keeping the Fabian view of a League for limited purposes before its readers and, it was hoped, a wider audience as well.

In sharp contrast to the views of the Fabians were those of H. N. Brailsford. Brought up as a Liberal, he waited to join the ILP until it appeared to be receptive to middle class intellectuals like himself who continued to write for Liberal newspapers. He was a gifted and prolific journalist and commentator on world affairs. Brailsford had finally abandoned the Liberals for the ILP in 1907. Shortly after the beginning of the war he published a third edition of his influential book, *The War of Steel and Gold.* In an appendix, he sketched a plan for a world federation, made up of regional bodies and including, as many League plans did not, enemy states as well as the present allies. Far from the limited League envisaged in those plans, Brailsford's proposals outlined a wide range of powers to be given his world authority. It should have control of trade routes, ships canals, and free ports and police the high seas in peace and in war. It should regulate trade with the unfree colonies of member states and control the competition for concessions and spheres of influence. In principal, it should have authority over emigration and for the protection, in grave cases, of racial minorities. Additionally, he proposed the development of international arrangements for standardizing national legislation on dangerous trades, child labor, white slavery, and the like. To these, Brailsford added the conventional defense against external aggression and the "consequent" regulation of armaments.

Later, Brailsford published the most far-reaching plan for international government to appear during the war. In *A League of Nations* he modified some of his earlier views on the machinery of a League, perhaps as a way of reaching a measure of accommodation with some of the less radical League advocates with whom he frequently cooperated throughout the war.[37] He continued to make the argument for economic cooperation through the League, outlining a "charter of commercial freedom" in terms which included most favored nation treatment in all home markets, tariffs (if any) for revenue only in non-self-governing colonies, the open door to all foreign enterprise in developed regions, such as China, and the appointment of an International Commission under the League to ensure freedom of access for the trade of all signatory powers to raw materials and other natural resources. Finally, Brailsford was concerned for the rights of nationality, proposing that League members agree to give all racial minorities in Europe full liberty to use their language, develop their culture, and exercise their religion. Only in this way could there be hope to keep the peace in areas of Europe where national strife was so likely to break out.

When the Labour Party conference met in Manchester in January 1917, it may well be that the most important action regarding foreign affairs was in a proposal that was not yet implemented. As part of a resolution on imperial and foreign questions, the Dock, Wharf, Riverside and General Workers' Union and the Ipswich Labour Representation Committee called for the formation of an Advisory Committee "whose duty it shall be to specialise upon Diplomatic questions and Foreign Policy, and acquaint the Labour Movement with all developments." Arthur Henderson's suggestion that the issue be turned over to the National Executive was accepted and the matter was remitted for consideration to the Joint Sub-Committee on International Affairs of the Executive Committee and the Trades Union Congress. Eventually, a committee on international issues was appointed with Sidney Webb as its chairman and Leonard Woolf as secretary. It met for the first time on May 30, 1918 and undertook to analyze some of the generalizations aired in the labour movement's policy statements.[38] In the years between the two world wars the Advisory Committee on International Questions played a useful role, particularly when the Labour Party was out of office—which was for most of the period—in exposing a number of complex issues to a variety of points of view. As Leonard Woolf, who was to serve for many years as secretary of the committee, was later to put it, at the end of the war the ignorance of foreign affairs in the labour movement was almost as deep and widespread as its ignorance of imperial affairs. The committee's dealing with such matters came to play a useful educational function both in the Parliamentary Labour Party and in the movement as a whole as well.[39]

In any case, the Manchester conference signaled a substantial shift in the Labour Party's attitudes and policies. Previously, support for the war had meant, for one thing, substantial restrictions on speculation about the shape of the postwar world. At the same time, the trade unions had been suspicious of the postwar plans of such a body as the Union of Democratic Control, fearing "middle-class subversion" of the working-class movement. By the spring of 1917, conditions had changed. Increasing war weariness, complaints over the administration of conscription, fears that "dilution" in industry by unqualified workers would wipe out the gains achieved by the trade unions, all contributed to the dissatisfaction of a growing minority of Labour Party members, many of whom now appeared more receptive to the consideration of matters of foreign policy.

Dissatisfaction was tempered briefly by the optimism that greeted the March Revolution in Russia, which shortly became the pivot about which much subsequent consideration of foreign policy revolved. In the House of Commons on May 16, for example, Philip Snowden and Ramsay MacDonald joined with such Union of Democratic Control activists as Charles Trevelyan and Arthur Ponsonby to welcome the declaration of the new provisional government in Russia repudiating all proposals for imperialistic conquest and aggrandizement.[40] While there was obvious relief at the fall of the hated tsarist regime, there was also perplexity about next steps. The Labour Party's National Executive looked to Arthur Henderson, who had worked in tandem with MacDonald for years since before the founding of the Labour Party. Seen as a carthorse as against MacDonald's race horse, he was a rock of steady strength whose gift for detailed administration was essential to the development of the party. Until the war he had had little interest in foreign affairs. But the horrors of the war, including the death of a son, turned his mind increasingly to the organization of the postwar world. His membership in Lloyd George's coalition cabinet made it difficult for him to take an independent stand. When neutral socialists proposed the holding of an international conference in Stockholm, the Labour Party's National Executive, influenced by the views of Arthur Henderson, voted not to participate. At the same time, Henderson traveled to Russia as a representative of the government to make contact with the new socialist regime. He quickly realized the volatility of the Russian situation. The moderate Kerensky government viewed the Stockholm initiative, designed to clarify the war aims of the respective combatants, as an essential step in counteracting their Bolshevik opponents who were implacably opposed to the whole project. Henderson's conviction that it was important to support the provisional government and to keep it in the war led him to reverse his position on the Stockholm conference. When he advocated Allied participation in the proposed meeting of the Second International, his colleagues in the war cabinet not only refused permission, but treated him like an errant schoolboy in so doing. [41] His resignation from the government and a special Labour Party conference's approval of the Stockholm meeting gave evidence of the shift of Labour Party policy from official support of the coalition government to an increasingly critical stance. Such criticism was heightened when the new Leninist regime in Russia published secret documents and telegrams outlining in particular the territorial arrangements agreed among the Allied nations—annexations without regard to the claims of nationality, as Charles Roden Buxton put it in an assessment in the *Labour Leader.* [42]

Henderson's resignation made it easier for him to collaborate with Ramsay MacDonald and Sidney Webb in drafting a Memorandum on War Aims that reflected the work of a number of committees and the approval of the Executive Committee of the Labour Party and the Parliamentary Committee of the Trades Union Congress. The Memorandum, ratified by a special Labour Party conference on December 28, was a moderate document proposing many of the terms of peace suggested by the Union of Democratic Control earlier that year.[43] It called for the complete democratization of all countries and an end to secret diplomacy, the abolition of the private manufacture of arms and the abandonment of conscription, self-determination of peoples, and above all else the creation of an international body to give effect to the changes demanded in the postwar world. On one issue, the Labour Party's memorandum, which was substantially accepted by the Inter-Allied Labour and Socialist Conference that met in London in February 1918, differed from the formulation of the UDC. Labour's League of Nations went well beyond the instrument for the pacific settlement of international disputes contemplated by most of the leaders of the UDC. Many of those UDC leaders were active also in the League of Nations Society and the Bryce Group. Both those groups, significantly influenced by the views of the Radical cohort in the Liberal Party, envisaged, as has been noted, a League of limited functions devoted almost exclusively to dealing with international conflict once it threatened.[44] Labour's League, too, was limited but much less so than those of the League of Nations Society or the Bryce Group. The Inter-Allied Memorandum, largely the work of the British labour movement, insisted, for example, that the establishment of a system of international law and the guarantees afforded by a League of Nations ought to eliminate any insistence on the possession of strategic territories. It argued that maritime communications should be open to the ships of all nations under the protection of the League and it condemned the notion of an economic war—against the defeated enemy—after the peace.[45]

The Memorandum on War Aims clearly represented a compromise among the various strands of Labour opinion. Despite its differences from the more cautious proposals of the Liberal proponents of international change—it envisaged, for example, a settlement of territorial questions by an international body acting under a system of international law—its major elements did indeed parallel many of the ideas of the Union of Democratic Control to go along with those of the Fabian Society. Together they embodied the moderate views of those who hoped for an effective means of settling international quarrels without recourse to war. For the most part, the Memorandum minimized the aspirations of the minority who looked forward to a more ambitious system of world government. As time went on, however, the differing cross-currents of thought, especially in the ILP, increasingly affected the international views of the Labour Party. Those convictions tended in some ways to offer alternative approaches to dealing with the outside world. Suspicion of any arrangements made by capitalistic and imperialistic governments led some to insist that little could be achieved until socialism had triumphed in most of the major countries at least in Europe. Others looked to a powerful international body itself to help guide individual nations towards the utopias of peaceful economic intercourse and democratic government, and finally to the abandonment of the armaments upon which they had depended for their security. Not infrequently these convictions were mutually contradictory, particularly when they were accompanied by a widespread reluctance to deal with the use of force as an element in the functioning of any international system.

Many of these ideas were presented in the words of such highly individualistic spokesmen as Ramsay MacDonald and Philip Snowden. Neither had any great affection for the other. Indeed, Snowden often acted as if the whole world was arrayed against him. He had suffered a crippling illness as a young man and seems by sheer force of will to have taught himself to walk again. His relations with some of his fellows were often tense, but his financial expertise, which became more and more orthodox as the years passed, was considered too great to be abandoned when it was in short supply. Both MacDonald and Snowden were skeptical about the world that might emerge from the ashes of the world war.

Although MacDonald was a founding member of the Union of Democratic Control and one of the chief authors of the Memorandum on War Aims, his thoughts on a League of Nations were a good deal more questioning than the assumptions of many with whom he collaborated. Among the advocates of the League of Nations, he wrote, were some with whom the ILP could cooperate, but also those whose notion of a League to Enforce Peace might result in the promotion of militarism. The men who had controlled the governments of the world hitherto were hardly likely to abandon their methods, their traditions, their conception of policies. For the most part, MacDonald offered little in the way of concrete and detailed alternatives to schemes that were being aired. He did, however, propose that an international conference, not a peace conference of government officials, should be called to develop an international court of arbitration and one of conciliation, elected by the various parliaments with departmental officials only as advisers, to prepare international laws regarding commerce and labour. He warned, too, that the socialist party in each parliament would need to be in close touch with its fellows in other countries in order to foster common international policies: "If these things are done, we shall want no League to Enforce Peace, with its dangers and its surrender to militarism." Consistently, both openly and by implication, MacDonald made clear his view that it was an illusion to believe that peace could be enforced by the use of force, whether national or international. [46]

For his part, Philip Snowden, like H.N. Brailsford, stated the case for a more far-reaching statement of Labour's principles. Concerned about the possibility of postwar protectionism and the exclusion of Germany from sources of essential raw materials, Snowden warned, in his *Labour Leader* columns, that such a policy was inconsistent with any kind of League of Nations and made a mockery of the possibility of reducing armaments. Brailsford, in turn, joined the editors of the *Herald* in being concerned about the territorial clauses of the Memorandum and in calling for much greater attention to the development of a viable international economic organization which alone could be the basis for a peaceful world.[47]

Much that appeared in these various statements had been reflected in the statement of policy issued by the ILP at its annual conference at Leeds in 1917. Arguing that plans thus far aired implied an armed alliance of capitalist governments that could threaten the workers, the ILP had called instead for a "world-wide alliance of the common People." The conference doubted that peace could be secured by the threat of war. Instead, enunciating a position that was to run like a thread through Labour discussion of international affairs for the next two decades, it called for a new league of peoples based on trust rather than on force. Military sanctions, rejected here by the ILP, were to become the King Charles's head of the labour movement all through that period.[48]

Some of the positions expressed in the Memorandum on War Aims, then, did not sit well with the Labour left. In February, the *Labour Leader* featured an evaluation by Noel Buxton, another of the ex-Liberals making his way into the labour movement via the ILP. Pointing out that the whole war situation had been modified by events in Russia and the publication of the secret treaties, Buxton centered his criticism on the Labour Party declaration that "territorial readjustments are required." He condemned the Memorandum's support for Italy's claims in the Trentino and parts of the Balkans, as well as its demands for great changes in Alsace-Lorraine and Poland. In addition, he labeled proposals for international administration of parts of Turkey and the German colonies a form of territorial annexation so long as they were not balanced by compensations, such as Germany's administration under such international control of a larger share of tropical Africa. Most puzzling, he concluded, was the incompatibility of the official Labour Party Memorandum with the recent leaflet, *Labour's Peace Terms*, issued by Arthur Henderson. That document clearly stated that Labour's "irreducible minimum" aims, in addition to a League of Nations and Peoples for International Cooperation, Disarmament, and the Prevention of Future war, included such demands as absolute freedom and integrity of Belgium, Serbia, Rumania, Montenegro. If that was the attitude of the Labour Party, as Henderson stated it to be, then why had not the War Aims Memorandum been officially revised?[49]

When the ILP met at Leicester in April 1918 it took issue more formally with some of the positions expressed in the Memorandum on War Aims. Praising the sections on the League of Nations, the rejection of economic warfare, and proposals for the economic rebuilding of the world, the ILP nevertheless charged that the document limited the principles of self-determination and self government to territories in the possession of the Central Powers. It appeared to deny such rights to subject peoples of the Allied nations. Still, on the understanding that it was a contribution to the consideration of the peace settlement and not an "irreducible minimum," the ILP was pleased that it had been produced. [50]

Meanwhile, Lloyd George had responded to Labour's demand that the government issue a clear statement of its war aims. His contention to a conference of trade unionists on January 5 that the government's aims were congruent with those of Labour was greeted with satisfaction, as were the Fourteen Points outlined by President Wilson on January 8. Nevertheless, when it met at Nottingham for the vital purpose of adopting its new constitution, the Labour

Party accepted unanimously an international policy resolution presented by Henderson and MacDonald for the Joint Council of the Trades Union Congress and the party's National Executive. Its central point was to call upon the Allied governments to formulate and publish a joint statement of their war aims, not merely the individual national aims outlined by Lloyd George and Wilson. As MacDonald affirmed in his seconding speech, the recently revealed secret treaties among the Allies were not in accord with Labour's war aims, nor were they consistent with the pledges given to the men who joined the colors. The acceptance of the resolution by the ILP, which withdrew amendments it had earlier sent in, revealed a determination to achieve at least a measure of agreement on matters of international policy.[51]

The effort of various sections of the movement to reach accommodation can be observed in the continuing discussion of Labour's views of international organization. To illustrate, the *New Statesman*, which early in the war had advocated the very limited League of Nations proposed by the Fabian Society, by 1918 was lending its pages to the support of the substantial economic functions outlined by the Inter-Allied Labour and Socialist Conference. Those functions included enforcement in all countries of factory legislation, a maximum eight-hour day, various measures to protect workers against exploitation and oppression, and the prohibition of night work for women. Such a catalogue of functions suggests that towards the end of the war the Fabian Society for the moment had much more in common with visionaries such as H. N. Brailsford than had been the case earlier on.[52]

By the end of the war, the Labour Party had formulated, perhaps for the first time, a reasonably coherent approach to relations with the external world. On issues such as the future of territorial arrangements or the aspirations and needs of various nationalities or even the "democratic" control of foreign policy at home, it shared the views of the Radicals who made up the major part of the leadership of the Union of Democratic Control. On the issue of postwar international organization, however, Labour went substantially beyond both the UDC and the mainly Liberal leaders of such bodies as the League of Nations Society or the Bryce Group. By the end of the war, the Labour Party had come to accept much of the basic outlook sketched by the Independent Labour Party at its conferences, in its press, and by individual spokesmen. The result was a proposal for a League of Nations as the central core of international intercourse. Such a League, of course, did not come into existence, but in varying ways and with sharply differing perceptions, the role of the League, judgments on its viability and its failures, projects for its revision, all were at the center of Labour's approach to foreign policy in the next two decades.

3

Labour and the Paris Settlement

Disillusionment and despair followed as the peace conference in Paris made a shambles of Labour's hopes for the future.[1] Once war had broken out, Labour had not only slowly accepted the need to be an active player in international affairs but had begun to fashion its foreign policy around a new international agency that would provide the framework for a stable world. It had seen that body, the League of Nations, as central not only to furnishing peaceful ways to settle disputes, but also to promoting self-determination for peoples and countries, and fostering equitable economic and social policies worldwide. The punitive nature of the treaties that ended the war, the decisions those treaties reached about the disposition of territories in Europe and the colonial world, and the reluctance of the war's victors to use the League as a force for positive change all frustrated that vision. However, as they attempted to deal with those frustrations, some of Labour's leaders began to make the case for a more pragmatic and realistic foreign policy.

As the end of the war had approached, Labour's leadership had stepped up the campaign for a new order based upon international cooperation and understanding. But it is likely that neither Arthur Henderson, representative of the main current of Labour Party policy, nor Ramsay MacDonald, more or less expressing his own version of the outlook of the ILP and the UDC, reflected the prejudices of the average party member so well as Robert Blatchford, whose anti-German convictions persisted into the postwar period. In the general election campaign of December 1918 international policy formed a large part of the argument advanced by Labour candidates.[2] The result was a debacle. Despite the increase in the number of MPs over 1910, virtually every articulate spokesman for a peace of reconciliation was defeated, leaving the parliamentary cadre relatively weak and ineffective.

Labour's mood of hopelessness led to an almost complete rejection of the impositions of the Allied governments, coupled with the view that only a radical reconstruction of the institutions for the conduct of international relations offered any hope for the future. Middle-of-the-road Labourites joined more out-and-out pacifists in urging concessions to the fledgling German Republic as the foundation for Franco-German reconciliation, while a significant section of the movement argued that a peaceful and equitable world could only be achieved after capitalism had disappeared and socialism had triumphed.

During the last months of 1918 and into 1919, the new Advisory Committee on International Questions prepared a series of memoranda dealing with colonial questions, the freedom of the seas, and above all with the shape and functions of a prospective League of Nations. For the most part, the Advisory Committee analyses merely sharpened the rationale for positions already developed during the course of the war, but on one issue there was a warning that troubled British Labour for the next two decades. A major Committee memorandum pointed out that so long as nations remained armed, the League of Nations, if it was to be effective, must have the capacity to call upon armed force to resist armed aggression. Support for military sanctions was coupled with the need for gradual disarmament as the League demonstrated it ability to maintain the peace.[3] The emphasis upon coercion did not reflect the views of all of the members of the Advisory Committee nor was it welcome to many, in both the ILP and the UDC, who pictured a League of Nations, insofar as they accepted it at all, as a substitute for arms and their use in international intercourse. Reflecting ILP suspicions, for example, neither the politician Philip Snowden nor the publicist H.N. Brailsford was enthusiastic about the prospects for a "capitalist" League and both warned against putting too much faith in the effectiveness of President Wilson, upon whom, for a time, some Labour Party spokesmen rested their hopes.[4] Distrust was increased by the fear that the Allied leaders were more interested in destroying the new Bolshevik regime than in seeking a broadly based international collaboration.[5]

At the Labour and Socialist Conference that met in Berne in early February, British Labour's contribution was central. Hope for a reconstruction of the old Second International was frustrated, but on territorial issues and international organization, the Berne recommendations and the decisions taken subsequently at Amsterdam to bring them to the attention of the principals of the Peace Conference substantially followed the British position. Little heed, however, was given to that position when decisions were made in Paris.[6] From the publication of the Draft Covenant of the League of Nations in February through the airing of preliminaries of peace with Germany in May, Labour politicians and journalists recorded their shock at virtually all of the proposed terms. Territorial arrangements that ignored "self-determination," confining of the mandates system to ex-enemy territory, economic "war after the war," failure to abolish conscription, establishment of the League as essentially an alliance of the victorious Allies with no provision for an assembly representing peoples instead of governments, all were denounced in colorful terms by ILP and UDC spokesmen and only slightly more cautiously in official Labour Party circles.

Sidney Webb was one of the few among Labour's leaders who believed that the peace terms were somewhat better than might have been expected. But his wife demurred, noting in her diary that it was a hard and brutal peace, "made more intolerable by the contumely of circumstances deliberately devised, in the method of its delivery to the representatives of the German people." [7] Mrs. Webb's reaction was more characteristic than that of her husband. Even Arthur Henderson, whose pamphlet, *The Peace Terms,* was perhaps the most authoritative statement of official Labour Party policy, felt it necessary to phrase his analysis in terms very much like those of the more extreme critics within the labour movement.[8] The one major exception was the weak Parliamentary Labour Party, led for the time being by Will Adamson, a middle-aged Scot suspicious of all intellectuals, who was described as having "neither wit, fervour, or intellect." Adamson was decidedly not a leader and when the peace treaty with Germany came before the House of Commons, Labour voices were conspicuously muted. Only J. R. Clynes, recognizing that the treaty was an accomplished fact, argued pragmatically that the new League of Nations, flawed though it was, might be used in the future to correct some of the deficiencies in the treaty.[9]

Perhaps more fully representative of the official Labour Party position was *Labour and the Peace Treaty,* prepared as a handbook for Labour speakers. Taking issue with term after term of the final settlement, the pamphlet conveyed a spirit of discouragement and pessimism that belied its suggestion, like that made by Clynes, that the League of Nations might be revised into an effective organ of international cooperation. In a sense, Labour was arguing that only if the League were revised so as to become a different organization could there be any hope for a viable and peaceful future. Whether the Labour Party as a whole could shake off the impact of the failure of its wartime aims and its suspicions of the capitalist governments and their instruments in time to move towards a more realistic assessment of what was possible on the international scene was as yet an open question.

As the components of the labour movement confronted the postwar world, socialist theory, now embedded in clause four of the new Labour Party constitution, which had been accepted in 1918, offered little guidance for the clarification of international attitudes and policies. While the various strands of socialist thought had developed coherent, ideologically based positions on social and economic policies within Great Britain, there was little in its foreign policy stands that differentiated Labour from the Radical Liberals whose ethical views on foreign affairs had been nurtured in the Victorian milieu of an earlier century.[10] Because there was so little in the way of a genuinely unique "socialist" view of international affairs, the "foreign legion" of ex-Radicals who made their way into the Labour Party exercised a perhaps disproportionate influence for a few years, both through the Union of Democratic Control and in the Independent Labour Party which most of them used as their vehicle

of affiliation with the Labour Party. While the influence of some of the recruits—Ponsonby, Trevelyan, Charles Buxton, Brailsford—was especially
evident in the left of the labour movement, their stamp could be seen in the
early postwar period in the style and the opinions of even the more moderate
of Labour's spokesmen. As the years went by, their importance diminished. A
new generation, among whom figures like Philip Noel Baker, Will Arnold
Forster, and Hugh Dalton were most prominent, emerged as the advisers of the
moderates such as Henderson and MacDonald who, however much they differed from each other, both recognized that Labour's policy had to operate in
a complex world of independent states which demanded negotiation and compromise far more than the rehearsal of vague aspirations and illusory dreams.

In the early twenties, then, most of Labour's attention to the international
scene focused heavily on three issues: the integration of revolutionary Russia
into the Europe that had emerged from the war, the treatment of Germany and
its implications for the future, and the role, if any, to be played by the new
League of Nations in shaping that future. For a time, as has been noted, the
reaction to the peace settlement created a measure of agreement among the
various groups that customarily had differed both as to the timing and the
tactics of the search for the new order so hopefully described in the literature of
the movement. Even when the disagreements over policy and propaganda
persisted, the rhetoric of opposition helped paper over differences that were
less significant so long as there was little likelihood that Labour would have
to implement its aspirations in the exacting environment of the existing international society.

While neither Ramsay MacDonald nor Arthur Henderson had any illusions
about the rapid achievement of the "socialist, anti-capitalist, anti-imperialist"
utopia postulated in Labour's various materials, both men considered it important to reinvigorate the Labour and Socialist International that had been
broken by the consequences of war. The hope for an all-inclusive, revived
International comprised of diverse labour and socialist parties committed to
the promotion of working-class goals by democratic and gradual methods was
shattered with the creation of the Third International sponsored by Moscow.
Briefly, a Vienna "Two-and-a-Half International," which attempted to bridge
the gap between the Communist Third International and the Social Democratic Second, emerged. It was finally absorbed into the Second International
as the gulf between the communist movements and the more traditional parties of the left became apparent. But the hope that the international "working-
class" movement would have a significant influence on the policies pursued
by the various governments of the world was surely belied by the experience
of the next several decades.

British Labour was no less troubled about how to deal with the revolutionary regime in Russia than was the government whose policies Labour censured. Most of its moderate leaders had welcomed the early uprising that

seemed to promise the construction of a more-or-less social democratic regime, but the seizure of power by the Bolsheviks produced serious doubts.
Henderson, for example, who had gone to Russia after the March Revolution
with considerable sympathy for what had transpired, returned with grave concerns about the course of events and the leadership of the revolutionary cad-
res. Like MacDonald and Clynes and others who shared their view that socialism
would be achieved by the gradual gain of parliamentary strength, he recognized early on, as some within the labour movement did not, the enormous
chasm between a British labour movement and the Bolshevik version of the
inescapable road to what was also called socialism. Whatever their view of the
communist movement—and they rejected the British Communist Party's application for affiliation to the Labour Party for the first time as early as January
1920—they took the view that the internal affairs of Russia were the business
of the Russians. They opposed both the intervention of the Allied armies in
Russia and subsequent threats, such as the Polish war, of further attacks upon
the struggling new regime there. While it is evidently largely a myth that the
Councils of Action, organized by Labour Party locals and trade union groups
to put pressure on the government, forced Lloyd George to withdraw British
help from the White armies in Russia, there is little doubt about the systematic
opposition of mainstream Labour to any attempt to suppress the revolutionary
movement from without.[11]

One key figure who took a different tack from MacDonald and Henderson
was George Lansbury. Deeply religious, a pacifist, and a doctrinaire socialist,
he agreed with them in the demand that there be no intervention designed to
restore the old order in Russia—or even to strengthen an alternative, presumably democratic government. But his assessment of the Bolshevik regime was
strikingly different from theirs. He visited Russia in 1920 and was convinced
that the recently created Third International did not advocate violence, a view
that had substantial support among many in the ILP. The ILP, however, while
it insisted that there should be hands off the Russian experiment, took a strong
stand against the communist movement in the Labour Party at home. As for
Russia, the ILP's *Labour Leader* commented somewhat wryly near the end of
1920 that Lloyd George, in accepting the withdrawal of British troops, was
now following the policy of the Labour Party, but that did not hide the fact that
for two years the opposite policy had been pursued.[12] Lansbury was much less
discriminating. Throughout early 1920 his *Daily Herald* insisted again and
again that the "war lords" of the West were trying to destroy a popular and
progressive movement. While Lloyd George talked peace, he charged, "his
lieutenants are preparing war." A Polish exploration of a possible peace with
Russia was greeted with satisfaction, but as the rumors spread of a renewed
attack on the Russians, Lansbury saw it as an indication of "vultures gathering
round Russia." His view was more than a warmhearted sympathy for the victims of aggression. In Central Europe, he asserted, where there was a possibil-

ity of a "dictatorship of the military" leading to a revival of monarchy and a reborn imperialism, the alternative was a "dictatorship of the proletariat" leading, for its part, to the final overthrow of capitalism and its creatures.[13]

However unrepresentative the argument of a Lansbury might be, "hands off Russia" was a common theme. In mid-1920, for example, a joint meeting of representatives of the Trades Union Congress, the Labour Party, and the Parliamentary Labour Party was convened to consider the Russo-Polish conflict. Its deliberations resulted in a resolution declaring that war was being engineered between the Allied Powers and Soviet Russia on the issue of Poland and branding such war as a crime against humanity. It warned the government that the whole industrial power of the organized workers would be used to defeat such a war, and urged that affiliated organizations throughout the country hold themselves in readiness to drop tools in the event such steps were deemed necessary by the leadership of such organizations.[14]

As the years passed, the gulf, on the domestic scene, between the gradualist, "Labourist" view of the road to power and that of the communists became increasingly evident. But while the denial of Communist Party affiliation with the Labour Party appeared sound in the light of the Party's principles, most sectors in the labour movement continued to agree on the need for recognition and normalization of relations with the emerging Soviet Union. The reasons were varied. Suspicion of the purposes of the Western governments tended to be a common denominator among the component groups of Labour, but the influence of those who shared the somewhat idealistic views of Lansbury has perhaps been exaggerated.[15] To the belief that Russia, like any other sovereign nation, had the right to make its own decisions about its form of government, was added the argument that stabilization of Russia would be aided by recognition of its regime and that such stabilization would help open up Russia to the economic relations so essential to Britain's own future. In 1922, the Advisory Committee on International Questions pressed for *de jure* recognition "as a preliminary to the opening up of trade." Somewhat later, this position was supported by Ramsay MacDonald in the ILP's journal. He saw recognition as the path to the safety demanded not only by the cause of European peace but by Britain's economic interests as well. His position was endorsed by the Labour Party throughout the postwar years.[16]

The terms of the postwar treaties continued to be seen as an unmitigated disaster by virtually the entirety of the labour movement. The *Daily Herald* summed up the consequences for Germany especially. Handing over the coal mines of the Saar to French administration, ceding large areas inhabited by German-born populations to Poland, preventing Austrians from joining their German brothers and sisters if they wished, surrendering all the German colonies—these all added up to the dismemberment of Germany. Worst of all was the "insane" indemnity imposed in flat contradiction to the Fourteen Points and some four or five times greater than the maximum Germany could possibly pay.[17] In short order, Labour's critics were joined by the brilliant polemic of the young economist John Maynard Keynes, whose *Economic Consequences of the Peace* was greeted in the labour press as a confirmation of all that it had been maintaining.[18] Over the next several years virtually all of Labour's voices joined in the demand for the revision of the postwar treaties. Regularly, those demands were augmented by condemnation of policies of militarism and imperialism and paralleled by arguments for economic policies that included the "open door" for the development of the resources of the world, the abandonment of tariffs and other barriers to the free flow of commerce, the tutelage of the "non-adult" peoples leading to the earliest possible achievement of self-government, and the end of secret diplomacy and Parliamentary ratification in advance of any treaty or convention. Such proposals, more often than not, originated in ILP and sometime UDC circles, but when brought before the mainstream trade unionists and "moderate" delegates at Labour Party conferences were usually accepted without serious dissent and often without discussion.[19]

More specific than the general castigation of "capitalist" and "imperialist" machinations was the conviction that the French were determined to destroy Germany in their mistaken search for military security. Some of Labour's leaders—Henderson was one example—understood the demographic and military reasons for French concerns, but believed that they could be addressed as the new institutions of international relations matured. For the most part, however, suspicion of France was axiomatic if not always clear-headed.[20] When the possibility of an Anglo-French alliance surfaced, the Labour Party conference unanimously denounced the proposal, affirming that such an agreement would be based on the mutual concession of a free hand for imperialist expansion in certain spheres. It would be wholly opposed to the spirit of the League of Nations whose object it was to render such partial alliances unnecessary. The conference's resolution, which was passed unanimously, expressed the intention to maintain fraternal relations with the French workers, but also the conviction that an alliance would be no less injurious to their interests than to those of the workers of Great Britain.[21]

From the very beginning of the postwar period, Labour portrayed the struggles of the infant German republic as the direct result of the Versailles Treaty. From the right-wing Kapp Putsch in 1920 through the French occupation of the Ruhr in 1923, British Labour looked upon the German Socialists as the one hope for the achievement of democratic institutions in Germany, but saw restrictions in the treaty combined with the persistence of French ambitions as the roadblock in the way. Writing to Arthur Henderson in September 1920 as an individual, but also as a member of the Advisory Committee, H. N. Brailsford reported that on a recent trip to Berlin and Vienna he had become convinced that the future there would be out of all control unless the German Socialists had faith in the will of the British Labour Party to work effectively for the amendment of the treaty at an early date. He offered to speak at the forthcoming party conference about what he had seen and heard, but it is clear that his was only one of many voices making the same observations and emphasizing the same fears.[22]

Most vehement in support of Germany and assault upon France was E. D. Morel. Already well known for his exposures of the cruel exploitation of the natives in Leopold II of Belgium's Congo, Morel had turned his mind to the iniquities of the diplomacy of the Great Powers before the war and had concluded that Britain and France bore as heavy a share of the blame for the conflict as did the German enemy. Born of a French father and an English mother, he was particularly critical of the French politicians, whom he saw as determined to wipe out Germany as a rival for political and economic supremacy in Europe. In the pages of the UDC's *Foreign Affairs*, which he edited, but in public speeches and other writing as well, he carried the strictures of a Keynes or an Angell, or even the charges of a Brailsford to an extreme that again and again went beyond UDC policy in describing the Versailles Treaty as both ineffective and criminal. It had been deliberately shaped, he insisted, to destroy the German people, economically and physically, in the interests of the French lust for power. The most striking example of Morel's impassioned accusation of the French is well known. His pamphlet *The Horror on the Rhine* painted a lurid picture of black troops ravaging the civilian population as part of a deliberate attempt by the French to break the will of the Germans. Even Arthur Ponsonby, who agreed with Morel about the treaty and its effect on the German people, pointed out that most of the allegations in the pamphlet could not be substantiated when investigated.[23]

Nevertheless, Morel continued his campaign well into the period when Labour unexpectedly took over the administration of policy. When the French and Belgians occupied the Ruhr in 1923, Morel wrote that a crime for which it would be hard to find a parallel in history had been in process of perpetration for four and a half years against a helpless people. Now the results might well be that multitudes of starving workers, maddened by famine, would destroy in their urgent need whatever was left standing after those years of external persecution and international acceptance of deliberate wrong.[24]

If E. D. Morel was less than evenhanded in his judgment of both Germany and France, George Lansbury's *Daily Herald* was, if anything, more extreme. Trying desperately to reconcile his Christianity and Christian pacifism with the revolutionary socialism of the Soviet Union, he condemned the German Socialists for fighting their own people. They preferred, he charged, even French occupation to the possibility of revolution at home. And British politicians, having seized the German colonies and destroyed German trade, now were intent to use the German government to destroy Bolshevism. Otherwise, unlike the French, they had realized their ends.[25]

Even before troops marched into the Ruhr, Labour spokesmen, particularly those of the left, had been predicting that reparation demands would result in further French persecution of Germany. Several articles by Charles Roden Buxton, one in the ILP-supported *Socialist Review*, the other in the more mainstream *Labour Magazine,* outlined the case quite cogently. The payment of reparations had done little to repair the devastated areas of France because virtually all of those payments had been eaten up by the costs of occupation. If Britain remitted the debt owed her by France, the French might be persuaded to join in the revision of reparation payments and the consequent withdrawal of the armies of occupation from Germany.[26]

Not only the revival of the French countryside, but the economic health of Britain as well were tied to the reparation question. At a Union of Democratic Control conference presided over by Ramsay MacDonald, the case was made that the collection of reparations had contributed heavily to the decline in British industry and the malaise of the British working class. The conference condemned any further occupation of German territory, proposing that Britain renounce its share of reparations and cancel its share of the French war debt. All of this was included in a long composite resolution that ventilated the customary array of UDC policies.[27]

For the first several years after the war, Labour's official efforts with regard to Germany also centered about the demand for the revision of the peace treaties. That demand was shared by those who increasingly came to view a League of Nations as a possible vehicle for international change as well as by those who were somewhat more than skeptical of the utility of the present international organization. For the most part, Labour's views were promoted in conference resolutions and other manifestos, along with a variety of articles in the modestly few organs of press and periodical opinion. Until the election of November, 1922, the Parliamentary cadre was small and generally ineffective, but with the return of most of the political leaders of Labour, above all Ramsay MacDonald and, after he was returned in a by-election, Arthur Henderson, the Labour voice in the House of Commons was, at the very least, somewhat more audible. That did not mean, however, that there was necessarily agreement among the Labour M.P.s. Clynes and Henderson, for example, differed markedly from Morel and Snowden, while MacDonald tended frequently to put his own individual stamp on the policies he promoted. Still, Labour's impact on Parliamentary business in the field of foreign affairs was minimal until the occupation of the Ruhr precipitated a major discussion of reparations and the future of Germany.

Once the Ruhr occupation was an accomplished fact, the various organs of opinion and the official bodies of Labour rallied to oppose the action. The UDC's Executive Committee, this time agreeing fully with Morel, issued a manifesto calling attention to the "fantastic sum" for reparations and calling upon Britain to dissociate herself from such mistaken ways to obtain security for France or any other country. The UDC called for a world conference, if possible with American collaboration, to revise all the peace treaties, promote a general scheme of disarmament, and establish machinery to ensure free access to undeveloped mineral deposits. All this was to be preceded by withdrawal of all troops from Germany.[28]

Various voices echoed the outlook of the UDC. On the left, Brailsford saw the invasion as the start of a new war, while Roden Buxton branded the exactions upon Germany, and especially upon the German workers who were living on starvation wages, as the real betrayal of Europe. Somewhat more to the center, F. W. Pethick Lawrence, who had earlier been most conspicuous in Labour circles as a fervent supporter of the campaign for women's suffrage, had already argued that just as prisoners received no wages and thus could "undersell" manufacturers on the outside, so the coalition government had made Germany a prison nation through the Treaty of Versailles and the reparation clauses. Ironically that had ruined the competitive labour of Britain and the neutral countries. "Our workers," he insisted, "by supporting this policy at the General Election in 1918 prepared a rod for their own backs by which they have been flagellated ever since." And Arthur Henderson summed up the case with a litany of actions taken by capitalist governments which failed to understand the economic interdependence of nations. The treaties were tissues of elaborate and contradictory provisions designed to extract from the defeated countries impossible sums as indemnities while denying them the bare essentials of State life. Germany was deprived of most of the iron ore upon which her industry depended. Her coal resources had been cut to less than what was needed for home consumption, while she was deprived of agricultural land which yielded a surplus of food and various essential raw materials. Her colonies were taken away, along with her large oceangoing ships. Her river communications were placed under Allied control, along with foreign trade and some of her chief industries. Intercourse with Russia, as well as with her former allies, was blocked as much as possible and she was compelled to grant the most-favored- nation treatment to the Allies that was withheld from her. Finally, weakened and impoverished, Germany was required to pay impossible sums and was sinking closer and closer into national bankruptcy.[29]

What to do? Norman Angell, often a voice of temperance and moderation, had no doubts. Labour should urge an immediate revision of the Treaty, cessation of all cooperation with France, complete and immediate peace with Russia, and a social and economic "triple alliance" of England, Germany, and Russia, among other moves. Would this increase the danger of war? Less, argued Angell, than any other policy.[30]

Angell's uncharacteristically drastic proposals sharpened the public expression of underlying differences within the labour movement. Before the Ruhr crisis, the generalized and essentially negative protests against British and Allied actions tended to conceal a growing rift on international issues. Despite the comparative moderation of Lloyd George's policy in 1921 and 1922, various wings of Labour could fairly comfortably engage in criticism without having to depart from the somewhat theoretical proposals for action of a minority party with little prospect of having to undertake responsible government. Little was made of the fixing of a final sum for reparations, since the policy itself was held to be at fault. It was easy to condemn the failure of the Cannes conference, where Lloyd George and his French counterpart Aristide Briand came close to accommodation about reparations and the future of the Anglo-French *entente*. When delegates from some twenty-nine European states, including Germany and Russia, failed when they gathered at Genoa to make constructive progress towards the postwar reconstruction of Europe, Labour's criticism was, in the long run, more effective in helping to undermine the position of Lloyd George as head of his postwar coalition than in providing any realistic alternatives to his efforts at international pacification. Similarly, when fear of a war with Turkey led to condemnation of Lloyd George's support of Greece in the tangled Greco-Turkish conflict in the eastern Mediterranean, Labour's position was richer in censure than it was in specific and concrete proposals for action. An exception, perhaps, was the outcome of the Washington conference of November 1921 to February 1922. Arthur Balfour, as head of the British delegation, agreed to a scrapping of capital ships under construction, a ten-year moratorium on all new construction and a ratio in capital ships of 5, 5, 3, 1.75, 1.75 for the United States, Great Britain, Japan, France, and Italy respectively. Concern that Britain was abandoning her long-time insistence on naval supremacy and accepting parity with the United States was not shared in Labour circles where there was satisfaction at the modest limitation of naval armaments, but even here comment was relatively meager when compared to the repetitive sweeps of general denunciation.[31]

The question of how to deal with the German default of reparation payments and the Franco-Belgian occupation of the Ruhr sharpened the differences within the labour movement. Approaches to both the revival of Germany and the integration of Soviet Russia into the European system depended upon the evaluation of the new international institutions that had emerged from the war. Labour had played a key role in campaigning for the creation of a League of Nations, but the body that came into existence was much more limited than most Labour advocates had wished. The fact that it had no provision for "popular" representation, that Germany and Russia were excluded, and that the United States did not participate, its limited purposes, even its inclusion in the hated Versailles Treaty, all contributed to a widespread suspicion that informed virtually all components of the labour movement. On the left, mistrust of capitalist governments and the conviction that the League was simply an alliance of the victorious Allies prompted either a total rejection or the call for so drastic a revision of the organization as to make it an entirely different body. Disapproval of the use of force as an instrument of coercion, even in the hands of an international body, continued to sway large sections of the left throughout the two decades leading up to the Second World War. Many of the more moderate elements shared in the disapproval. Even the few who accepted the need for military sanctions in the conduct of international affairs did so only reluctantly and often with the implied caveat that they would probably never have to be used.

From early on, a few of Labour's prominent spokesmen had insisted that it was essential to work within the system that actually existed, rather than dream of some perfect new world which would be long in coming. They were assisted by several of the members of the Advisory Committee on International Questions, including Leonard Woolf, its secretary, and Will Arnold Forster, whose contribution was to be increasingly important as time went on. Like a number of other young recruits to Labour, Arnold Forster came from a staunchly Tory middle-class family but had been driven by the failures of conventional diplomacy to seek surcease for the world in the new, League-oriented system of international organization. Both advisers tended to be cautious and limited in their proposals, no doubt because of the differences within the committee itself. Once the French had made their move, Arnold Forster explored, in a pamphlet published by the UDC, a number of solutions to the Ruhr impasse and suggested that a possible approach might be a reciprocal agreement so that both Germany and France could be reassured. Significantly, his proposal resembled the later Locarno agreements sponsored by the Tory government a couple of years later.[32] Subsequently, the Advisory Committee, submitting that the French had committed an act of war, argued that the British government should have invoked the League of Nations and called upon the French to turn to the League before acting alone. While the Committee outlined in some detail what a Labour government might have done if it had been in office, its positive contribution was to counsel against any precipitate British withdrawal from the Rhineland, while at the same time advising against a settlement of the reparations question so long as the French remained in the Ruhr. For the most part, the Committee refrained from offering controversial and combative suggestions, certainly a far cry from the demands of much of the Labour left.[33]

Not only the left, however, censured the French action. To be sure, the most passionate condemnation throughout the period of occupation was to be found in the pages of ILP organs such as *Forward,* the *Bradford Pioneer,* and especially the *New Leader,* but they were joined by the *Daily Herald* and even by the *New Statesman*, which as yet usually reflected the moderate right of Labour opinion.[34] Above all, E.D. Morel, in *Foreign Affairs,* kept up a barrage of attack on France and support for Germany.[35] Neither these organs of opinion nor the spokesmen of both the ILP and the UDC had very much use for the existing League of Nations as an instrument for dealing with either the occupation or the reparations issue itself. The ILP, in particular, was beginning to draw away from the majority of the Labour Party who were coming to accept that responsible policy required negotiation and compromise, concepts to which the ILP's National Administrative Committee (NAC) gave relatively short shrift. Instead, in addition to its usual attack upon the whole European settlement, it attempted to make common cause with the Socialist and Labour parties of Germany, France, and Belgium. As was usually the case during this period, such proposed collaboration was strong in rhetoric, but, perhaps predictably, less than persuasive regarding possible concrete courses of action. On the issue of British withdrawal of troops from the Rhineland, as a way of putting pressure on the French and Belgians, some of the pacifists in the party questioned whether the party should support a policy that might in the long run require the use of force if the French refused to leave the Ruhr. One such critic was John Wheatley, a Glaswegian Catholic who had been prominent in the fight for better housing for the working classes of the Clydeside. His appearance as a mild, avuncular figure behind thick glasses belied the sharpness of his intellect and the passion of his concern for the popular welfare. A future cabinet member, he argued that an aggressive British military policy to get France out of the Ruhr would simply serve the economic interests of British capitalists who wanted to substitute their own interests for those of the French. Wheatley and those pacifists who supported him, such as the fiery James Maxton, were a small minority when the ILP met in conference and adopted, despite NAC opposition, an amendment, which the minority considered dangerous, calling for British withdrawal from the Rhineland.[36]

For its part, the Labour Party in conference accepted a long resolution on foreign policy, moved by Ramsay MacDonald, that included a protest against the French occupation as an act of aggression and of war. It called upon the British government to use every effort to induce the parties concerned to come together in negotiation or to submit their differences to an impartial tribunal. It further insisted that reparation payments should be limited to what was required to restore the devastated areas of France and Belgium, that a generous attitude be taken in the matter of inter-Allied war debts, and that all the Allied armies should be withdrawn immediately from Germany. As usual, there was the call for a world peace conference to revise the peace treaties in accordance with the needs of European political and economic reconstruction. In supporting the relative moderation of the Ruhr statement, MacDonald noted that it would be very easy to go at it "like a bull at a gate," but that would not have helped the Ruhr, nor would it have helped the party, nor would it have helped Europe. What was needed was not a demonstration or a general resolution, but proposals and propositions that had a precise bearing on the problem as it was at present. Whether or not the Labour Party resolution was as precise as MacDonald suggested, it differed from the position of the ILP, of which MacDonald was still nominally a member, especially when it viewed with alarm the possibility of a division between the British and French people.[37]

Beyond the issues of European security and the balance of power between Germany and France that the Ruhr accented, its basic economic implications were high on the list of Labour's criticisms. In typical Fabian fashion, Sidney Webb had used his presidential address at the conference once again to brand the treaty settlement a "factory of international inefficiency" on a quite calamitous scale. Five years after the Armistice, the complicated organization of Europe as a commercial whole had not been restored, additional barriers to the free movement of goods, people, and communications had been set up, no unified transportation system had been ventured, and penury and privation almost universally prevailed. The treaties had failed because they ignored both morality and economics. To make the weakest pay for the war was self-defeating. What was needed was a policy of mutual service, not the deliberate pursuit of profits whether for the individual at the expense of other individuals or for the nation at the expense of other nations.[38]

Conference action was paralleled by a long resolution adopted by the Parliamentary Party which declared that no settlement could be reached which assumed that Germany should be dismembered further, that German sovereignty should be limited by outside authority, or that it should be kept permanently in a state of economic vassalage. The resolution further called for the immediate fixing of the German financial responsibility, an international loan secured on German resources to enable reparation payments to be made, and a special session of the League of Nations to arrange for the admission of Germany and to settle conditions of national security in Europe. To promote such a settlement the Parliamentary Party declared that Britain should be prepared to be generous in regard to war debts, mandates, and forfeited property. Finally, the MPs welcomed counter-proposals made by the German government as a basis for negotiation between the German and Allied governments and urged that a conference be called immediately to deal with the reparation issue.[39]

Whatever may have been the general sense of the Parliamentary Party's resolution, the differences that underlay it had been made evident in an earlier debate on the address in the Commons. There, J. R. Clynes, in particular, made it his business to insist that the League of Nations could be used to promote Labour's purposes. It was right and proper to battle for improvement, but meanwhile it made sense to help make what existed as efficient as possible. Clynes had made that point as early as 1919. Now that the general election of 1922 had made Labour the official opposition in Parliament, it was imperative to address the Ruhr invasion and the crisis it had engendered. That could only be done through the League of Nations, which was the instrument through which revision of the peace treaties could take place. Britain should try to improve the League, not to substitute some other body or create a rival body.

Neither Philip Snowden nor E. D, Morel showed the same concern for the use of the League as did Clynes. Morel essentially bypassed the League in calling for a world conference to deal not only with the Ruhr issue but the whole postwar settlement. Snowden, for his part, seemed to see such a conference as being called not only to deal with the peace treaties, but also to reconstruct—or indeed to construct—a new and efficient League. Even Ramsay MacDonald spent most of his time outlining the failures of Bonar Law's government and the inadequacies of the League rather than in any argument for its use in dealing with the Ruhr question. In much more sharp contrast to the Morels and Snowdens, Arthur Henderson summed up for Labour by insisting that he could not understand why the Ruhr issue had not been referred to the League of Nations. He agreed that the League was not all that it should be and that it needed to be reformed, but surely it was better to use the international body than to deal with the problem as was being done by the French government.[40]

By now Henderson and MacDonald were beginning to make the case for working within the existing international system while pressing for its improvement. However much they differed in their interpretation of how Labour should approach the task, both recognized the constraints that limited the freedom of action of any policymakers and both were determined that Labour must be prepared to play its role responsibly, at home through the instruments of the parliamentary system, abroad in collaboration with actors with whom they might often disagree but with whom it was essential to reach some measure of accommodation. Given the temper of so many of his followers, MacDonald showed real courage when he greeted the response of the Bonar Law government to the French invasion with a degree of approval. It was poor spirited, he wrote, and might not be pursued to the end, but in all honesty Labour must admit that it dealt with the big problems and uttered the true warnings. What was needed now was for an impartial committee of experts to work out the economic problem—and that was the only point that should be of concern. Such a view, however obscured it was in the almost impenetrable verbiage of MacDonald's prose, was a far cry from the almost total negativism that still flourished in large portions of the labour movement.

MacDonald's approach to both the economic and the political ramifications of the Ruhr issue demonstrated how substantially he was beginning to modify his earlier assumptions. During the war, most particularly in an important little book called *National Defence,* he had argued, and continued to believe, that the only way to provide for national security was "to remove the fears and arbitrate upon the misunderstandings and rivalries which grow into conflicts when armies are available and the possession of force is an inducement to rulers to be unbending." Consistently, he remained skeptical of the use of force, whether employed by an individual nation or even under the control of an international body. But he had also argued that the only way to deal with those fears and misunderstandings and rivalries was to do away with the secret diplomacy that enabled foreign offices, and ministries of war, and the newspapers that supported them to rouse the public which in times of peace was always against war. He did not assume that "open diplomacy" would do away with the causes of war, but he argued that it would enable those causes to dissipate themselves without an explosion. "Secret diplomacy" he wrote, "acts upon national rivalry as a confining chamber acts upon a high explosive." Capitalist rivalries and pressure for national expansion would provide plenty of causes for future wars, but open diplomacy would prevent those causes from generating disruptive force. Now, as the Tory government struggled with the complexities of the European impasse, he had less and less to say about the virtues of open diplomacy and more about the technical decisions, however made, that needed to be addressed.[41]

As for Henderson, as secretary of the party he was in close touch with the advisory committees which on the whole bolstered his conviction that Labour must accept the reality of working within a system of national governments which often had different priorities and certainly a different outlook from those of Labour. This required negotiation and compromise, both of which could increasingly be pursued through the existing League of Nations. It was not a perfect instrument; it needed revision, particularly to be more inclusive, but if the world was to escape from the cycle of tension, armaments, alliances, and war, the League, however flawed, was the one real hope for international cooperation in the future. One other difference was to become increasingly important during the course of the next few years. Unlike MacDonald and many others who consistently suspected the use of force by an international body no less than by national governments, Henderson was, step by step, becoming firmer in his conviction that any international body would require the ultimate sanction of military force in order to be effective in its task of keeping the peace. Doubtlessly, he frequently skipped over his conviction that effective sanctions, in the final analysis, implied resort to military action because the sharp differences within the labour movement made such caution tactically inevitable. The differences of approach, while significant, were not seriously disruptive so long as Labour was a tiny minority whose only effective weapon was the rhetoric of dissent. But as Labour came closer to the position of a viable alternative to the majority Conservatives, the issue of sanctions was one which virtually tore the party asunder over the next fifteen years. Nevertheless, the reality of the Paris peace treaties had forced the party leadership to shift its position on foreign policy. Slowly, between the end of the war and Labour's first assumption of office in 1924, some of Labour's spokesmen had begun to supplant a highly idealized vision of the postwar world with a more pragmatic program. By the time Labour assumed office, they were more ready than before the war to confront a series of prickly foreign policy issues with more realistic approaches.

4

The First Labour Government

The first Labour government faced daunting tasks as it assumed office in 1924. Almost immediately, it had to deal with German default of reparations and French occupation of the Ruhr. As the fledgling administration moved to follow through on the Tory government's tentative initiative on the reparations question, the customary critics muted their concerns for the time being. For the most part, the doubters waited to see how effectively their leaders would carry out the policies they took to be those of the larger labour movement. Foreign policy took a back seat.

In the circumstances of the time, MacDonald's decision to combine the foreign secretaryship with his prime ministerial duties was probably a wise one. Sidney Webb later pointed out that this left MacDonald as foreign minister without the advantage of "experiencing the check of consultation with the P.M." [1] On the other hand, it may well be that in the international arena the ambiguities of MacDonald's personality and philosophy were assets. Over the years he had made few close connections within the labour movement. He was not a trade unionist, but neither was he a natural member of the affluent classes whose social company he increasingly appeared to enjoy. Each section of Labour could see him as its man, prepared to fight for its particular version of the foreign policy of a Labour government. [2] By now MacDonald shared the conviction of a Clynes or a Henderson that Labour had to accommodate its policies to the real world in which it had to operate. At the same time, though his estrangement from the ILP was well under the way, he continued to share many of its convictions, including a suspicion of the use of military power for whatever reason and considerable skepticism about the value of the current League of Nations. The ambivalence of the movement he was leading was perhaps best symbolized by the appointment of Arthur Ponsonby, pacifist and one of the stalwarts of the UDC, as his undersecretary for foreign affairs, while the quite differently minded Arthur Henderson went off to negotiate at the League of Nations in Geneva.

The healing of the wounds over foreign policy since the wartime split in the labour movement has probably been exaggerated. The restraint from criticism, particularly from the left, was as much the result of unwillingness to undermine the authority of the first-ever Labour government as a reflection of any underlying agreement on fundamental issues of policy. In addition, many of the same critics would have agreed with the *New Statesman* when it warned against pushing the French too hard and running the risk of ensuring the return of the intransigent Raymond Poincaré in the forthcoming French elections.[3] For the most part, the doubters waited to see how effectively their leaders would carry out the policies they took to be those of the broader labour movement. [4]

For example, H. N. Brailsford, often the most penetrating of the critics of the official leadership, praised MacDonald for undertaking a policy of persuasion and constructive adjustments that might bring the dangerous quarrel with France to a successful resolution.[5] The *Daily Herald,* still often negative and suspect by much of the leadership despite being taken over by the party, continued to damn the policies of the French, but it nevertheless expressed its confidence in the intentions of the new government and praised its influence on the psychology of European diplomacy.[6] Even Morel's *Foreign Affairs* marked time, although its editor's comments continued to be typically acerbic.[7]

The reparations issue was concerned at bottom with the difficult matter of the balance of power between Germany and France. The Baldwin government had begun the task of reconciling the French insistence on security with the German need for economic revival quickened by a realistic assessment of her reparations obligations. The foreign secretary, Lord Curzon, had supported the setting up of an expert body to examine the reparations question. His advocacy had helped trigger the establishment by the Reparations Commission of two committees of experts for that purpose. MacDonald moved pragmatically and with patience to follow through on his predecessor's initiative.[8] In doing so he was not favored by any unanimity of opinion among his officials. Among them both Sir Eyre Crowe and Sir John Troutbeck, long-time fixtures in the Foreign Office, saw German aspirations as continuing to pose a real threat to the peace of Europe, while others, such as Sir Arthur Nicolson and Sir Miles Lampson stressed German weakness as making dubious her capability to challenge the status quo. Troutbeck, in particular, argued that the Germans were not ready for democratic government, that they needed to be led and drilled, and that soon they would find a new leader and the new Germany would again prove a danger to Great Britain.[9] Most of the officials, nevertheless, supported a policy of conciliation as the best hope for a viable Europe in the future.

Not only the civil servants in the Foreign Office but the Labour Party's own Advisory Committee on International Questions also offered its views on the

Ruhr quandary. Its first suggestion was that the British should use their position at Cologne, where British troops served in the Allied occupation of the Rhineland, as a bargaining counter with France while attempting to mobilize "world opinion" behind a reasonable settlement. Optimistically, the committee proposed that the Labour Party issue a "Manifesto to the Peoples of the World" designed to demonstrate the superiority of Labour's democratic methods of diplomacy to those of other parties and other governments. With the passage of time the Committee became more aware of the realities of the international situation, which required working with other nations towards effective compromise. A long memorandum entitled "Labour, the League and Reparations" now argued that success could only be achieved by approaching some middle ground. Nothing could be done unilaterally. While the memo outlined a long-term policy of supporting the League of Nations, it also advised that the time for the League in the matter of reparations was not yet ripe. Any attempt of the League to force a settlement was likely to be an obstacle rather than a help.[10]

Whatever use he may have made of the varied advice—and the British Treasury did not share his enthusiasm for the work of the British and American bankers who helped draft the report of the international committee established under the chairmanship of the American General Dawes—MacDonald proceeded with great skill to deal with that report.[11] He recognized, of course, the validity of the French fixation on security and took into account the Service departments' conviction that France and Britain were mutually dependent on one another from a military point of view. But he was no more willing than any other British statesman to offer France any clear-cut military guarantee against Germany. Instead, he insisted on treating reparations as a technical question, to be dealt with in advance of any formal consideration of the issue of security. His approach to Raymond Poincaré, the French premier, was cordial but firm, and his position was made substantially more viable when the more flexible Edouard Herriot succeeded the intractable Poincaré after the French elections. Another factor, the threat of a group of allies ganging up on France and isolating her, was strengthened by the vulnerable position of French finances which made continuation of the Ruhr occupation less and less attractive.[12] Far from holding to the often easy certainties of his party when it was in opposition, MacDonald handled the delicate discussions with tact and sensitivity, achieving most of his desired settlement while appearing to offer significant concessions to the requirements of the French. Once the Dawes Report proposed a financial framework within which Germany might be able to meet reparation payments, he was able to facilitate the implementation of the program and to negotiate with the French for their withdrawal from the Ruhr, not after two years, as the French desired, but after a delay of only one. In all of this, he was close to the thinking of the majority of the officials in the Foreign Office.

Perhaps for that reason, once the shape of the reparations settlement became public, criticism from within the ranks of Labour began to surface. Morel, for example, denounced the conclusion of the Committee of Experts set up by the Dawes Committee on Germany's capacity to pay. The Report, in his view, could have no other consequence than total disaster. As usual, his proposals argued that any settlement should have been made with Germany as an equal and should have included the evacuation of troops from German soil. In addition, he repeated earlier demands for the cancellation of all French and Italian debts to Britain, the immediate entrance of Germany and Russia into the League of Nations, and the calling of a world conference to discuss disarmament. The UDC Executive Committee, for its part, advised the French and German governments to accept the Dawes Plan. At the same time it followed Morel in his various demands and made no bones about the fact that it considered the Dawes scheme a miscarriage of international justice. [13]

Paralleling the ambivalence of the UDC, Brailsford in the *New Leader* suggested that the labour movement had accepted the Dawes Report with many mental reservations. It was a typical bankers' scheme, threatening the German workers in a variety of ways and in the interest of private capitalism. Yet, somewhat like the UDC, he expressed the hope that MacDonald would be able to turn the Report into a viable settlement.[14] And Lansbury, while he kept many of his doubts to himself, confessed to Beatrice Webb that he felt somewhat like a criminal for doing so.[15] More serious, perhaps, was the criticism from within MacDonald's cabinet itself. Philip Snowden, reflecting the financial conservatism that was to continue to characterize his future political career, openly criticized the Dawes agreement, seeing it as a betrayal of British trade interests and infuriating the French by his denunciation of their policy.[16]

The government's actions created substantial uneasiness among some of the leaders of the Trades Union Congress. A somewhat moderate delegation, for example, waited upon the prime minister to protest the fact that German workers were to have 10 percent deducted from their wages to pay for reparations. In like fashion, the General Council's statements at the TUC's annual meeting hardly concealed its doubts about the settlement. While the left-wing strictures of A. A. Purcell, who was president of the 1924 meeting, might have been taken for granted, they served as the prelude to a resolution, in part designed as a signal to the government, which instructed the General Council to convene a special congress to consider industrial action in the event of the danger of war.[17] A few dissenting voices were even heard at the conference of the Labour Party when it met in London in October. There the report of the Parliamentary Party, which of course had accepted and propagated the policy of the Dawes plan, was censured by one or two delegates (including the communist member for St. Pancras, S. Saklatvala), who contended that the scheme would lead to slavery for the workers of Germany as well as those at home.[18]

Otherwise, the Party supported the government in its steps to implement the Dawes proposals.

Concern over the handling of reparations was paralleled by suspicion that the government had abandoned Labour's commitment to the policy of "open diplomacy." The Union of Democratic Control had been founded in 1914 in large part to insist on the jettisoning of the old-style diplomacy which was held to be largely responsible for the coming of the war. By the end of the war the labour movement as a whole, at least nominally, had come to accept the rhetoric of open diplomacy. But it was the UDC, partnered by the ILP, which insisted, now that Labour was in office, that the government should establish a Foreign Affairs or Foreign Relations Committee in the Commons on the American model and that no treaties and agreements should be entered into without the prior consent of Parliament.

Although he had been one of the founders of the UDC and had occasionally written in support of open diplomacy, MacDonald in office showed no enthusiasm for the policy. To be sure, Ponsonby informed the House of Commons that treaties and agreements that might imply certain obligations on Britain's part would now be placed before both houses of the legislature for twenty-one days to permit discussion under the normal procedures of Parliament.[19] While accepted as a first step, the Ponsonby declaration was a far cry from the Parliamentary resolution that Morel and others wanted time to introduce, proposing sweepingly that no diplomatic arrangement or understanding with a foreign state which involved national obligations, whether direct or indirect, should be concluded without the consent of Parliament. The resolution further intended that no military preparations with the staffs of a foreign country be permitted unless subsequent to Parliamentary approval of the diplomatic arrangements or understandings. Both the General Council of the Trades Union Congress and the Executive of the Labour Party agreed to petition the prime minister for time to be given in the House to discuss the Morel resolution.[20]

By now Ponsonby was sensitive to the difficulties of a policy which he too, as one of the UDC's original five, had trumpeted over the years. Parading the objections in a letter to Morel, he now insisted that demonstrations or resolutions would be of little help. Instead democratic control required education, watchfulness, discussion, and parliamentary intervention.[21] When the government noted in the House of Commons that no time could be found to debate the Morel motion, the Parliamentary Party approved a resolution expressing deep regret that "in view of the unanimous support given by the Party to the request...the Government has not seen fit to accede to the request." It went on to ask that if necessary the session be extended by one day in order that the question be discussed in the House of Commons.[22] Despite the concerns of the Parliamentary Party, however, the government was not prepared to go beyond the Ponsonby statement to the House. What it meant was that any treaty would be placed in the House of Commons Library where MPs could read it.[23] Nevertheless, the so-called Ponsonby Rule helped in the Parliamentary ventilation of some issues of foreign policy, while the Labour government's positive response to Morel's campaign for the publication of the documents on pre-war diplomacy led to the appearance of G. P. Gooch and H. W. V. Temperley's important volumes on the *Origins of the War.*

Significant differences within the labour movement over reparations and open diplomacy were reflected when the Draft Treaty of Mutual Assistance was taken up. It may be stretching a bit to say that the Labour Party's wartime split over foreign policy had gradually healed during the five postwar years,[24] but it does seem clear that the need to support a Labour government, in office for the first time, created a tendency to downplay differences which earlier would have precipitated sharp conflict. A case in point may be found in the reaction of the *Bradford Pioneer* to the Draft Treaty. The northern paper, a firm supporter of the ILP, was reluctant to condemn the Draft Treaty in an unqualified fashion. Admitting the proposal's faults from Labour's point of view, the *Pioneer* nevertheless argued that the project was the only practical one likely to lead to a measure of disarmament. Precisely because MacDonald was the leader of a party that had supported the use of the League of Nations to ensure security, it would be dangerous for him to reject the first major scheme devised by the League to deal with issues of security and disarmament.[25]

The *Pioneer*'s reluctant acceptance of the Draft Treaty was nevertheless something of an anomaly. There is no doubt that the Draft Treaty was regarded with substantial suspicion in all quarters of the labour movement. Lord Robert Cecil had been involved in the formulation of the proposal and it had been adopted by the League of Nations Assembly in 1923. The crux of the Draft Treaty was the obligation of signatories to come to the aid of the victims of aggressive war. It was left to the League Council to decide when such aggression had occurred. There was a regional aspect to the proposals. Only those states in the same region as the injured party were to be required to provide military assistance, while the arrangements, in turn, were to be conditional upon the institution of a measure of disarmament within a period of two years. Clearly, the Draft Treaty echoed the position of most French leaders on the issue of national security, but it was almost universally suspect in Britain, not only in labour circles, but among virtually all of the official and Service advisers to the government as well.

A long Advisory Committee memorandum mirrored a statement issued by the Executive Committee of the UDC, which argued that the Draft Treaty would turn the League of Nations into an organ to maintain the balance of power, "reposing, as before, upon armaments and inspired, as before, by the conception that peace can be secured by preparing for war."[26] The preparation of the Advisory Committee document by Morel and Lowes Dickinson, the Cambridge don who by now had completed his journey from Conservatism through Liberalism into the Labour Party, ensured that it would give short shrift to the assumptions of the Draft Treaty. Morel and Dickinson argued that there was no way to achieve common acceptance of definitions of aggressive and defensive acts of war. By providing for the establishment of sectional military alliances, the Draft Treaty, far from acting to abolish war, which ought to be the main function of the League of Nations, was instead going to prepare for war and ratify the maintenance and perfection of armaments in the future. Their recommendation was that the Labour Party dissociate itself from the policy of the Draft Treaty, seek the admission of Germany and Russia into the League, and work to secure widespread international opposition to the policy of the one bellicose power—France. Morel and Dickinson seemed unconcerned over the possibility that such a policy might drive France from the League. If so, they argued somewhat disingenuously, the French people might then bring in a more satisfactory government.[27]

Within the Advisory Committee the Morel-Dickinson position was subjected to a devastating critique by the American political scientist, Professor James T. Shotwell, one of the Western world's leading authorities on international organization and a strong supporter of the League of Nations. His point-by-point refutation of the memorandum noted that the document, while criticizing the Draft Treaty, offered no concrete alternative. Practically, he argued, the French had at least made a definite proposal which could be used as a basis for negotiation.[28]

The two memoranda were contributions to an extensive debate within the Advisory Committee which ultimately resulted in a decision to issue both a minority and a majority evaluation of the Draft Treaty.[29] The minority, who agreed with the Morel-Dickinson analysis of the undefined definition of aggression and the vague obligations of military action, feared that to proceed with the ideas of the Draft Treaty would run the risk of destroying the League of Nations system in its infancy. The majority, on the other hand, while it had reservations about some of the terms of the Treaty, considered that it would be disastrous to reject the result of years of international debate and compromise. Instead, they suggested amendments, the most important of which was to get a definition of aggression into the text of the Treaty itself. To that end, they proposed that each state agree to submit any dispute either to the International Court or to a court of arbitration, or alternatively to the Council of the League. Meanwhile, this group recommended, states should commit themselves to avoiding warlike actions for a limited period of time, and any state which refused to use the procedure should be deemed the aggressor. A handful of other measures reiterated suggestions that had long been part of Labour's prescription for international peace and security, but the attempt to link the willingness to submit a dispute to international consideration with the definition of aggression was by far the most important element in the majority's policy proposals. In it was to be found a central feature of the later Protocol for the Pacific Settlement of International Disputes—the Geneva Protocol.[30]

MacDonald's own views on military alliances and the use of force were probably more attuned to those of the minority of the Advisory Committee than to the conviction of the majority that some accommodation to the concerns of the French was essential. He believed that any military agreement with France—and the Draft Treaty could by implication be interpreted as such—was the worst possible way to provide security. Eventually, he believed, such an approach would result in war.[31] Nevertheless, when he wrote to the secretary general of the League of Nations a letter rejecting the Draft Treaty, he took a more traditional approach. His arguments followed in large measure the assessment of the Committee of Imperial Defense (CID) that the Treaty's naval, military, and air commitments for the British Empire would be almost limitless. Because of her worldwide interests, Britain, and especially her navy, would be called upon first for action, whatever the regional character of a particular dispute. The CID had listed a whole host of technical objections to the Treaty arrangements and commented that any preparation in advance— and such preparation would be essential—was hardly different from the old system of alliances. Objecting to the augmented role proposed for the League Council, the Committee had made clear its judgment that the Council was an inappropriate body to control military forces in operations against any state or states. It had been especially critical, as had been most Labour commentators, of the fact that no acceptable definition of aggression was provided as the basis for implementing the procedures of the Draft Treaty. Whatever his own views, MacDonald was able to use the CID rationale as the case for British rejection of the League initiative.[32]

Rejection of the Draft Treaty appeared to make it imperative to reach out in some way to the advocates of a more active League role in the search for a stable international order. One possibility was the promotion of the Optional Clause of the Permanent Court of International Justice, which provided for the Court's compulsory jurisdiction in "justiciable" issues. Adoption of the Optional Clause was almost universally supported in the labour movement, although the purposes of such adoption often differed sharply. For some, at this stage quite clearly a minority, recourse to the Court was seen as a supplement to the possible coercive features of the international system anchored by the League of Nations. For the majority, however, the use of the Court was regarded as a substitute for the use of force as a sanction of the international system.

Most of the Labour government's official advisors were as opposed to the Optional Clause as they were to the Draft Treaty of Mutual Assistance. The Admiralty in particular feared for the exercise of the Navy's belligerent maritime rights in the event of war, while Maurice Hankey and Sir Eyre Crowe outlined the same budget of objections that had surfaced in the consideration of the Draft Treaty.[33] Hankey, who later was to serve as minister without porfolio in Neville Chamberlain's wartime government, exerted considerable influence in the deliberations of the politicians. He had been secretary to the Committee of Imperial Defence and then secretary to the cabinet and more than most officials took an aggressive stand in presenting his arguments for firm adherence to the conservative tenets of a traditional foreign policy strategy. MacDonald himself seems to have been willing to consider the Optional Clause, although he was equally willing to use the demurrers of the Admiralty and the Foreign Office in his dealings with the League.

MacDonald's visit to the League Assembly in the fall of 1924 was intended to be a gesture of cooperation and by all accounts it was notably successful. Like so many of MacDonald's public appearances this one was characterized by the quality of its rhetoric rather than by the substance of its content. Indeed, Lord Robert Cecil, not an unbiased observer to be sure, later complained that MacDonald had addressed the Assembly delegates "as if they were an English public meeting." [34] Still, MacDonald's defense of a new approach had begun before the general election of October and continued after the seating of the new government. Repeating at Geneva the reasons for his government's rejection of the Treaty of Mutual Assistance, including the danger of returning to the prewar system of alliances, he did suggest, in somewhat general terms, that the use of arbitration might be the key to the vexing question of how to identify and control the problem of aggression.[35] While the Labour press gave high marks to MacDonald for his effort, an underlying concern was evident in some of the reactions to the British appearance at Geneva. Brailsford in the *New Leader* did indeed praise both MacDonald and Herriot for their frankness at the Assembly, but he nevertheless noted that any possible use of British forces in the service of the League must be contingent on drastic disarmament by all the Allies and the abandonment of sectional alliances, and ought to take effect only when Germany at least had joined the League. Even arbitration and disarmament, Brailsford argued, would be ineffective, so long as "economic imperialism" was not addressed. Somewhat similarly, the *New Statesman*, already moving to the left, pointed out, despite its considerable differences from the *New Leader*, how difficult it would be to apply the principle of arbitration in actual practice.[36]

MacDonald's deft handling of the reparations negotiations was not paralleled as the League of Nations explored alternatives to the Draft Treaty. Once he had departed from Geneva, it was left to the various committees of the League to attempt to work out a substitute for the unacceptable Draft Treaty. It is perhaps one of the many ironies of this period that it should have been the Czech Eduard Beneš along with the Greek Nicolas Politis, both of whose countries were savaged in the failure of the international security system in the years ahead, who played a leading role in proposing a new and different approach. Essentially, they offered the unwillingness to resort to some form of peaceful settlement—arbitration, conciliation, mediation—as the test of aggression. They were supported from the British side by Lord Parmoor and

Arthur Henderson, who appear to have had an almost free hand in helping to devise that approach. Parmoor, former Conservative M.P. and father of Sir Stafford Cripps, had joined the Labour Party after the war. He was now lord president of the council and had been given special responsibilities for League of Nations affairs. Henderson, whom MacDonald had hoped to persuade to remain in charge of the Labour Party's organization and not a member of the government, was now the home secretary. Nevertheless, since the end of the war he had increasingly played a role in the formulation of Labour's foreign policy. Step by step, he had strengthened his conviction that no system of international peacekeeping would be viable without effective provisions for enforcement, a notion that MacDonald accepted, if at all, with great reluctance. Henderson's views developed during the postwar period and indeed fluctuated as he felt it necessary to respond to the conflicting currents of the divided coalition that made up the labour movement. While he was far from sharing the French elevation of military power to the central position in the provision of national security, he came to insist that an international system based on good will alone was likely to be a prescription for disaster. As a consequence, he sought some means of reconciling the British distrust of automatic and excessive military commitments with the French requirement for national security.[37]

The answer, hammered out in the Third Committee of the League's Assembly, was a proposal to substitute arbitration, accompanied by a substantial measure of disarmament, for the recourse to war in international affairs. "Arbitration" was shorthand for any of a variety of methods for the settlement of disputes. Included, of course, was the use of the Permanent Court of International Justice, where appropriate, so that the Optional Clause was in effect to be folded into the new procedure. From the beginning, however, British officials and the British cabinet approached the Committee's work with great caution. Little advance preparation or study had been given the Protocol in Whitehall. MacDonald had sought some information from Geneva, but evidently did not consult his colleagues. The Service representatives at the League were also not consulted and, as might have been expected, immediately raised many of the same objections as had been made to the Draft Treaty.[38] It is not clear whether MacDonald's dual role as prime minister and foreign secretary ensured that he would devote less than full attention to the formula emerging at Geneva. His enthusiasm for the Protocol was at best lukewarm, and it may well be that he hoped to use the Service objections, as he had concerning the Draft Treaty of Mutual Assistance, eventually to make the case that he favored for other reasons. However that may be, when the proposals were aired, Parmoor was instructed to urge that they take the form of recommendations to the member governments rather than as hard and fast commitments.

When the Protocol was presented to the Assembly, both Parmoor and Henderson spoke in its support. The latter had some reservations about particular aspects, but he was convinced that it marked a major step forward in the construction of a viable League of Nations system. Admitting that as yet the League had not won full acceptance of its moral authority and peaceful intentions, Henderson therefore understood that some states would insist on retaining the military tools to ensure their own security. The Protocol was designed to suspend the use of force to the last possible moment, and then only to protect the international community against the "criminal activity" of an aggressor state. Basically, however, he recognized that the use of military force, even if exercised as an instrument of international order, was a reality that could not be denied and should not be glossed over. Supported by the British delegation, the Protocol for the Pacific Settlement of International Disputes was accepted by the Assembly and signed by a number of countries, most notably France.[39]

The Geneva Protocol, as it came to be called, proposed to define aggression as the unwillingness to agree to some form of pacific settlement of an international quarrel. Once such aggression had been certified, the members of the League were to be pledged to use all their resources, including military force, to prevent the aggression and curb the offending state. By the time action had been completed at Geneva, the first Labour government was approaching its last days. Although Henderson in particular made it his business to promote the Protocol in a variety of venues, there was little opportunity for public discussion before the Labour Party had to face a general election at the end of October 1924. The Service Departments, as has been noted, remained as unpersuaded about the safeguards of the Geneva Protocol as they had been about the Treaty of Mutual Assistance. Their arguments continued to center about the reluctance of the Dominions, the potentially unlimited commitments that might be required, particularly on the part of the British Navy, and the impossibility of effectively defining not simply aggression, but the threat of aggression.[40]

Within the cabinet, there were evident differences of opinion. MacDonald himself was no enthusiast for sanctions. His views on the "organic" development of society spilled over, at least in theory, to his approach to international affairs. He tended to emphasize the gradual improvement of the international "atmosphere" and looked with skepticism on the use of force by the international community. Henderson, on the other hand, had by now come to believe that the League could be used effectively in the struggle for peace, but only if there were genuine teeth in its Covenant. He was sensitive to the opposition to any contemplated use of force in a substantial—perhaps even a majority— segment of his party. For tactical reasons, he sometimes deemphasized the coercive features of initiatives such as the Geneva Protocol, but there is no doubt that until the emergence of spokesmen such as Hugh Dalton, Ernest Bevin, and Walter Citrine as advocates of the use of collective force to deal with threats to international peace and security, Henderson's role in reshaping

Labour's approach to foreign policy was central.[41] In 1924, however, he faced formidable resistance to his views. In the cabinet, not only MacDonald but others demurred for a variety of reasons, some of them, reflective of Service Department's concerns, quite foreign to earlier Labour notions regarding external affairs.

Given his prewar experiences as the reorganizer of Britain's military establishment, Richard Haldane's concurrence with the opposition of the Service Departments, for example, was to be anticipated. Josiah Wedgwood and Arthur Ponsonby still clung to an earlier Radical and Labour refusal to accept that international stability might require the use at some time of the sanction of force. Even Philip Snowden, reflecting his earlier stands as an ILP stalwart, showed no great eagerness to move beyond an essentially pacifist stand.[42] Whether the first Labour government, had it remained in office, would have eventually ratified the Geneva Protocol is at best dubious. Once Labour was again in opposition, it was easy to criticize the Tory government for its rejection of the initiative. Comments by leaders of both the Union of Democratic Control and the Independent Labour Party, both before and after the change of government, are illustrative. While Ponsonby, once he was out of office, reverted to the full-fledged pacifism which he had not trumpeted in 1924, others tended to compromise their views in criticizing the new government for abandoning the lead of the League of Nations. C. R. Buxton, for example, who was later to split with colleagues in the Advisory Committee on International Questions in part over his opposition to the acceptance of coercion, concluded that the Protocol did indeed commit nations to the application of force. The price was worth paying, he concluded, in a world in which pure pacifism was not yet a reality.[43] Helena Swanwick, a key figure in the UDC, had been like Buxton a British delegate to the League's Fifth Assembly. She was what has been called a "pacificist" rather than a pacifist. She believed that while war was always an irrational and inhuman way to settle disputes, it might sometimes be necessary. Despite her record of opposition to almost all forms of sanctions, she now concluded that neither the reduction of armaments nor the abandonment of the balance of power would be achieved unless the powers could be guaranteed the international sanction of force. Her departure from the ranks of the opponents of armed sanctions was short-lived and, after the new Tory government had taken office, she soon was emphasizing disarmament and arbitration as substitutes for the use of force rather than as part of a system that ultimately might require some measure of coercion.[44]

By far the most penetrating of the left-wing assessments of the Geneva Protocol came, as frequently was the case, from the pen of H. N. Brailsford. Labeling it "the biggest and happiest thing which has happened in the world since the peace was marred at Versailles," he nevertheless pointed out that its function was essentially to defend the status quo. Its procedure for the prevention or outlawing of war was perhaps the best that conventional thinking could devise, but, he asked, did it make provision for the need for peaceful change in the world? As he read the proposal, any one state in the Assembly could veto any change in the existing—often unjust—international treaties.[45] At the moment the issue of peaceful change, which had been raised in Labour circles especially at the end of the war, was hardly in the forefront of Labour's immediate agenda, but in the years of opposition after 1924 it was to loom somewhat larger in Labour's redefinition of the aims of its foreign policy.

These somewhat qualified individual acceptances of the Geneva Protocol were paralleled by the UDC when its twenty-third General Council met as the Labour government was approaching its end. Included in a budget of resolutions, such as the usual ones on secret diplomacy or the evacuation of the Cologne area, was a long section on the Geneva Protocol. The arrangement, declared the Council, constituted a substantial amendment of the League Covenant in that it (1) greatly extended the principles of arbitral, judicial and mediatory settlement and (2) defined and limited the use of the sanctions already to be found in the Covenant. Since the Protocol would give a universal guarantee of security under the League it was greatly to be preferred to any form of partial defensive alliance outside the League. Accordingly, the UDC Council urged the government to recommend ratification to Parliament, in order that a Disarmament Conference might be held, and that the next League Assembly might consider, and if necessary enact, the amendments to the Covenant proposed in the Protocol.[46] The position adopted by the UDC was a considerable change from earlier postures. In the early postwar years—indeed until the assumption of office by the Labour Party—the UDC, while paying lip service to the League, was quite clear that its priorities did not include vigorous support for the existing international organization. Whether a reform such as that proposed in the Protocol would have significantly altered the posture of the UDC and others on the Labour left is conjectural, but highly unlikely in the light of positions adhered to in the years that followed.

MacDonald's handling of the Geneva Protocol tended to be more characteristic of his approach than was his treatment of the reparations issue. In the latter case, his hand was evident in every step of the complicated negotiations designed to implement the recommendations of the Experts' Committee. This was different from his procedure on most issues. Generally, he abstained from taking part in the early stages of foreign policy formulation and instead put a premium on rapid decision making once a matter was brought to his attention.[47]

Perhaps this helps explain Labour's embarrassments in dealing with the Russian Bolsheviks, embarrassments that helped lead to the withdrawal of Liberal support from the minority Labour government. Recognition of the Soviet regime, which had the support of all branches of the Labour movement, came quickly. Most of the rank and file had little access to the sources of information which early on persuaded most mainstream leaders of the movement that the new Soviet regime had little in common with the democratic socialism they espoused. But many of those same leaders, for their part, were equally persuaded that Russia, just as was the case for Germany, must become a full-fledged participant in the international affairs of Europe if there was to be a real chance for normal relations to be developed. Beyond that, many viewed the substantial population in Eastern Europe as potentially a very profitable trading partner.

Recognition was followed by a conference to deal with various issues that separated the two countries. Most important were the claims of British bond-holders over tsarist government's debts that had been repudiated by the Bolsheviks and the Soviet demand for a loan to be guaranteed by the British government. MacDonald was more than fully occupied with the Reparations Conference, to say nothing of a crisis in Ireland, so that he left it to his undersecretary Ponsonby to handle the negotiations in London for a possible treaty. Ponsonby appears to have been less than a subtle and skillful spokesman, although it must be said that in C. G. Rakovsky, the chief Russian representative, he found an opposite number of substantial rigidity, largely because the Russian delegation was not authorized to make any but the most minor of decisions.

When Rakovsky returned to Moscow, whether for instructions or as a negotiating tactic, Ponsonby called upon colleagues outside the government for help. Writing to E. D. Morel he suggested that it would be useful if Morel could get in touch with Rakovsky in Moscow "from yourself or your group" to urge him to do his utmost to conclude an agreement—and whatever else they might want to add.[48] The Morel group complied and also asked George Lansbury to send a wire. Subsequently, when negotiations broke down, several MPs led by Morel and A. A. Purcell, the left wing TUC activist, once again intervened and the deliberations were resumed. MacDonald was kept informed of the course of negotiations, but there is no evidence that he knew of the overtures to Morel and the others. While there is no suggestion of venality or even inappropriate behavior on Ponsonby's part, his judgment, in the delicate circumstances of the time when Labour was so dependent on Liberal support in the House of Commons, can be faulted.[49] Although the initiative appears to have come from Ponsonby, both Conservatives and Liberals portrayed the issue as one in which a group of pro-Soviet extremists in the Labour Party had put pressure on the government to reach an agreement with the Russians. When taken together with the handling of the Campbell case—in itself a relatively inconsequential issue involving a communist editor—by both Sir Patrick Hastings, the attorney general, and MacDonald himself, the Russian question prompted Liberal withdrawal of support and the subsequent assumption of office by the Tories.

As for the Russian arrangements themselves, one document provided for a commercial treaty with the unusual feature of giving diplomatic immunity to a number of representatives in the Russian trade mission to Britain. The second made a guaranteed loan to Russia contingent upon a general treaty signalizing some measure of movement on the question of obligations to bondholders. For the most part Labour circles saw the agreement as a major step in the normalization of relations with Russia. For Ponsonby, who subsequently wrote the introduction to a Labour Party pamphlet of explanation, the treaties helped stabilize the Anglo-Russian connections and would contribute to the fight against unemployment, while others, such as J.R. Clynes, took satisfaction from the fact that Russia was no longer a threat to the peace and would take her place in the diplomatic give and take of the European world. [50]

Altogether, given the inexperience of most of its members and its vulnerable minority status, the performance of the first Labour government on matters of foreign policy was impressive. MacDonald's handling of the reparations question, in particular, was both skillful and balanced, working to give Germany the financial stability she so desperately needed, while providing France with the concessions that made it possible for her to withdraw from an almost impossible position. The success, to be sure, was short-lived, but for the moment it helped in the appeasement of European tensions until the impact of the world economic collapse once again changed the terms of reference within which the issues of international relations were played out.

For the moment, as well, there seemed to be a lessening of the differences that had divided the labour movement so sharply during and immediately after the First World War. When Labour took office, the disparate elements of the movement had tended to downplay their disagreements. The underlying tensions, however, still remained. On such issues as Parliament's part in the making of foreign policy or, more urgently in the years ahead, the role of force in the conduct of international affairs, there were significant challenges to beliefs long taken virtually for granted in the labour movement. In the five years before Labour's next assumption of office, the case for a foreign policy based upon support for and cooperation with the nascent League of Nations began to be developed by a group of young activists. They faced serious challenges from other Labourites who saw the League of Nations as simply a conspiracy of capitalist and imperialist states to maintain their own power and the positions of their ruling classes. Still others rejected what they saw as the contradiction of the use of force to ensure the peace, especially in the hands of a League they mistrusted. As it tried to reach agreement among its various elements, Labour attempted to refine its prescriptions for dealing with the external world.

5

The Locarno Era

Most Labour leaders were increasingly convinced that a sound international order required the fullest use of the League of Nations and an accommodation with other nations. Arthur Henderson, in particular, turned to a group of younger men to help him argue for the pursuit of British interests through collaboration with a strengthened international organization backed by the sanction of adequate force. By the general election of 1929, in large part under the leadership of that group, Labour had continued its journey away from the almost total repudiation of capitalist and imperialist governments that had stemmed from the disillusionment of the immediate postwar period. Slowly, Labour was moving into the mainstream of European and indeed world politics.

Henderson's prescription for the international order was not shared by MacDonald. Despite MacDonald's quite evident foreign policy success in his brief tenure of office, his leadership was questioned in various quarters of the labour movement. Henderson himself confided to Beatrice Webb that some thirty MPs, including Lansbury, Wedgwood, Trevelyan, and a number of Clydesiders, were planning to force MacDonald out of the leadership. At the same time, Ernest Bevin of the Transport and General Workers Union also led an initiative with the same purpose. Although his chief scorn was reserved for the left of the labour movement, Bevin had little use for "intellectuals," by which he meant most politicians. He gave his trust slowly and had little use for conciliation, yet by sheer force of character—and the weight of his trade union position—he increasingly played a role in the shaping of Labour's political positions. More than a "working-class John Bull," he was mercurial in his moods, at one point displaying deep sensitivity to the problems of other human beings, at another striking out at opponents with anger and prejudice. He was uncomfortable with the give-and-take of the House of Commons, where indeed he did not serve until he took his place in Churchill's wartime government.[1] But increasingly, from the 1920s, he was a major force to be reckoned with as British Labour moved towards political maturity.

Bevin, checked by Henderson—who regarded MacDonald as indispensable to the labour movement, however much they clashed both as personalities and on matters of policy—next attempted to have the Labour Party pledge not to take office unless it gained a Parliamentary majority. He argued that without such a majority the party could not carry out the policies demanded by the British working people. Nor was Bevin alone in the trade union movement to question the leadership of MacDonald. The left-wing A. J. Cook of the Miners Federation, for example, garnered substantial support among the trade unions when he branded the Dawes Plan a conspiracy of Anglo-American capitalists. Although major trade unionists endorsed the reparations settlement, and Bevin's view was overwhelmingly rejected at the Liverpool conference of the Labour Party in 1925, the very fact that it was considered was testimony to the tensions which characterized the debates within the ranks of labour, not the least on matters of international policy.[2]

During the course of the five years between the first and second Labour governments, it continued to be clear that major differences of assumption separated the various groups that made up the labour movement. Many on the left continued to look to the international working class, despite its failure to act as a deterrent to the outbreak of the world war, as the only basis upon which to build a viable international order. Pacifists and quasi-pacifists—sometimes identified as pacificists—were reluctant to countenance the use of force, even in support of the organs of a League of Nations, while others looked to the development of habits of cooperation and mutual adjustment as a substitute for armaments and the arbitrament of war. Many of these attitudes harkened back to the days when Labour was a tiny propagandistic minority with only a vague dream of assuming the responsibilities of government. Now Labour's role had changed as it became realistic to aspire to the assumption of office once again. Henderson was fearful of a new system of alliances that mirrored the combinations that had helped precipitate the recent war, while at the same time he argued that popular oversight of foreign policy was necessary in order to keep diplomats and self-serving financial interests under control. MacDonald, too, despite his suspicion of the League and reluctance to envisage the use of force, nevertheless had shed many of what he regarded as the illusions of his former comrades of the left. Both men made use of the new Advisory Committee on International Questions, Henderson, in particular, turning to the group of younger men who used the committee, as well as the press and party meetings, to argue for the pursuit of British interests through collaboration with a strengthened international organization backed by the sanction of adequate force.[3]

Like Will Arnold Forster, Philip Noel Baker and Hugh Dalton came from Conservative or Liberal families. A gifted athlete, Noel Baker had been a member of the British Olympic Games team in 1912. After serving in an ambulance unit during World War I, he became a member of the British delegation at the Paris

Peace Conference. As an academic and then as a politician, he became a consistent and indefatigable advocate for the use of the League of Nations in dealing with international issues and, after World War II, received the Nobel Prize for his long-term contributions to world peace.

Beginning in the 1920s, Dalton, along with Ernest Bevin, became the most effective political figure in the transformation of Labour's foreign policy outlook. Educated at Eton and King's College, Cambridge, he had been taught by John Maynard Keynes and, as he put it, learned about socialism from Keir Hardie and Beatrice Webb. He had been sensitized during the war by the loss of numerous friends, the privations of the fighting men, the bigotry of senior officers, as well as the callous arbitrariness of the war cabinet and the high command. From the beginning, he was often accused of insincerity, cynicism, and malice, yet to his friends he was a man of feeling, humanity, and unshakable loyalty. Physically ungainly, with a great bald head too large for his shoulders and a booming voice that commanded attention, he, more than any other single figure, helped move Labour from an essentially pacifist position to supporting the armed deterrence of aggression.[4]

The expanding role of Arnold Forster, Noel Baker, and Dalton was paralleled by defections from the ILP, often for reasons having nothing to do with foreign affairs. The ILP malaise was symbolized by the split between James Maxton, who viewed MacDonald's editorship of the *Socialist Review* as drifting farther and farther away from the socialist credo, and Clifford Allen, who pleaded for tolerance in defending MacDonald's freedom of thought. The victory of the Maxton faction highlighted a trend that had already witnessed Snowden's resignation from the ILP and now resulted as well in the dismissal of Brailsford from the editorship of the *New Leader* and the transfer by both Charles Trevelyan and C. R. Buxton of their Parliamentary candidacies from the ILP to their Divisional Labour Parties.[5]

Shortly after assuming office, the Baldwin government made clear that it would have nothing to do with the Geneva Protocol. Although some, perhaps even a majority of Labour's major spokesmen had reservations about the Protocol sponsored by Henderson and Lord Parmoor, once Austen Chamberlain, the new Tory foreign secretary, moved on to explore other means of fostering European pacification and security, the virtues of the Protocol loomed larger in the eyes of many in the labour movement. Still, as Chamberlain moved to promote the western security arrangements that resulted in the Treaty of Locarno, a pact of non-aggression between France, Germany, and Belgium, guaranteed by Great Britain and Italy, there was considerable doubt as to how best to respond to his initiative. Brailsford argued in the *New Leader*, for example, that since the Baldwin government would not have the Protocol at any price, the substitute of a Western pact had to be considered on its own merits. It must include Germany and also guarantee against aggression from the French side. Although Locarno appeared generally to meet those criteria,

Brailsford was soon convinced that Chamberlain had crushed the hopes of Europe and had authored a scheme similar to the discredited alliances of past European history. As time went on he saw the pact as hazardous in the extreme. There had been risks in the Geneva Protocol, he conceded, but the conception that underlay it was the general disarmament of Europe. The Locarno Pact was neither Western nor mutual. It hoped to separate Germany from Russia, undoing the rapprochement achieved at Rapallo in 1922, when they had signed a pact of mutual understanding. Altogether, Locarno had to be regarded as both a danger and a sham.[6] Nevertheless, recognizing the reasons for the French concern for the protection of the Polish frontier, Brailsford commended Chamberlain for insisting on German participation in any pact of guarantee and for resisting French pressure to extend guarantees to France's Polish and Czech allies. France felt insecure, he concluded, only because of her resolve to dominate the European continent.[7]

Most ILP organs of opinion were less nuanced in their criticism of Tory policy. One contributor to *Forward* condemned the "fatuous faith in the League of Nations" which so many Labourites professed, while another warned his readers to get ready for the next war.[8] The *Bradford Pioneer*, even as it praised the efforts of Henderson and Parmoor, deplored the fact that the League was at present inspired by no more than traditional Liberal ideas, while the *Socialist Review* professed to see foreign policy turning again to the parceling out of the world among the Great Powers. It faulted the Parliamentary Labour Party for failing to make clear the difference between the policy of Labour and that of its opponents.[9] And George Lansbury, although he conceded in the pages of his short-lived *Lansbury's Labour Weekly* that the Protocol could "at considerable cost" be supported by Labour, deplored the way in which the Protocol had been killed by Austen Chanberlain far more than he regretted its demise.[10]

But even for those who did not share the ideology of the ILP and the Labour left, the agreements being explored by Chamberlain posed vexing problems. Concerned about the drift in foreign affairs under the Baldwin government, the Parliamentary Party insisted that the country should do everything in its power to obtain the acceptance of the principles of the Geneva Protocol and the holding of a disarmament conference. When Chamberlain defended his policy and outlined his proposals for a pact of security, the Parliamentary group carried a resolution at its regular meeting in which it charged that the proposed security pact, "having regard to its limited scope, its grave military commitments, and undefined responsibilities, and its failure to make provision for a mutual and general reduction of armaments," was not calculated to secure Franco-German conciliation or a stabilized European peace. Instead the pact conformed more to the system of partial alliances against which the workers had so often protested, and was inconsistent with the spirit and ideals of the Covenant of the League of Nations to which Britain adhered. Repeating its frequent demand for the admission of Germany and Russia to the League, the Parliamentary Party urged as a substitute to Chamberlain's plan the setting up of an "all-inclusive" pact of security based on the principles of arbitration, security, and disarmament, as contemplated by the Geneva Protocol.[11]

A majority in the Parliamentary Party represented the moderate element in the labour movement, heavily influenced by the views of the leaders of some of the strongest union affiliates. Yet it continued to be clear that, even on the right, many Labour spokesmen were skeptical about the Protocol, even when they remained supporters of the League of Nations. *Clarion* emphasized the reservations that would have to be insisted upon by Britain in order to accept the Protocol, while the *New Statesman* was more than content to pronounce the document dead before it was born.[12]

As yet, the National Executive of the Labour Party and the General Council of the Trades Union Congress held fast to the support of the Geneva Protocol of the League Assembly. A special sub-committee meeting of the two bodies passed a resolution that read

> Resolved: That the Party holds that this country should do everything in its power to obtain the acceptance of the principles of the Protocol and the holding of the Disarmament Conference. It stands by the Protocol on the ground that it furnishes the only practical plan at present for obtaining disarmament and substituting arbitration for war as the method of settling disputes. The Party should strongly oppose any suggestion of substituting for the Protocol any form of limited military alliance or guarantee.
>
> Every effort should be made to get all non-signatory States to sign and ratify.[13]

By now Arthur Henderson had established himself as the leading advocate of a League of Nations policy including, if necessary, the use of force to support its decisions in case of international disputes. In the House of Commons, where MacDonald placed his emphasis on the development of a new habit of mind, that of thinking in terms of arbitration, Henderson spoke more concretely of "pooled security" and pointed out that the Geneva Protocol, whatever its deficiencies, recognized the need to ban war as an instrument of *national* policy and depended upon resort to sanctions only when peaceful settlement of disputes was refused. Dealing with the criticism that the Protocol tended to freeze the status quo, he insisted that its only new requirement was that changes not be made by the use of force. Supported by Dalton, who pointed out that none of the terms of Geneva were intended to come into operation until some measure of disarmament was effected, he went considerably beyond MacDonald in addressing the criticisms levied against the Protocol which he had helped to draft.[14]

In the Advisory Committee on International Questions, a majority as yet saw the Chamberlain proposals as no more than a set of traditional partial alliances. This group advised the Labour Party to insist that Britain should not make any military commitments under their terms unless prior provision had been made for the limitation of national armaments and general agreement had been reached on a convention of mutual arbitration and guarantee, in other words, a system very much like that envisaged in the Geneva Protocol. On the other hand, a minority of the Advisory Committee proposed a much more flexible approach. They suggested a series of tests—the arbitration of all disputes, or the offering of military guarantees only to the victims of aggression as defined by League of Nations machinery, or the prior achievement of a scheme for reduction and limitation of armaments—by which any international proposal brought before Parliament should be judged.[15]

The difference of opinion in the Advisory Committee was mirrored at the meeting of the Parliamentary Party on November 17, when Josiah Wedgwood suggested an amendment to the forthcoming government resolution approving the ratification of the Locarno Pact. His proposal, which considered it undesirable for Britain to be committed to guarantee by force of arms the frontiers of any European nation or to enter into any sort of partial alliance which could be construed as hostile to other powers, was defeated by a narrow 16 to 14 vote. It was replaced by an official party amendment agreeing to the ratification of Locarno and expressing satisfaction at the impending entry of Germany into the League of Nations and the improvement in international relations. The Parliamentary Party nevertheless warned that the real test of the treaty depended on whether it was followed by disarmament. It urged that steps be taken to bring Russia into the League of Nations and to encourage her participation in European arrangements.[16]

Whatever the views of the party's MPs, MacDonald was still its leading spokesman. In the spring of 1925, he published an article in a series that was clearly intended to establish Labour's posture towards the negotiations among the Western powers. Other authors were Philip Noel Baker and G. N. Barnes and all three took their stand on the superiority of the Protocol to the policy being pursued by the Baldwin government. MacDonald was particularly condemnatory. "I doubt," he wrote, "if any greater calamity could have happened to Europe in these days than the declaration made by Mr. Chamberlain at Geneva that the British Government had torn up the Protocol, had decided against the outlawry of war, had no support to give to the attempt to make arbitration in national disputes general, and wished to return to military alliances and separate understandings." [17]As late as November 7, just before the Locarno Agreements came before Parliament for ratification, he asserted in his column in *Forward* that Locarno was of little value as an achievement for peace and indeed, because it was based on old assumptions, an actual danger, Nevertheless, he concluded somewhat lamely, it helped people think about peace and that should be built upon.[18] His performance when the Locarno Pact was debated in the House of Commons was much more impressive. Here he followed the advice of the minority of the Advisory Committee, accepting the Pact as a first step towards the idea of the Geneva Protocol. It contained all the elements of the latter, but without disarmament it posed risks far greater than those imputed to the Protocol. Its negotiation and conclusion outside the orbit of the League of Nations was disturbing. One prescient comment noted that the major flaw in Locarno was its failure to deal with the Eastern frontiers: "The lighting of the match will take place, if it takes place at all, in Middle and Eastern Europe." His skillful Parliamentary performance enabled MacDonald to argue that Locarno presented an opportunity to go on to the building of a viable European system, in effect keeping open Labour's options for the time it might again be in office.[19] Following his lead, the Labour MPs voted overwhelmingly for ratification of the Locarno Agreements, the exception being thirteen MPs mostly from the ILP ranks, who joined Ponsonby and Lansbury in deploring the concessions made by Labour's leadership to the initiatives of the Tory government.

When the Executive Committee of the Labour and Socialist International met in London in early November, it substantially accepted MacDonald's argument. Persisting in the view that the security of European peace could most effectively be achieved by means of the Geneva Protocol and regretting that the Tory government of Great Britain had wrecked it for the time being, the International committee nevertheless greeted the Locarno agreements as a first move towards the pacification of Europe. The steps that it outlined as necessary corollaries were unanimously adopted by all the national representatives, except those of the ILP, who abstained in protest against a paragraph which deplored the "self-isolation" of the Soviet Union.[20]

The complex differences that continued to characterize Labour's approach to foreign policy were no more sharply illustrated than in the role played by Arthur Ponsonby. Increasingly, and especially after the defeat of the General Strike in 1926 had put the labour movement on the defensive, he moved beyond the conventional left-wing support of disarmament by international negotiation to an insistence that if Britain showed the way to disarmament by her example, she would soon be followed by other nations and would be more secure than if she remained armed. Ponsonby attempted to gain the support of both the ILP and the UDC for his intensifying crusade for unilateral disarmament. His position was particularly embodied in his campaign to gather signatures for a Peace Letter to be addressed to the prime minister indicating the intention of its signatories to refuse to take part in war. That he was not alone was suggested by a war resistance rally at the Royal Albert Hall at which ILP officials and MPs made up a majority of the speakers, as well as by a pamphlet, *Why We Will Not Fight!*, which presented the arguments of Fenner Brockway, J. H. Hudson, George Lansbury, and others along with those of Ponsonby.[21]

Ponsonby persisted in his campaign for a British initiative in giving up its arms despite the fact that the press, even the labour press, took virtually no account of his efforts. A handful of correspondents, both in Britain and Germany, encouraged him in his pacifism, but when he attempted to win the

Union of Democratic Control to a policy eschewing the use of military sanctions in any circumstances, he was soundly defeated. His motion to give the UDC's stamp of approval to unilateral disarmament was opposed by Arnold Forster, along with Delisle Burns and J. A. Hobson. Their amendment, rejecting the view that the organization's hands should be tied in advance on the matter of sanctions, was carried. Shortly thereafter Ponsonby resigned from the Executive Committee of the UDC, of which he had been a founding member in the first year of the Great War.[22]

The strength of the pacifist position in the Labour Party was dramatized by the role of Ponsonby. Having served as MacDonald's second at the Foreign Office during the first Labour government, he continued from 1924 to 1929 as one of Labour's front bench speakers, even as his position in the party became increasingly tenuous. Twice he was defeated—by Hugh Dalton and Sidney Webb—in his bid to serve on the Executive of the Labour Party, but he often took MacDonald's place in presenting the views of the opposition on matters of external policy. Despite his own opposition to any use of arms, he understood that his was a minority position and that disarmament by example was not likely to be achieved in the foreseeable future. Given that fact, he believed the Labour Party's position was the one most likely at least to reduce armaments and avoid all wars. He was prepared to support its program as a first step towards the more comprehensive abandonment of arms that he advocated.[23]

Ponsonby's position was an extreme example of the dilemma facing the pacifists in the ranks of Labour. He realized how little likelihood there was that his views would soon become a matter of public policy. Until then he was, if not content, at least resigned to supporting the less far-reaching program of his party, while reserving the right to fight privately and publicly for his more root-and-branch position. It would seem that George Lansbury, who shared Ponsonby's rejection of the use of force, was substantially less willing to accept the implications of the fact that he was a leader of a party that frequently questioned his assumptions about the international order.[24]

Ponsonby, however, was increasingly to be marginalized within the labour movement, while Lansbury, after the General Election of 1931 had resulted in a debacle for the Labour Party, eventually became, almost by accident, its leader. Meanwhile, MacDonald, more than sensitive to the differences among his colleagues, wished deliberately to avoid being too specific about Labour's "peace policy." He feared losing the confidence and good will he believed the party now enjoyed.[25]

Arthur Henderson was largely responsible for the fact that the general thrust of the Protocol remained for a few years alive in Labour Party policy statements. He and his advisors looked upon Chamberlain's substitute initiative with considerable suspicion. The writings of Noel Baker were particularly prominent in the mid-twenties, although there is little evidence that they enjoyed a wide circulation. In a series of books, especially *The Geneva Proto-*

col and *Disarmament*, he forcefully made the argument for the accommodation of international differences through the instrumentality of the League of Nations, emphasizing his conviction that such a League system could only come into being as a concomitant of a mutually agreed reduction in national armaments. Unlike many Labour advocates of the Geneva Protocol—even Henderson from time to time for tactical reasons minimized the Protocol's Article XI which provided for international force as the final support of the proposed new system—Noel Baker made no bones about the fact that the Protocol would require its signatories, at the demand of the Council of the League, to employ their troops if necessary to implement the decisions of that body. If Britain took the lead, the central bastion of the enemy defences would be captured and from that moment the forces of progress would march forward, irresistible and even perhaps unresisted.[26]

Skepticism about Locarno did not prevent Noel Baker from declaring himself optimistic about the system of international peacekeeping. In his little book on *Disarmament*, which he published in 1926, he outlined his reasons: "America stands ready, ardent if doubting; Germany, eager for the equality which only disarmament can bring; France, democratic France, ready to take a risk for reconciliation; Russia, using fair words, fairer than could have been expected; all the smaller powers enthusiastic for results for which they have been waiting long."[27] He conceded that the struggle against the age-old misery of war would be a long and difficult one. But if Great Britain took the lead who could doubt that it would be decisive?

Like Noel Baker, Arnold Forster and Dalton marshaled the arguments for an international system to replace what they regarded as the dog-eat-dog aspect of earlier arrangements. Both were increasingly prominent in the twenties as spokesmen for the growing group in the labour movement who recognized, sometimes reluctantly, that an international system required some form of genuine sanction if it were to be effective at all. The world had come a long way in the development of international institutions, they reasoned, and it was now time to take the next steps forward. As for the Locarno proposals, which Hugh Dalton later described as a "nine days' wonder which led nowhere," neither Arnold Forster nor Dalton accepted the view that they would contribute to the pacification of Europe. Only the prospect of Germany's admission to the League of Nations was seen by them as a positive step forward. Together, Arnold Forster, in a cogent pamphlet, and Dalton, in an important book, supported disarmament, but warned that, before any nation would agree to disarm, it would have to be assured of a guaranteed substitute. Only if there was ultimately force behind a League of Nations to which was assigned the settlement of disputes was there any possibility that a new international order might come into being. Dalton, in particular, attacked head-on one of the shibboleths of earlier Labour belief—that before peace could be assured the existing frontiers of Europe needed to be revised. That view was totally unrealistic, he argued. No nation would willingly agree to revision that might result in the loss of territory. Instead, attention should be addressed to the creation of a system in which frontiers would eventually be regarded as less volatile and less important. Above all, Dalton insisted that it was an ostrich policy to deny the need for coercion behind the workings of the international order. Like any legal system, the international one could not rely on good will alone. It must have the protection of forcible sanctions, however sparingly they might be used. [28]

Deliberations in the Advisory Committee on International Questions made it abundantly clear that Henderson and the younger men who supported his views did not have the field to themselves, even in the inner circles of the Labour Party. There the Quaker Charles Roden Buxton began the reconsideration of his reluctant acceptance of sanctions as part of the Geneva Protocol. Now he offered a paper in which he listed the various objections. American opposition and Dominion resistance; growing pacifism in the Labour Party; progress in the direction of disarmament and arbitration, all this he viewed as an indication that the Labour Party would never agree to military or naval action even in support of the League of Nations.[29]

Quite clearly, the issue of sanctions had the possibility of tearing the party apart, although Buxton's description of the opposition to the leadership's position at the 1926 conference was somewhat exaggerated. There a motion from a Glasgow constituency party—holding that until the capitalist class was overthrown there would be no security against war—was diverted by an amendment presented by the National Executive. It welcomed the admission of Germany to the League of Nations and urged that Russia be encouraged to become a member, supported the moves towards a world disarmament conference and deplored the reluctance of the British government to consider various forms of arbitration agreements. Short of the revival of the Geneva Protocol, it called for adherence (with reservations if required) to the Optional Clause of the Permanent Court of International Justice which provided for submission of all justiciable—that is, legal—disputes to that body.[30]

David Mitrany and Arnold Forster took issue with Buxton. In the Advisory Committee on International Questions Mitrany insisted that sanctions could not be abandoned without running the risk of destroying the League. Just as domestic order required some support, so the international order could not keep the peace without sanctions. The firmest supporters of force for the League were those nations who feared most for their security. To reject them would be to reject the League system. Perhaps, he suggested, there could be a compromise. All members of the League could agree on the application of economic sanctions, but it would be left to each individual government to agree—or not to agree—in advance to be committed to the use of its armed forces if needed by the League to implement a decision.[31]

Arnold Forster would have nothing of the compromise. A sanctionless League, he declared, would be much less effective in dissuading a would-be attacker or in stopping aggression once it had occurred. At the same time, policy should be directed to the abolition of private war and to dealing with the causes of war, for example by the use of Article XIX of the League Covenant, which provided that the Assembly might from time to time advise the reconsideration of treaties which had become inapplicable and the consideration of international conditions whose continuance might endanger the peace of the world. [32]

Henderson followed the argument developed by Arnold Forster when he wrote a major article on foreign affairs for *Labour Magazine* late 1927. Still committed to the Geneva Protocol, he denied the allegation that it implied unlimited obligation of a military character that might well split the Commonwealth. Instead, the Protocol made provision for the geographic location and particular situation of member states. But in the final analysis, Britain must become part of a system—whether through the Protocol or some similar instrument—that considered war an international crime or become an empire that might maintain peace within its own borders, but remained organized for war against all other states. Playing down the coercive features of the Protocol system, he emphasized Labour's program for the peaceful settlement of disputes and its aspiration for the abolition of competitive armaments. That program would certainly have more chance of succeeding than one in which the British Empire maintained a "unitary" system that it deemed threatened by either the Protocol or faithful adherence to the obligations of the League Covenant. For Henderson disarmament was increasingly becoming the major goal of his approach to external affairs. He was convinced that it would be an evident impossibility so long as there were no guarantees of security for governments in the face of what they regarded as potential threats. While he sometimes downplayed the coercive features of his "pooled security," he nevertheless again and again made clear his view that for the foreseeable future the mailed fist of coercion might sometimes be necessary to reinforce the velvet glove of arbitration and the peaceful settlement of international issues. His proposed program came closer to what later came to be called collective security than that of any of his major political contemporaries.[33]

Whatever the differences on the matter of sanctions, there was little Labour Party disagreement on the need to press for international disarmament and some form of security guarantee. As late as its 1927 conference, for example, the delegates accepted a resolution criticizing the opposition of the Baldwin government to any limitation of the expenditure on armed forces by international treaty, castigating its rejection of every proposal for a general treaty of arbitration and security, and continuing to declare Labour's support for the principles, if not the letter, of the 1924 Geneva Protocol.[34] Similarly, in the House of Commons, the party offered resolutions, invariably defeated of course, during discussion of air force and navy estimates, deploring the failure of the government to take the initiative in pressing for the reduction of air and naval armaments.[35]

When the American secretary of state, Frank Kellogg, transformed a French proposal—that France and the United States sign a treaty abandoning war between them as an instrument of national policy—into a more universal international proposal, the various wings of the Labour Party grasped at the suggestion with varying degrees of eagerness. In the discussions of the Advisory Committee, it was clear that the possibility of involving the Americans more fully in issues of international policy loomed large. The American proposal for an agreement to outlaw war as an instrument of policy rested substantially on two resolutions presented to Congress by senators Arthur Capper and William Borah respectively. The Capper resolution was the more far-reaching, proposing a treaty between the United States, France, and other countries outlawing war, agreeing to all-out arbitration, and defining an aggressor as a nation that flouted its agreement to submit disputes to arbitration, conciliation, or judicial settlement. Most Labour commentators preferred the Capper resolution to that of Borah, which was more general, essentially a statement of international good will. For Leonard Woolf, Capper's proposals were in complete accord with the policy of the Labour Party and he urged that the party press the government to respond favorably to the initiative.[36]

Others in the Advisory Committee likewise urged full support for the American plan, and MacDonald followed their lead. In Parliament he too argued that British acceptance would foster Anglo-American relations and bring the Americans more into touch with the practical peace problems of Europe. Anticipating the reaction of the government, he declared that to accept the proposals with reservations would be the worst possible approach. Austen Chamberlain's reply took note of MacDonald's warning, but made no commitment before the Dominions were consulted.[37]

In the Labour press the enthusiasm was rather more muted. Both the *Daily Herald* and the *New Leader* would have preferred the proposal, which the Russians had recently thrown out, for completely doing away with armies, navies, and air forces. And *Clarion*, where Robert Blatchford still held forth, professed not to understand the American initiative, but warned nevertheless that it would not result in disarmament and so not abolish war.[38]

Press critics were evidently more realistic, from the first, than were some of Labour Party's political advisers. When the British government threw cold water on the scheme by indicating that it could only accept the Kellogg proposal with a series of reservations, there was almost universal condemnation in the Labour press.[39] By now members of Labour's Advisory Committee were no less critical and their disappointment was mirrored in the statements of Labour spokesmen in the House of Commons.[40] At the same time, the criticism received formal expression at the 1928 Labour Party conference. There, a long resolution on foreign policy repeated many of the charges made at the 1927 conference and added additional deficiencies attributed to the Conservative government. Introduced by MacDonald and seconded by Sir Oswald Mosley, it rejoiced in the condemnation of war by the governments of the world, but expressed profound disappointment that the declaration had been made with reservations. The resolution charged that many of the governments were pursuing, in a prewar spirit, a policy that was preventing any progress being made towards disarmament and which assumed that neither the Covenant of the League of Nations nor the Pact for the Outlawry of War and the Locarno Treaties had contributed anything to the security of the world. In all of this, the resolution went on to emphasize the responsibility of the British government. It had weakened the significance of its signing of the Kellogg Pact by reserving its own right to go to war, by its refusal to sign the General Act of Arbitration, Conciliation and Judicial Settlement recently approved by the League Assembly, by creating a deadlock in the disarmament discussions by opposing limitation of expenditure on arms, by torpedoing the Three Power Naval Conference of Great Britain, the United States, and Japan in 1927 by insisting on an increase of cruisers and then making an agreement with France that essentially was an agreement not to limit armaments, and finally by opposing an early meeting of the Preparatory Disarmament Commission in order that negotiations might be continued outside the machinery of the League of Nations.[41] In effect, the National Executive of the Labour Party was firing the first gun for an election campaign that was due to be waged no later than the following year.

Both Henderson and MacDonald were involved in drawing up the election manifesto labelled "Labour and the Nation," but on matters of foreign policy it clearly bore the stamp of MacDonald much more than that of Henderson. The document reiterated the stands Labour had assumed in the years since the war, supporting the policy of the Kellogg Pact, urging the reduction of armaments by international agreement, and in general advocating the systematic use of the organs of the League of Nations. While "Labour and the Nation" demanded the immediate signature of the Optional Clause of the Permanent Court of International Justice, it did little to promote the view that an international body must ultimately be backed by the threat of force as it insisted on the employment of the League's various procedures for the peaceful settlement international questions. Instead, "Labour and the Nation" made tepid endorsement of sanctions "to the minimum required for police purposes." All in all, the document was hardly an improvement over "Labour and the New Social Order," produced at the end of the war.[42]

Despite MacDonald's undoubted charisma, the years between the first two Labour governments were largely influenced by the campaign of Henderson and his younger advisers to persuade their Labour comrades that international peace and security could only be achieved by the use of the fledgling League of Nations in the give-and-take of compromise and negotiation among the nations. By the end of the decade of the twenties, the self-defeating negativism of the tiny splinter group of an earlier period had become a minority position, although the issue of the use of force continued to divide the party and often to vitiate its effectiveness in presenting its case. Still, by 1929, the Labour Party had become an advocate for a League of Nations policy in international affairs, although the parameters of such a policy remained to be determined.

6

The Second Labour Government

The second Labour government that assumed office in 1929 faced serious problems at home and abroad. It had to deal with the ravages of the Great Depression, which soon became worldwide. At the same time, as other nations themselves became more aggressive in responding to the spreading economic crisis, Labour had to confront an increasingly complex and thorny world of foreign affairs.[1]

As it tried to handle those issues, the longstanding tension between Arthur Henderson and Ramsay MacDonald continued, and the foreign policy moves of the Second Labour government turned into failed initiatives.[2] Agreements that had once appeared promising dissolved and opened the way for Britain and the world to be drawn, step by step, ever closer to another war. As that happened, plans for the growth of the League of Nations as the major instrument of international cooperation and the guarantor that international disputes would be settled in peaceful ways foundered. For the resurgence of national ambitions around the world brought with it the rejection of the assumptions upon which the League project had rested.

When Labour took office after the summer election of 1929, prospects for the future appeared favorable. The Kellogg Pact for the "outlawry' of war had been signed by a substantial number of nations, the League of Nations had seemed to operate successfully in pushing Mussolini out of Corfu, Gustav Stresemann in Germany and Aristide Briand in France appeared ready to cooperate in the search for peace, preparations for a disarmament conference were being discussed, and the Young Plan was being presented as a practical solution to the troubling issue of reparations.[3]

MacDonald was reluctant to make Henderson his foreign secretary and when he grudgingly did so, he insisted on keeping the conduct of relations with America in his own hands. From time to time the public utterances, to say nothing of diplomatic actions, of one made the work of the other more difficult. The fault rested especially with MacDonald's low opinion of Henderson's abilities, a low opinion fueled perhaps by the resentment he felt at the support he had received from Henderson over the years. Whatever their differences, Henderson continued to believe that MacDonald's public leadership was indispensable for Labour, even as he was often frustrated by the latter's contempt and obstructionism.

The team Henderson organized to advise him was a strong one. Aside from the officials of the Foreign Office, his parliamentary under-secretary was Hugh Dalton and his parliamentary private secretary, Philip Noel Baker. The fact that the two were now in government meant that their influence was exercised more directly rather than, as often was the case when Labour was out of office, indirectly through the Advisory Committee on International Questions via the National Executive of the party or the Joint Council of the national party and the Trades Union Congress. To Dalton and Noel Baker, Henderson added the Conservative Lord Robert Cecil, leader of the League of Nations Union, who served as an adviser on League of Nations affairs and was given a room at the Foreign Office despite the opposition of the permanent officials. Cecil's appointment brought Will Arnold Forster, who had served as his secretary at Geneva and was active in the Advisory Committee on International Questions, into even closer touch with the foreign policy makers in Whitehall. Henderson did not see eye-to-eye with Sir Ronald Lindsay, the permanent under-secretary (who soon went on to Washington and was succeeded by Sir Robert Vansittart, with whom Dalton in particular got on very well). There is general agreement that Henderson gained the respect as well as the affection of most of the permanent officials. To be sure, Vansittart sometimes went to MacDonald over the head of Henderson, but on the whole their relations seem to have been professional and even cordial.

Almost immediately Henderson came into conflict with Lord Lloyd, the British high commissioner in Egypt, who disagreed significantly with Henderson's attempt to pursue a policy of moderate conciliation on questions at issue with the Egyptian government. When Henderson decided to ask for Lloyd's resignation, he had the support of most of the permanent officials of the Foreign Office and was able to point out that Austen Chamberlain had had similar problems with Lloyd, whose function it was to represent British Government policy in Cairo. Despite the probably ill-advised Parliamentary support of Winston Churchill, Lloyd was unable to make his case successfully when he returned to London and was replaced by Sir Percy Loraine, a career diplomat.[4]

Whatever his victory over Lord Lloyd, Henderson was no more successful than Austen Chamberlain had been in reaching agreement with the Egyptians. MacDonald had little sympathy for Henderson's policy and the latter himself, while conciliatory, was as determined as had been Austen Chamberlain, to protect British interests, such as its military base in the Suez area, and to resist Egyptian claims to control of the Sudan.[5] After extended negotiations, once the Wafd party was returned to office in Egypt, it became impossible to conclude a definitive treaty, although the Labour press took comfort in its perception that at least the two sides had come to respect, to know, and to understand one another better.[6] A later commentator concurred and judged that the "character of relations with Cairo showed a marked improvement" as a result of Henderson's efforts and approach.[7]

Much more central to Labour's concerns was the question of the status of Germany. For some years after the 1914 war, Labour opinion, particularly opinion on the left, had insisted that the treatment of the defeated enemy was both wrong and self-defeating. Parallel with sympathy for Germany was the view that the French desire to dominate the European continent posed the most serious threat to the European order and must be resisted if a viable balance of power was to be achieved. The Baldwin government's policy of cooperation with Paris was looked upon with suspicion in most Labour circles, a suspicion somewhat tempered when Germany was admitted to the League of Nations after the conclusion of the Locarno agreements. More than most of their Labour colleagues, Henderson and his advisers rejected the demonization of France as they concluded that Franco-German reconciliation was essential to the peace and harmony of the European world. Certain key issues demanded attention—stabilization of reparations payments, their possible reduction, and, more generally, the better reintegration of Germany into the international economic order, as well as the search for a measure of parity in military armaments, ideally by the reduction and limitation of the weapons of war along the lines imposed upon Germany by the Versailles Treaty. As the years passed, mainstream Labour rhetoric continued to identify the League of Nations and its Article 19 as the instrument for peaceful change of the Versailles settlement. In practice, however, specific revision of the postwar treaties tended to give way to emphasis on the use of League machinery for peaceful settlement of international quarrels as well as on its role in the organization of economic cooperation among the nations.

These changing views pointed up an optimism about the state of international relations that was to hold the stage for a very few brief years. Hugh Dalton reflected that optimism when he told the House of Commons,

> I myself hope and believe that we are now entering upon a new and more hopeful phase of history. I think we now have an opportunity to go forward which, if we miss it, may not come again in our own day. Therefore, I hope and believe that we shall be able, in the months and years that lie ahead, to make a forward movement in the direction of arbitration, disarmament, the better economic organization of the life of the world, and the general establishment of reconciliation between old enemies and former friendship between old friends. [8]

To be sure, this rather sanguine point of view was not really supported by MacDonald, who earlier in the decade was convinced that the French were determined to ruin Germany and to dominate the continent without regard to the interests of others or the future consequences for "European sentiments."

His British misgivings were shared by the American banker, Owen D. Young, who was to lead the next attempt to regularize reparation payments as a contribution to the pacification of the postwar world.[9]

When the Dawes Plan was adopted in 1924, it had been intended that subsequently a limit, both in the amount and the duration of reparations, would be set. By the time the second Labour government took office, the cost of remaining in the Rhineland as a guarantee for the fulfillment of Germany's treaty obligations was deemed too high to be maintained any longer. For France, the occupation dealt with security from a future German threat. Reparations were one instrument for the control of Germany and protection against the experiences of 1870 and 1914. The search for the next steps to deal with the complex and intertwined issues of reparations and security was put in motion in 1927. From the beginning it was evident that the quid pro quo for Germany's acceptance of a final reparations figure and a revised schedule of payments was withdrawal from the Rhineland. By the middle of 1929, a conference was assembled at The Hague. The British made it clear that they were prepared to withdraw unilaterally from the Rhineland if no mutual arrangement could be achieved.[10] The Young Plan that emerged called for about a 20 percent reduction in Germany's annual payments and a limitation of those payments to fifty-nine years. A Labour Party pamphlet, designed to in part to quiet fears that a revived Germany would become a dangerous competitor, assured its readers that what was important was that the arrangements had succeeded in wiping out the past: "In brief, all that has happened in the Rhineland since the Occupation of the Ruhr on January 11th, 1923, has been undone, except the ineffaceable memories." [11]

The plan was almost derailed by Philip Snowden's insistence that Britain's share of the German payments be increased, a position which gained widespread approval at home. Henderson was convinced that to reject the new plan would deal a severe blow to Britain's policy of reconciliation and cooperation and seriously damage relations not only with Germany but with the United States.[12] He had developed good relations with Aristide Briand, the French foreign minister, and feared that too inflexible a stand would jeopardize what had been achieved. He was hard put to persuade the adamant chancellor to accept a compromise that did increase the British share but not quite as much as had been demanded. Henderson believed that the slight difference in British reparation payments was trivial when compared to the importance of fixing the schedules in order to proceed with the evacuation from the Rhineland of the Allied troops who formed a constant irritant of European tensions. As he later explained to the Labour Party Conference, it was only possible to complete the political agreements at The Hague when agreement was reached on the financial issue. [13]

Gustav Stresemann, the German foreign minister, had insisted that withdrawal was a condition of acceptance of the Young provisions. Once the financial issue was settled, Henderson was able to persuade the French to advance the date of departure by some five years to June of 1930.[14] All in all, the arrangements were a significant triumph for British diplomacy, although the impact of worldwide depression soon undermined the economic assumptions upon which they were based. By November, for example, not long after the retreat from the Rhineland had been implemented, Henderson expressed misgivings about German hints that they might have to appeal for a moratorium in the working of the Young plan. He could imagine, he told Horace Rumbold, the ambassador in Berlin, no action more calculated to sow suspicion of Germany than any such development. In the interests of the policy of appeasement on which the British government was now engaged he hoped he would hear no more of the proposal.[15] His hope was not fulfilled. The economic crisis ensured that the future of reparation payments would continue to plague the European governments, while, in addition, the ubiquitous issue of the relation of war debts—owed by Britain and owed to her—to reparations remained in abeyance.

Just as the reintegration of Germany into the European economic and political order was a tenet of Labour policy, so too was the normalization of relations with the Soviet Union. Those relations had been cut off by the Tory government during its tenure of office. The leaders of the Labour Party believed that only if Germany and Russia became full-fledged participants in the development of the new international instruments could there be hope for mutual economic benefits along with the achievement of disarmament and the substitution of methods of peaceful accommodation for the horrors of recurrent conflict. They had few illusions about the nature of the Soviet regime, however much some of their left-wing followers wanted to believe in the accomplishments of Russian "socialism." MacDonald's gradualism had very little in common with the revolutionary authoritarianism of the Soviets and Henderson, from the time of his visit to revolutionary Russia in 1917, was deeply suspicious of the policies and the practices of the Soviet government. Nevertheless, the Labour government moved, although quite slowly, towards regularization of relations with the Soviet government, a policy that was accepted as necessary by moderate Conservatives as well as by a majority of the Labour Party. The Foreign Office believed that there were strong reasons for the resumption of diplomatic relations and the foreign secretary agreed. The difficulties in dealing with the Soviets were precisely the reason for more regular contact, he judged, so that problems could be explored and perhaps resolved. Assured by the legal advisers to the Foreign Office that relations with Russia had been suspended rather than terminated by the previous Tory government, he proceeded to negotiate for their resumption. The negotiations were far from smooth, made more difficult when MacDonald announced in Parliament that the government would not exchange ambassadors with the Soviet Union without Parliamentary approval, thus putting off implementation at least until the next session of Parliament.[16] A little storm in a teacup was provided by some of the opposition press when Henderson left the party conference being held at Brighton to meet with the Soviet ambassador to France at nearby Lewes. In the negotiations the issue of Soviet propaganda in Britain was an especially thorny one. The Soviet government maintained, quite implausibly, that they had no control over the actions of the Comintern. When a document was finally agreed upon, Henderson made clear that he considered the propaganda of the Third International the responsibility of the Soviet regime although nothing to that effect appeared in the formal document finally agreed upon. While he had little hope that propaganda would cease, he insisted at the party conference and in Parliament that the benefits from the resumption of relations far outweighed its problems. He emphasized the importance of promoting Anglo-Russian trade relations and in the House of Commons argued, along with Noel Baker, that unless the Russians were included, there was no hope for the achievement of general disarmament. In Central Europe, for example, disarmament was essential and could hardly be achieved without Russian involvement.[17] In the event, neither the economic nor the political advantages of the Russian rapprochement were realized. Communist propaganda continued unabated and the increase in trade in a troubled world was modest at very best. As Hugh Dalton later put it, the best that could be said was that Labour's policy made Anglo-Russian relations less unsatisfactory than might otherwise have been the case.

Steps to regularize the positions of Germany and Russia went hand in hand with the effort to promote the international role of the League of Nations. Henderson continued to be convinced that the Geneva Protocol had held the most promise as a peacekeeping instrument, but, given what had transpired in the five years since 1924, he moved, in the first instance, to press for British adoption of the Optional Clause of the League of Nations Covenant. That clause made provision for the voluntary acceptance of the jurisdiction of the Permanent Court of International Justice in the settlement of justiciable, that is, legal disputes. It has recently been argued that the gulf between Labour and the Tories on the matter of the Optional Clause was not as wide as often depicted.[18] However that may be, Henderson had to deal with the repeated concerns of some of the Dominions, concerns that an international body not be given the right to interfere in intra-Imperial questions nor to thrust the Dominions unnecessarily into continental quarrels. The reservation of certain questions, even of a justiciable nature, from the purview of the International Court was the price paid for British acceptance of the Optional Clause.[19] In effect, it proposed to take one of the alternative methods posited in the Geneva Protocol—arbitration, mediation, conciliation, judicial settlement—as a start towards the desired goal of step-by-step developing the peace-keeping machinery of the new international body. Indeed, in presenting the British government's views to the Tenth Assembly of the League in September, 1929,

Henderson made clear that "arbitration"—often used as short-hand for a variety of methods of settlement—was looked to as the vehicle for bringing about just settlement of troubled questions in place of reliance upon the use of national armed forces. At this stage, he downplayed his differences with MacDonald, who had made a somewhat general statement of support in a brief appearance at Geneva. The foreign secretary had little to say about the enforcement of the commitment to use the International Court, instead emphasizing that any real progress depended on moving ahead towards a measure of disarmament as the essential precondition for the acceptance of non-violent substitutes for war among the nations.[20]

Henderson was not so naïve as to believe that the road to disarmament was an easy one. He warned the Labour Party conference that unilateral disarmament—the "disarmament by example" increasingly being promoted by the Labour left—was a practical impossibility. The world—and human nature— would have to be much further advanced before it could do without police forces. [21] His reaction to Briand's somewhat tentative proposal at Geneva for the exploration of a European Union reflected these views.[22] Responding cautiously so as not to alienate the French foreign minister with whom he had a good working relationship, he nevertheless accepted the Foreign Office view that the proposed body, whether it was largely political or economic in nature, might be seen as opposed to the United States or other non-European area and that, like other proposals, it might weaken the links between Britain and the Commonwealth. Above all, he argued that such a federation might undermine the role and the usefulness of the League of Nations. After considerable discussion in the Foreign Office and the Cabinet, the course taken was to assure Briand of Britain's interest while at the same time recommending that he bring his proposal before the League for its consideration. There it was turned over to a Committee of Enquiry for European Union where it was quietly forgotten.[23]

Even more troubling to the British was the initiative of some of the continental governments with regard to perceived deficiencies in the League Covenant. At the 1929 League Assembly, British leaders, MacDonald and Henderson among them, had called for a "closing of the gap" in the Covenant to do away with the right to make war and to bring it into conformity with the Kellogg Pact outlawing war. But the approach suggested at Geneva gave them pause. When a League committee brought in a report that urged that the League Council be permitted to compel the implementation of arbitral awards in certain circumstances, Cecil at Geneva went along with the recommendation. The British government, on the other hand, was strongly opposed. Not only the officials of the Foreign Office and Cabinet members but a number of prominent commentators took issue with a proposal that they saw as possibly calling upon Britain for military action when her own interests were not involved. When Philip Kerr (later Lord Lothian), a member of Alfred Milner's "kindergarten" and a former private secretary to Lloyd George, denounced the emphasis upon force in the pages of the *Times,* Austen Chamberlain seconded his warning, arguing that the more the League concentrated on sanctions after war had broken out the weaker it would be. Prevention of war, not punishment, should be the function of the League.[24] The intervention of Kerr and Chamberlain effectively destroyed any chance of British support for the proposals emanating from Geneva, since it spelled out the opposition that might be anticipated in Parliament.[25]

Actually, the concern was widely shared in Labour circles, where a critic in the *New Statesman* somewhat heavily likened the emphasis upon "security" to the actions of a cat fortifying itself against the aggressiveness of Mickey Mouse.[26] Interestingly, in commenting upon the interventions of Kerr and Chamberlain, Brailsford, perhaps the most incisive of the internal critics of the Labour government, wondered what the French would make of it when both Kerr and Chamberlain, no less than Prime Minister MacDonald, seemed to place reliance not on the League but on the Kellogg Pact as the guarantors of a future peace. He wondered, too, whether all this meant that the British government was drawing close to the American version of "entangling alliances." [27] In any case, the wide range of opposition, especially to the notion of the use of force, ensured that "closing the gap" was no longer a matter of practical politics, although just before its demise in 1931 the Labour government did sign the General Act of Arbitration, Conciliation, and Judicial Settlement, subject to the same reservations that had been attached to the Optional Clause.[28] As the *Daily Herald* explained, such arrangements were rendered absolutely necessary by the signing of the Kellogg Pact. By signing that document, that paper pointed out, Britain had pledged itself not to attempt to settle disputes by arms. And since disputes did not settle themselves, some alternative method must be provided. Hence the General Act.[29]

In retrospect, MacDonald's American initiatives, like Henderson's efforts at Geneva, appeared more significant than a disintegrating international order proved them to be. MacDonald's anxiety to promote Anglo-American cooperation was paralleled by similar concerns on the part of American Secretary of State Henry Stimson and, perhaps to a somewhat lesser extent, President Herbert Hoover. Since the Washington naval agreement of 1922, which had provided for a moratorium on capital ship building and set ratios among the battleship fleets of the major naval powers, the question of further limitation had been repeatedly raised. Differences of opinion with regard to auxiliary vessels stemmed from the different requirements of the two countries. Put oversimply, the Admiralty, given Britain's worldwide interests, felt the need for a large number of smaller cruisers, while the Americans considered a smaller number of large cruisers better suited to the defense of the Atlantic and Pacific approaches to the United States. In 1927, the so-called Coolidge Conference had failed to reach agreement, largely, in the view of the Americans, because of Anglo-French intransigence. MacDonald's first step towards the remedying of the resulting tensions was to take up the proposal of a British visit to Washington that had been made by the Americans while the Baldwin government was still in office. In preparation for a discussion of naval issues care was taken not to give the French or Italians the impression that there would be bilateral understandings designed to disregard their approach to the reduction of naval armaments. Instead Britain agreed to call for a five-power naval conference to include representatives from Japan, France, and Italy along with those of Britain and the United States.

When MacDonald did sail to the United States in the fall of 1929, his visit was a public relations triumph and he was greeted with enthusiasm by American crowds.[30] On substantive matters he was less successful in reaching agreement with President Hoover. No progress was made on the cruiser question, nor was there any meeting of minds on the reduction of battleship strength. Similarly, while MacDonald was willing to discuss the matter of belligerent rights at sea, the horror of Maurice Hankey, the influential secretary to the cabinet and the Committee of Imperial Defence, and the opposition of members of the cabinet soon ensured that such discussions would come to nothing. They feared, to put it simply, that the operations of the British Navy would be seriously hampered in time of war if they had to be justified to an international body.[31]

Despite the failure of the Americans and British to reach agreement before the start of the London Naval Conference in January 1930, the willingness of both governments to cooperate seemed to bode well for the shoring up of the postwar security system—on land and sea as well as in the financial sphere. The conference soon demonstrated, however, how difficult the achievement of an agreed upon security system would be. As it proceeded, "like a wounded snake drags its slow length along,"[32] the French, who continued to make clear that they considered naval reduction intimately tied to land disarmament, were unwavering in their opposition to the Italian demand for theoretical parity in naval forces. They became even more adamant when the British rejected out of hand a proposal that signatories agree to take up arms against a state resorting to hostilities in violation of the Pact of Paris. Unless the League Council should decide otherwise, the French proposed, such resort should be considered an act of war according to the meaning of Article 16 of the League Covenant. In the event, it was impossible to reach accommodation between the French and Italians, although a surface impression of cooperation was presented by a Franco-Italian agreement to continue negotiations on the questions that divided them. Despite all efforts on the part of the British to find a modus vivendi between the two countries and the insistence in the Labour press that some gains should come from the naval conference, no solution was found by the time the Labour government left office in the debacle of 1931.[33] More to the point, the British insisted on an escalation clause in the treaty to take into account the possibility of an increase, rather than a decrease, in French naval forces.

All five governments signed those parts of the London Treaty dealing with a battleship holiday, the scrapping of some battleships, and several measures relating to submarine warfare. Once Japan was accorded parity in submarines and destroyers and a rather favorable percentage of American and British strength in small and large cruisers, the United States, Japan, and Britain accepted the provisions dealing with so-called auxiliary vessels. It is of some interest that the agreement made no provision for enforcement or even for verification of its agreed ratios.[34] Nevertheless, for the moment success in minimizing the possibilities of future conflict through Labour's various initiatives seemed attainable. Even Dalton, who, like Henderson and Noel Baker, had few illusions about the difficulties ahead, confided to his diary after the signing of the General Act, "A Historic event! Now we have done everything in *Labour and the Nation* (international policy), except General Disarmament."[35]

From the beginning of Labour's second term in office, its foreign affairs experts came to understand the difficulties posed by the various proposals for land disarmament. Dalton and Noel Baker, as well as Cecil, served on the Committee of Imperial Defence sub-committee on the reduction and limitation of armaments. Here they quickly learned the difficulty of equating Britain's need for effective armed forces with arms reductions. The three came to appreciate that Britain required a minimum armed strength to meet its obligations, from collective security under the League of Nations to support of the civil power and Imperial policing.[36] At the same time, on the importance of proceeding with the search for a sustainable formula, they agreed with Henderson, who virtually had the area of arms reduction to himself because of MacDonald's (and Snowden's) absorption in dealing with the economic crisis. Early optimism on the issue was soon undermined as the impact of the worldwide slump along with threats to the European and Far Eastern balance of power began to be felt.

Henderson's impressive performances at Geneva led to his designation as president of the World Disarmament Conference now scheduled to begin in 1932. Despite the awkwardness of a sitting foreign minister holding the post (and despite MacDonald's attempt to throw cold water on the invitation) Henderson accepted a task that he considered the most important he could undertake. He believed that a successful disarmament policy depended in large measure on the unfolding of the German situation. As the months passed, the German response to the British policy of appeasement was hardly promising. Once the Rhineland was evacuated, other demands quickly arose. Control of the Saar and the "lost" territories in the east were among the issues raised by various German cabinet members. British advisers warned that Germany was already contravening the military terms of the Versailles Treaty. In a prescient memorandum, Vansittart pointed out that not all of Germany's objectives had been achieved and should be assumed to be inevitable.[37]

The result was a tempering of optimism as Henderson came to feel that he was waging a struggle against time in the effort to pacify Europe while meeting some of Germany's legitimate demands. When German foreign minister Julius Curtius suggested that the Young Plan might possibly be revised, Henderson pointed out, with characteristic firmness, that Britain had probably suffered more from the depression than Germany. Curtius, he cautioned, was playing into the hands of nationalist ambitions in Germany which in turn might heighten tensions with her European neighbors.[38] At the same time he recognized that if the Brüning government should fall, it was likely to be replaced by a much greater threat to European stability. When the Germans and the Austrians rather heavy-handedly raised the project for a customs union, he regarded it as a not very subtle method of indirectly moving towards the *Anschluss* that had been forbidden after the war. Rather skillfully he maneuvered the issue so that the Permanent Court of International Justice was asked to rule on the compatibility of the customs union with the postwar obligations of the two countries. By the time the Court ruled unfavorably, the Austrians had backed off, but the whole incident had further embittered the relations of the countries that were charged with collaborating to find a method of reducing the burden of arms in their world.

Whatever may have been Henderson's views of the financial stringencies of Germany, its plight remained a touchstone of international relations. By the summer of 1931, President Hoover's proposal for a moratorium on all international obligations had surfaced, but further action to deal with the German crisis came to naught. Neither the Americans nor the British felt themselves to be in the position of extending further loans to Germany, while the French, consistent as ever, searched for compensations which were as much political as economic. A conference which finally convened in London managed to achieve virtually no agreement on how to handle Germany's economic woes except to recommend a standstill on non-governmental international credits to Germany. This may have temporarily stemmed the financial draining of Germany, but it did little to address the fundamental malaise not only of the German but of the European economy as a whole.[39]

By the time the Disarmament Conference met in February 1932 after years of preparation, the Labour government was no longer in power. Henderson continued as president of the Conference, but he was handicapped by overwhelming odds. For one thing, despite his personal stature, his alienation from the national government that had come into being after the split in the Labour government, particularly over cuts in unemployment benefit, inevitably diminished his influence at Geneva. For another, his role in the restructuring of the truncated Labour Party was a demanding one that inevitably attenuated his work as a major facilitator of the disarmament negotiations. He was not well and it may not be too much to hazard the guess that his life was shortened by his attempt to undertake more than might reasonably have been expected of him. At any rate, as the conference haggled its way its way through impasse after impasse it became clear that little in the way of real agreement was to be expected. Germany's first withdrawal and ultimate departure from the conference, along with the victory of National Socialism, spelled defeat not only for disarmament but for the League of Nations system as well.

Though criticism of Labour's leadership in foreign affairs was relatively muted when the party was in office, fundamental differences on essential matters remained, most importantly on the use of force even in support of the international organization. A diminishing group within the movement regarded a body created and controlled by capitalist governments as inimical to the working classes. In their view, a peaceful world depended upon the ascent to power of socialist governments and their subsequent collaboration. Many more accepted the new League of Nations, but believed, or wished to believe, that it could do its work by providing such substitutes for armed force as moral suasion and the gradual development of the habit of cooperation rather than conflict.

During the 1920s, Arthur Henderson and his team insisted that Labour could not simply impose its dogmas upon the governments of other nations. They understood that compromise and accommodation were the lifeblood of international intercourse and that a Labour government must be prepared for the give and take that fueled the international system. Increasingly, as a result, they became the advocates of a League system that accepted the need for sanctions—ultimately the possible use of force—to undergird a developing League of Nations. While they believed that the underlying differences among nations that were the cause of international tensions had to be addressed, they also argued that, in the world that existed, armed force continued to be necessary. Of course, until well into the 1930s, when the international environment changed dramatically, they were less than enthusiastic for the kind of military alliances that the French, in particular, sought to develop. Moreover, for obvious domestic reasons, they downplayed the possible use of military sanctions even in support of League actions. Nevertheless, their position toward the use of force was undergoing a significant shift as the years went by. Their policy of reliance upon the League, of appeasement designed to remedy some of the inequities of the postwar settlement, and of disarmament or the reduction of armaments was, at least, an early version of what came to be called collective security. For the decade ending in 1930 it was a forward-looking policy. But in a few short years, the attack upon the international order—by Japan, by Italy, and, above all, by Germany—changed all the assumptions upon which the policies of Henderson and his supporters rested.

7

The Early 1930s

Throughout the 1930s, Labour struggled with a number of issues: resisting challenges to the international order, dealing with its mistrust of the Conservative-dominated National Government, and tempering pacifism among its rank and file. Labour's ambivalence about the use of force to maintain worldwide peace in the thirties was no less striking than that of the National Government. But, in that decade, the heirs to the Henderson initiative, along with such outspoken trade unionists as Ernest Bevin and Walter Citrine, ensured that Labour's official policy was one that eventually made it possible for Labour's leaders to take their place as effective members of the wartime coalition finally put together by Winston Churchill.

The tangled, not to say confused, character of Labour's foreign policy in the early years of the 1930s can only be understood in the light of the debacle of 1931. The defection of MacDonald and a handful of supporters followed by the disastrous general election of October left the Parliamentary Party rudderless. Henderson had to split his time between preparing for the Disarmament Conference and restoring stability to the political wing of Labour. The major spokesmen for the international policies he had advocated, Dalton preeminent among them, were for the time being out of Parliament. In fairly short order Henderson gave up the leadership to George Lansbury, whose sincere attempts to speak for the party on issues of foreign policy while at the same not compromising his own pacifist views inevitably created misunderstandings and tensions. Lansbury's Deputy Leader, Clement Attlee, had come close to taking a pacifist line as early as 1923 and until about 1934 appeared to be significantly influenced by the left-wing views of Sir Stafford Cripps. Attlee's "tergiversations" mirrored those of the party, and as a leader he continued to voice the uncertainties and ambiguities in Labour thinking.[1]

Given the defection of MacDonald and his followers along with the overwhelming defeat of Labour in the general election of 1931, it is not surprising that the General Council of the Trades Union Congress should begin to wield greater influence in the labour movement through the National Joint Council (later National Council) established in 1932. Eventually, for example, Ernest Bevin and Sir Walter Citrine joined Hugh Dalton as the most outspoken of the champions of a policy of "collective security" through the League of Nations in the face of Japanese aggression in China and then of the growing threat of fascism on the European continent. Even here, however, political prudence often appeared to dictate minimizing the danger that force might be necessary to implement the peacekeeping functions of an international body.

Once again in opposition, the first test of the diminished Labour Party came when the Japanese army used the fabricated sabotage of a railway in Manchuria to seize control of that Chinese province. Britain had had serious differences with the Chinese, in large part because of the inability of the Chinese government to control the divisive elements in that country. Labour's representatives, like the members of the National Government, in the first instance did not see the Japanese aggression as jeopardizing British interests in the area. While they came to recognize that Japanese actions posed a test of the effectiveness of the machinery of the League of Nations and criticized the National Government for its failure to take a stand against them, their own stand was hardly characterized by more than a tentative reference to economic deterrents as a means of changing Japanese policy. Critics probably went too far in emphasizing the negative aspects of Labour's reactions to the Far Eastern crisis, just as Labour apologists, then and later, tended to exaggerate the firmness of the party's position. [2]

Almost on the eve of the Japanese move, Lansbury left no uncertainty about where he stood as he commented in the House of Commons. What would the people of the East think of the League and the other Great Powers, he queried, if they could not exercise "moral influence" over Japan to prevent her continuing on her path? As if to make his point clear, he hoped the government would do all it could to persuade the Japanese to bring their case to arbitration or judicial settlement. "I do not want to be considered," he assured the Commons, "as urging that the moment has come for the application of sanctions."[3] This was a position that was not significantly different from that of the foreign secretary, Sir John Simon, who rejected the doctrine of nonrecognition proposed by the American secretary of state and made clear his opposition to any form of sanctions in the case.[4]

The farthest that the National Joint Council would go in the early stages of the Japanese action was to urge the British government to request the League of Nations Council immediately to consider the advisability of calling upon all members of the League and signatories of the Kellogg Peace Pact to withdraw their representatives from Tokyo. "We trust this withdrawal will not be necessary, and hope and believe that a manifestation of world opinion that the war must cease will not go unheeded in Japan." What if the Japanese, in defiance of the public opinion of the world, refused to cooperate? The Joint Council then called upon the British government to propose whatever "cooperative and graduated" measures of financial and economic constraint as might be necessary, in association with the United States and members of the League, to restore peace and ensure a just settlement.[5] This was hardly a full-throated endorsement of international action, but it remained for some months the major statement of Labour's position.

The report of the Lytton Committee, which had been commissioned by the League to investigate the Sino-Japanese controversy, sympathized with Japan's grievances but condemned the invasion of China. Once that report had been issued, the General Council of the TUC and the Executive of the Labour Party urged that economic sanctions be adopted to coerce Japan into accommodation in the Far East. At the same time, however, the Parliamentary Party would go no further than to advocate an embargo on shipment of arms to Japan. Even there, Lansbury illustrated the almost schizophrenic problem of the Labour leadership. In making the case for the embargo he indicated that the cutting off of arms shipments to Japan was the policy of the Labour Party, but that he himself would prefer not to send arms to either side.

While the labour movement, for the most part, marked time, both before and after the issuance of the Lytton Report, its few organs of opinion called in general terms for action. The *New Statesman,* for example, judged at the end of October that it was too soon to discuss the application of sanctions against the breakers of the League Covenant, but it argued that if the defiance of the Council were to be permitted, "we may as well put the Covenant and the Kellogg Pact into the wastepaper basket, and offer the Palais des Nations to the Russians to be made into a museum." By November the journal professed to see signs that the Japanese would "repent" and suggested that cooperation in the withdrawal of ambassadors to Japan might be effective in persuading the more moderate elements in Japan to oppose the militarists. If not, then there might be resort to economic sanctions, but to "that extreme" the *New Statesman* trusted it would not be necessary to go. As time went on, the paper argued that to concede Japan's claims would be to ring the death knell of the League and all it stood for. By February of 1932, when it seemed clear that the League was unlikely to take significant action, the *New Statesman* became somewhat bolder. "We do not want to see all the sanctions of Article XVI rigorously and instantly applied," but if the Japanese went on with their aggression, then sanctions would not worsen the situation. Japanese finances were already strained and the "big money powers" of Europe and the United States could, if they chose, put a heavy check on Japan. Finally, even as it called for vigorous action against Japan, the paper judged that a blockade of Japan would be unnecessary, but that economic and diplomatic pressure should be applied cumulatively and progressively. Thus, an oil embargo might be more effective than one on arms. It is hard to escape the conclusion that the editor of the paper, Kingsley Martin, was trying to carry water on both shoulders, calling for "action" but stopping short of the action that Henderson, Dalton, and some of their supporters had come to regard as the ultimate sanction of the international community.[6]

The official organ of the movement, the *Daily Herald*, devoted much less attention to the Far Eastern conflict. When the Lytton Report appeared, the *Herald* greeted its "cool and impartial" establishment of the facts and suggested that the Council and Assembly of the League must first make a supreme and final effort to secure a settlement by negotiation and consent on the lines proposed by the Lytton Commissioners. Since prospects of the success of such an approach were slight, the next step must be decided with the most careful consideration—but that there must be a next step was unquestioned. If not, then the whole League system built up since the war would be in ruins. The *Herald* had no proposals for action, but it took comfort in what it judged to be the fact that the League could count on the full cooperation of the United States in any measures it might take to vindicate the paramountcy of law.[7]

On the left, H.N. Brailsford was much less sanguine. By February of 1932, observing the hesitancies and rationalization of both London and Geneva, he came to the conclusion that the League, for all practical purposes was dead. Could anyone maintain, he enquired, after its failure to protect China, that any shred of belief survived in its capacity to avert war or to bring an offender before a court of the world's justice? Even in circumstances that were unusually favorable for action against Japan—she had no ally, America was ready to act with the League— nothing had been done. It was manifest that any Great Power bent on war could defy the League with impunity and not even suffer a verbal censure regardless of whether it had shattered every rule of humanity and broken the treaties that were a charter of order in the world. Realistically, Japan was vulnerable to economic pressure, but it was an illusion to believe that either the Council or the Assembly of the League would now do anything effective.[8]

By this time, Brailsford was presenting a point of view he shared with an ILP that was rapidly, if reluctantly, moving toward disaffiliation from the Labour Party and retreat to the margins of real effectiveness in both domestic and international policy. At a time when a significant number of intellectuals expressed their dissatisfaction with the politics of the gradualist left by joining, or at least flirting with, the Communist Party, the seceders who followed James Maxton out of the Labour Party increasingly found themselves bypassed in the struggle for the minds of the "progressive" forces in the British political spectrum. Probably more important in left-wing politics for a brief period of time after 1932 was the formation of the Socialist League by the group which opted to remain in the Labour Party and to attempt to influence its policy from within. Joined by the Society for Socialist Inquiry and Propaganda and the New Fabian Research Bureau, the new group chose E. F. Wise, who was to die prematurely, as its first chairman. As time went on Sir Stafford Cripps became its most prominent spokesman, as well as its major financial benefactor. Although he was a nephew of Beatrice Webb, Cripps, a distinguished and highly remunerated King's Counsel, appears to have been a conventional Conservative early in his career. Gradually, however, concern for the social question and the example of his father, Lord Parmoor, who had moved from Conservatism to Labour because he viewed the Labour Party as right in its international outlook, persuaded him to join Labour in the late 1920s. When he was made solicitor general in 1930, he was not yet a member of Parliament, but after the collapse of the second Labour government he came to be regarded as a possible future leader of the party. Deeply conscious of the poverty he saw about him in the years of the Depression, he drifted farther to the left in a somewhat unsystematic flirtation with a kind of ethically based Marxism, then step-by-step came to believe that the foreign policy of the National Government was the greatest threat to the safety of the British people.[9]

Along with Cripps, the leadership of the Socialist League included a mixed bag of pacifists, Christian socialists, some Marxists and ex-communists, as well as the ex-ILPers. Among them were Brailsford and Cripps, Sir Charles Trevelyan, Harold Laski, G.D.H. Cole, Ellen Wilkinson, D.N.Pritt, William Mellor, G.R.Strauss, and Aneurin Bevan. From the beginning there was tension with the middle-of-the-road chieftains of the Labour Party (and the TUC) as the Socialist League, quite like the ILP before it, tried, as it were, to function as a rival party within the ranks of the Labour Party.[10] In fairly short order, both G.D.H.Cole and Ernest Bevin, for quite different reasons, became alienated and distanced themselves from the Socialist League. Bevin in particular took the lead in setting up the National Joint Council through which the Trades Union Congress exercised a growing influence over the policies of the labour movment.

The Labour left, responding to the destruction of the working-class movements throughout a good part of Europe, was most successful in forcing through the 1932 Leicester conference of the Labour Party a series of resolutions in effect urging that any future Labour government apply genuinely socialist principles to the legislation it promoted. Arthur Henderson was disgusted by the lack of realism in the actions of the conference and Hugh Dalton commented that Henderson's reaction was one of the reasons for his giving up of the leadership of the party and surrendering it to George Lansbury.[11]

At the same time, Socialist League figures began to urge consideration of Communist International proposals for the formation of "United Fronts" to resist the march of fascism which some saw as the inevitable outcome of a capitalism in decline. A majority of the leaders of the Labour Party and the Trades Union Congress, like the Labour and Socialist International, were convinced that the United Front agitation was a scheme promoted by the British Communist Party as an entering wedge by which to undermine the Labour Party and promote the growth of communism.[12] The issue remained a matter of controversy within the Labour movement through most of the 1930s, illustrative of serious divisions even when the marshalling of the major big battalions of the trade unions gave overwhelming support to the mainstream positions of Labour's National Executive and the General Council of the TUC. In that sense, the resolutions at Leicester and, more dramatically, those of the Hastings conference in 1933 seemed aberrations subsequently rationalized away in the somewhat misleading explanations of the official leaders of Labour.

The Hastings conference was held while the Labour Party was still reeling from the consequences of the split in the party and the subsequent setback in the general election of 1931. There Sir Charles Trevelyan, in a kind of farewell gesture before his semi-retirement to his estate in Northumberland, presented a long composite resolution on the question of war and peace. After a preamble which viewed with disquiet the steady drift of the international system towards war and the failure of the governments assembled at Geneva to check such developments, it instructed the National Executive of the party, in conjunction with the TUC and the Cooperative Movement, to launch vigorous propaganda to counter the tendencies in the present social system which predisposed large sections to respond readily to war appeals. Stressing the growing awareness of the war danger, the appalling nature of the modern methods of warfare, the economic crisis and the deepening of capitalist and imperialist rivalries along with the growth of Fascism as a direct cause of war, the resolution called upon Labour to pledge itself to take no part in war and to resist it with the whole force of the labour movement. It urged the Labour Party to consult with the Trade Union and Cooperative movements to decide what steps, including a general strike, should be taken to organize the opposition of the working class movement in the event of war or the threat of war. Finally, the statement urged British Labour to take steps to secure international action by the workers along the same lines.

In presenting the resolution, Trevelyan conceded that the League of Nations would some day become the machinery for international safety, but only "when hearts are different and Governments are different." If the government would not use the League to check Japan, could Labour believe that it would itself be checked if it embroiled itself with other nations? He was certain that in the event of war there would be widespread refusal to have anything to do with it throughout all classes in society, but he called upon "the greatest democratic working class in the world" to take the lead in determining that war should not be. [13]

The notion that war might be avoided by rhetoric accompanied by a general strike had attracted the support of a minority in the labour movement since before the First World War. Keir Hardie had been persuaded not that a general strike was necessarily a feasible undertaking, but that the threat of such action at the very least would strengthen the propaganda of the advocates of peaceful settlement of international issues. Trevelyan too saw the conference resolution as a call to all classes to express their horror of war by a statement of combined resistance. Individual action was not enough to stop war in a rising tide of patriotism and fear: "We have got to make them listen next time and let no one say it is impossible."[14] While the Trevelyan resolution represented the long-held views of a minority in Labour's ranks it also reflected the frustration and the sense of defeat that clearly was to be felt among a much larger segment of Labour Party members.

Attention to that sense of defeat had been urged by the Advisory Committee on International Questions in an important memorandum earlier in 1933. Pointing to the deterioration of the international situation, highlighted by the war between Japan and China, the menacing position of Germany, the dangerous tensions in the Balkans, and the isolation of Russia, the committee noted especially the futility of the League in dealing with the Japanese action in Manchuria and its unproductiveness at the Disarmament Conference. Those facts had been accompanied by, and to some extent had caused, a change in public opinion with regard to the League. Certainly the feeling had been growing among the Labour rank-and-file that the League had failed and that it was not a reality. This change in attitude demanded serious attention for it meant that an increasing body of opinion among the supporters of Labour no longer was in sympathy with one of the main planks in the Labour Party's international policy. In other words, there was now in the party a considerable body of opinion in favor of a policy of isolation from any international embroilment, whether in Europe or elsewhere. Clearly, such a policy was not consistent with the official policy of the party, which had always stood for full and active support for the League and the Covenant obligations.[15]

The Advisory Committee's assessment throws light on why the Executive of the party accepted a resolution at the Hastings conference which surely Henderson and Noel Baker and Dalton found unrealistically self-deluding. Dalton later suggested that the Executive had gone along because it considered it a mere oversight that the Trevelyan motion had not excluded League sanctions from its rejection of war.[16] Technically, he argued as well, since the resolution was a composite one it could not be amended, but would have to be voted up or down. Not wishing to precipitate a floor fight with a debate on disarmament in the offing, the platform accepted the resolution, including the general strike, with fingers crossed and the determination so to interpret the will of the membership as to bend the statement to what the Executive viewed as a more realistic approach to the issue of war and peace. Noel Baker did warn that no delegate should vote for the resolution until he understood the personal obligations it meant for him. To him the statement was a declaration of Labour policy, a program of propaganda, the starting point for the foreign policy of the next Labour government, and a program for action of the Labour Party if war came while it was out of office. He regretted that the resolution was not based on the Kellogg Pact and the Covenant of the League of Nations, but he felt that it was a declaration that would go ringing through the country. For his part, Dalton also commended the pronouncement, only regretting that it did not go far enough in prescribing the economic and financial boycott of a war-mongering state—"Hitler, or any other person who may disturb the peace and murder the workers of the world." His call upon the delegates to accept the resolution was greeted by a unanimous vote of support.[17]

In the debate on disarmament that followed, Henderson took the lead, bluntly taking issue with Trevelyan by insisting that the task of organizing peace depended on one political instrument, and only one, the League of Nations. He realized that the League was far from being a perfect instrument, but it had the great merit of existing. He noted that he had outlined his own views on how the League could be improved in a recent pamphlet and emphasized the importance of bringing the United States and the Soviet Union more fully into the partnership for organizing the peace.[18] Here too, he asserted, the road to both Washington and Moscow lay through Geneva. The League had come into being largely because of the pressure of the Labour and Socialist movement and they needed to be vigilant in seeing that its purposes were realized. After his address to the conference, J.R. Clynes, who had from the first been a firm advocate of a League of Nations policy, proposed an Executive-sponsored resolution which was regarded, however much that might have been the case, as quite compatible with the Trevelyan statement just accepted. It read:

> This Conference favours the total disarmament of all nations throughout the World and the creation of an International Police Force, and calls upon the British government at the Disarmament Conference to abandon its retrograde attitude on the question of air-bombing, and to submit proposals for a large and immediate reduction in the expenditure of all nations on armed forces, for the general abolition of all weapons forbidden to Germany by the Treaty of Versailles, for the abolition of military aircraft and for the International Control of civil aviation, for the suppression of all private manufacture and trade in arms, and for strict International inspection and control of the execution of a Disarmament Treaty.[19]

Like the resolution incorporating support for a general strike, the disarmament statement was a composite of the proposals of a number of constituent groups. Clynes urged the delegates to vote for its spirit without too critical a concern for specific phrases. With relatively little discussion the resolution was accepted.

Whether a general strike against war or its threat was compatible with support for a war undertaken by an international police force or in support of the decisions of an international body was an issue not debated at Hastings. It was one on which there continued to be major differences of view, sometimes openly and clearly articulated, sometimes under the surface of positions for which the rationalizations spoke to only a portion of the perceptions of the respective advocates. As Clement Attlee noted in a letter to his brother Tom, the actions of the 1933 conference indicated that the party had not really made up its mind as to whether it wanted to take up an extreme disarmament and isolationist attitude or whether it would take the risks of standing for the enforcement of the decisions of a world organization against individual aggressor states.[20] It is clear that "disarmament" meant different things to different groups in the labour movement. For some it denoted unilateral surrender of national armaments, the "disarmament by example" that Arthur Ponsonby had been preaching for several decades. For others, it often was regarded as a substitute for the other instruments of international peacekeeping, at least until the triumph of socialism ushered in a new millennium of understanding and cooperation. Above all, for many in this heterogeneous group the use of force in any circumstances was anathema. So long as the official Labour Party position—negotiated multilateral disarmament and adherence to the League of Nations Covenant—showed little danger that the use of force was likely, it was possible for this group to go along with that policy. Hitler's rise to power, in particular, made the question of military sanctions a more urgent one and sharply divided the labour movement up to the very eve of a new war. [21]

The more pragmatic mainstream leaders assumed, for the most part, that disarmament connoted a reduction in the level of national armaments as part of an international system in which the machinery of accommodation through the League of Nations—arbitration, conciliation, judicial settlement of disputes—might act as complements for arms that, ideally, would be available only to the international body. As the international order deteriorated after 1931, the leading advocates of the latter position became more and more urgent in their insistence that it was imperative that the Disarmament Conference show some concrete results. Hugh Dalton noted that those who had framed the peace treaties and founded the League of Nations had foreshadowed such a gathering, but it had taken more than twelve years to bring it together. If it should now fail, the world would be left in an even more desperate and disillusioned and dangerous mood than at present. The labour movement, he contended, had done its best to rouse public opinion to the importance of disarmament, but "the nations to-day resemble men walking in their sleep, men walking unawares amid stupendous dangers, towards a precipice over which our civilisation may, if we do not soon change our direction, crash to destruction."[22]

Similarly, if less emotionally, as the Disarmament Conference argued its way from one impasse to another, Will Arnold Forster pointed out that the peace movement, especially the socialist parties, had again and again insisted that the system of disarmament would only be complete and durable if it was based on equality of rights and duties. That meant that nothing would be more fatal to peace than to claim that the victorious and vanquished nations could be kept indefinitely under different systems of armaments. Germany's "recalcitrance" was logical and to have been expected.[23] As yet, the full implication of the triumph of the Nazis was unclear. The *New Statesman*, for example, professed to believe that Hitler had overreached himself on Jew baiting, attacks on churches, and the irritation of capitalists and industrialists. Having destroyed the private army that had brought him to power, he would be forced to fight more bitterly still to retain any reality of power.[24]

By the time Henderson and Clynes had introduced the resolution to the Hastings conference that paralleled the position of Arnold Forster, Japan had left the League of Nations and Germany was about to do so. Responsibility for Germany's withdrawal was placed squarely on Sir John Simon, the foreign secretary, by the *Daily Herald*. He was blamed as the leader in the "take it or leave it" refusal of the major powers to compromise on German demands for arms equality.[25] Now any accommodation on the reduction of armaments appeared less likely and less realistic. The *New Statesman* urged Henderson to resign as president of the Disarmament Conference and not listen to those who urged him to remain in order to obtain some convention, however valueless.[26]

Henderson stubbornly continued until the eve of his death in 1935 to hope for some breakthrough on the disarmament front. He was, perhaps, supported in his view by a long memorandum drawn up for use by the Labour Party's National Executive Committee, which contended that the British government was largely responsible for the collapse of the European order. Failing to tackle the legitimate demands of a democratic Germany, it was now faced with the violent reactionary militarism of the Hitler regime. The memo condemned the Nazi government's destruction of democracy and the abolition of the rights of personal liberty and free speech; noted the beginning of rearmament in Germany by the incorporation of Storm Troopers and Steel Helmets into the armed police; and denounced the speeches of Hitler, Goering (spelled Goerling), and other Nazi ministers for statements that "the spirit of peace must be killed" or that "Germany's rights must be asserted by the shedding of blood" or that "Germany has now shown that the spirit of Locarno is dead." The memorandum went on nevertheless to warn that it was important not to exaggerate the consequences to which these factors were likely to lead. Though there was much talk of conflict, there appeared to be no immediate prospect of war in Europe. Those who regarded the situation as being as serious as in July 1914 were creating fears that were without foundation. The German General Staff was aware that it would take some time to rebuild the military strength of Germany, even if they were free from all armament restriction. In addition, the present French government of the left was more disposed in favor of the League of Nations and far more receptive to disarmament, arbitration, and international cooperation than any of its predecessors. So were Spain, the Scandinavian nations, and the Little Entente countries. Thus, the NEC was advised, there was still a period, to be measured in years not months, during which attempts could be made to recover lost ground and restore an atmosphere of confidence and peace. What then should the Labour Party do? First, asserted the advisory document, it should make plain to the country the responsibility of the British government for the deterioration in international relations. Second, it should emphasize its support for the whole panoply of international measures through the League of Nations. It should make that choice even if it should seem to involve some risks, and it should do so with the clear realization that the risks, whatever they might be, were far less than those of a return to the "old system of armaments competition and the chaos of conflicting alliances."[27]

This rather curious mixture of realism and wishful thinking was, it seems reasonable to conclude, a fair reflection of the approach of many of the official leaders of the Party in late 1933. By this time, however, Henderson's collaborators—Dalton, Noel Baker, Arnold Forster—along with key trade union representatives such as Ernest Bevin and Sir Walter Citrine increasingly were insisting that the aggressive challenge to the international order, particularly the looming threat of Nazi Germany, must be resisted, by force if necessary—and, as a corollary, that the military means to do so must be provided.

Even before the Labour Party met at Southport in October 1934, the National Joint Council (NJC) distanced the party and the TUC from the proposals accepted at Hastings. In April, the NJC carried a resolution deploring the dragging of feet on disarmament, noting the notice of withdrawal from the League of Japan and Germany, and observing that the United States and Soviet Russia still remained outside that body, while the world drifted towards international anarchy, indeed was drifting towards war. Urging that governments make a supreme effort to bring the Disarmament Conference to a successful conclusion, the Joint Council, for the first time, declared that it would wholeheartedly support the government in any risks or consequences that might ensue from its joining in world action to prevent or stop war.[28] Independently, the General Council of the Trades Union Congress took pains to make its position clear. In June, it adopted a memorandum on war and peace which insisted that it was necessary to distinguish between a war of an aggressive character and a war undertaken in defence of the collective peace system as organized under the League of Nations Covenant, the Optional Clause, and the General Act. The Council was emphatically opposed to any form of aggressive war, but recognized that there might be circumstances under which the government of Great Britain might have to use its military and naval forces in support of the League in restraining an aggressor nation which flagrantly used military measures in defiance of its pledged word. Finally, the General Council pointed out once more, in connection with the general strike, that responsibility for stopping war ought not to be placed on the trade union movement alone.[29]

At Southport, the Executive took its stand on Henderson's memorandum entitled "War and Peace," which had also been adopted by the National Joint Council in April.[30] Referring back to the Hastings requirement that the Executive consult with the trade union and cooperative movements regarding steps, including the general strike, to be taken in the event of war or the threat of war, the document rejected the general strike. Instead, it outlined the legal bases upon which the League system rested and suggested ways for making the world's commitments against war "watertight on paper and effective in practice." Henderson insisted that the Executive was not drafting a new policy, but merely restating Labour's aims and Labour's policy, while indicating methods by which that policy might be applied. Among them were bringing the United States and the Soviet Union into close cooperation with and as far as possible into membership of the League, suppressing the private manufacture of arms, and making a fresh start on disarmament by proposing such moves as the abolition of all weapons forbidden to the Central Powers by the 1919 treaties. Labour could support the total abolition of national military and naval forces, the internationalization of civil aviation, as well as a comprehensive and continuous system of control and the working out of a definition of aggression. All of this culminated in the demand for a Peace Act of Parliament to incorporate in the law of the land the principles to which Labour was committed under the "collective peace system." Opposition to "War and Peace" came from a variety of sources. It was led by figures in the Socialist League, who were joined, among others, by pacifists who were opposed to the notion of an International Police Force as proposed by Henderson. More than a third of the conference opposed the resolution, but the bloc votes of the trade unions, as was usually the case, carried the day for the Executive.[31]

As yet, whatever the position of the Joint Council, the issue of armaments and the use of force remained unresolved among the various constituents of the labour movement. As for the general strike, "War and Peace" had argued that in countries such as Germany, Italy, or Austria such a move was impossible and that even in Britain, as had been pointed out by the General Council of the TUC, the responsibility for stopping war ought not to be placed upon the trade union movement alone. The standing orders of the Trades Union Congress provided that a special conference should be called in the event of the danger of war. This, despite its obvious difficulties, provided the working class with the best means for dealing with the situation.[32]

The search for agreement on foreign policy continued as the international situation deteriorated. In February, a failed Nazi coup in Austria resulted in the murder of Chancellor Engelbert Dolfuss. A few months later, Hitler announced the resumption of conscription in Germany. In reaction, the British, French, and Italians met in conference at Stresa to make a brief display of unity. They condemned Germany's recent action, insisted on the maintenance of Austria's independence, and supported the Locarno agreements. The one failure at Stresa was the British silence with regard to Mussolini's intentions concerning Ethiopia. Much later, Dalton damned it as "one of the most criminal blunders in the whole course of British diplomacy in these disastrous years." [33]

Shortly before Stresa, the British government had issued an important White Paper on defence which announced a commitment to increased armament expenditure in the light of German rearmament. At that time, Dalton, for example, was less concerned about the danger of war than many of his Labour party fellows. Urging full support for the League of Nations, he was more inclined than most to assume that the government meant what it said.[34] But Dalton had been out of Parliament since 1931 and was not to return until the general election of November 1935. For those on the left, such as Stafford Cripps, both German Nazism and British Toryism were different manifestations of capitalism in decline. At this stage, they were unwilling to entrust a capitalist government, whose purposes they did not share and could not control, with augmented arms, even if used to balance the power of Nazi Germany or Fascist Italy. [35]

In short order, in any case, the so-called Stresa Front of Britain, France, and Italy, designed to keep Germany in check, collapsed under twin blows dealt by the British and Italian governments. The British signing of a naval agreement with Germany stemmed from a number of objectives: a desire to prevent a financially ruinous rearmament program; the need to deploy a maximum naval strength in the Far East in the event of war with Japan; a genuine wish to create some measure of arms control that might contribute to European pacification; the hope of promoting also some limitation on air forces in the light of Hitler's claim of parity with Britain; and, finally, the purpose of placating a confused public opinion which, though suspicious of large-scale rearmament, feared the possibility of a new war.[36] Whatever the motives, the treaty tore up a key provision of the Treaty of Versailles.

In urging the National Executive to condemn the Anglo-German naval agreement, the Advisory Committee outlined the reasons many had given for welcoming it—that it put some limit on German armaments, that the one-sided military provisions of the Versailles Treaty could not be maintained indefinitely, and that the policy made for a healthy break away from the weak subservience to France which had long paralyzed British policy on disarmament and collective security. Refuting each of the justifications, the committee called the agreement a triumph for Hitler's policy of dividing Britain from France. It advised that Party's spokesmen should strongly criticize the agreement on the ground that it injured the collective peace system, encouraged the Nazi challenge to Geneva, needlessly exasperated the French, and would contribute to an increase in armaments. To describe it as a contribution to reduction was a cynical piece of misrepresentation.[37] The argument was essentially the one that Attlee made in the House of Commons, but Labour's criticism was rather muted, perhaps because for so many years it had been arguing that Germany should be treated equally, preferably, to be sure, by scaling armaments down to her level, but in any case equally.[38]

Both government and opposition were evidently influenced by the results of the impressive polling of public opinion by the League of Nations Union in the National Declaration on the League of Nations and Armaments of 1934-5 which was much better known as the Peace Ballot. The Numerous peace and other voluntary groups which helped the League of Nations Union to poll the remarkable figure of 38 percent of the adult population in that Ballot were active in ensuring that the ballot showed overwhelming support for the control and reduction, and in some cases, abolition by international agreement of national armaments. Although its Question 5 (b) on military sanctions produced more "no" votes than any of the other questions, even that response showed almost a 7 to 2 support for such measures if necessary to contain an aggressor.[39]

At the same time, Mussolini's use of a border incident to prepare for the conquest of Abysssinia was a direct challenge to the League of Nations, to which Emperor Haile Selassie had appealed in early 1935. As the Italian dictator made his preparations for war, the political leadership of Labour was slow to make its position clear, despite the Advisory Committee's urging that there never had been any dispute between two powers in which the fundamental principles of the League Covenant were so clearly at stake—and in which those principles had been so deliberately set aside. As late as May 1935 the situation did not appear serious enough to warrant mention during the course of a major House of Commons debate on foreign policy.[40] In part, this may have reflected a growing unease about the emerging German menace. In April, for instance, the Bureau of the Labour and Socialist International (LSI), in expressing concern that the dangers to world peace were growing, had centered its attention on Germany. There, an important memorandum on the European situation declared that the German dictatorship had flung down a challenge to Europe and the world. It had repudiated the League of Nations, it had not abandoned its annexationist aims, it was in the process of achieving military preponderance in Europe, while the armaments race, an immediate consequence of German policy, augmented the dangers. Urging the cooperation of the Western democracies with the Soviet Union to prevent war, the LSI called upon working people in all countries to offer opposition both to the jingoism promoted by recent events and to war itself. The dangers of war in Europe would be averted only when it was known and understood that every member of the League of Nations must cooperate loyally and effectively, to an extent compatible with its military situation and geographic position, in support of the Covenant and in resistance to any act of aggression. Recognizing the equality of Germany, "an equality of duties, no less than of rights," the document called for equality of all countries, not through rearmament, but by the disarmament of all.[41]

Both the British government and Labour's leadership faced the dilemma of how to check Mussolini without driving him into the hands of Hitler. Just before Mussolini's legions marched their way into Abyssinia, the Advisory Committee once again took on the issue of the sanctions that might be employed in support of the League Covenant. If the peace was broken and sanctions were applied, it warned, then the efficiency of the economic sanctions that might be undertaken would be undermined, "if the Covenant were so interpreted as to justify the expectation that, whatever the circumstances and development, force would never be used." The Labour Party could not refuse, advised the committee's memorandum, to support any collective action, including the military sanctions of the Covenant, which might be found necessary to implement the league's purposes.[42]

The Advisory Committee's assessment reflected the views of only one segment of Labour's leadership. For a time Lansbury had managed to downplay his personal pacifism in speaking for the Labour Party, but the Abyssinian crisis made clear how deep was the gap between his position and even a moderate support for any League policy of sanctions.[43] On the left of the party, Cripps and some of his colleagues in the Socialist League rejected the League of Nations not for pacifist reasons but as the tool of imperialist British and French governments anxious to preserve the system that was the fundamental cause of war in the first place. Cripps' alienation from the thinking of the majority of the leadership impelled him to resign from the National Executive in order to free himself to argue his case for a change of policy.[44] Somewhere in the middle of the party's controversy were those like the deputy leader, Clement Attlee, who well beyond this period supported a League policy of collective security, but rejected both British rearmament and military sanctions.[45]

While the labour movement was virtually unanimous in condemning the impending attack on Abyssinia, most of the supporters of "collective security" nevertheless were careful to avoid the suggestion that to stop Mussolini might require more than good intentions or at most economic or financial pressure.[46] Sir Walter Citrine, the General Secretary of the TUC, was a major exception who made no bones about the implications of sanctions. In the fall of 1935, he outlined the meaning of economic and financial pressure, insisting that it was necessary "to put at the disposal of the League of Nations such a measure of force of a military, naval and aerial character as may be necessary to make the sanctions really effective." [47] Even Ernest Bevin and Hugh Dalton, who were the major voices urging resistance to the march of dictatorship, felt it necessary to minimize the possible use of force. The dramatic picture of Bevin lumbering up to the platform at the Labour Party conference in 1935 to attack George Lansbury has tended to obscure the rest of his remarks. While he bluntly supported Citrine's frankness at the TUC about sanctions, he concluded his speech by declaring of Mussolini, "he shall perish by *economic* [my italics] sanctions." And Dalton, while refusing to dismiss the risks involved, argued that the threat of sanctions might be enough to prevent war. If not, the use of economic and financial tools, without any military or naval action, might be enough to reestablish peace even if Mussolini broke it.[48] A similar position was adopted in the labour press, where the call for sanctions against Italy was accompanied by the assurance that neither military nor naval "acts of war" would be needed.[49]

Labour's caution was illustrated in the campaign for the general election of November, when virtually no mention was made of the possible recourse to military sanctions.[50]

Lansbury's resignation from the leadership of the Labour Party, precipitated by Bevin's assault, facilitated the determination of the "Dalton-Bevin-Citrine block" [51]to bring their followers around to support for the rearmament of Britain in the face, particularly, of the growing menace of Nazi Germany. Not until 1937 was the campaign to bear fruition. As yet any suggestion of collaboration with the national government was an impossibility given strongly held suspicions in all quarters of the labour movement.

As the Italian troops began their invasion of Abyssinia, the British government's brief flirtation with a League policy designed to restrain Mussolini was belied by the notorious Hoare-Laval plan, an agreement between the foreign ministers of Britain and France that would have given Mussolini substantially what he desired in Abyssinia. The National Council's opposition to the agreement was only part of a substantial wave of public opposition that compelled the government to repudiate it.[52] Repudiation, however, was not followed by serious collaborative measures to restrain Italy and in less than a year the conquest of Abyssinia was a fait accompli.[53]

Although Labour had been unsuccessful in frustrating the aggression of the Japanese in China and the Italians in Abyssinia, there had been a discernible change in the party's posture between 1931 and early 1936. For a minority of the party, the horrors of conflict outweighed revulsion at the admitted iniquities of the dictatorial regimes. These Labourites continued to believe, against all the evidence, that Hitler could be bought off by redress of the grievances in the hated Versailles Treaty.[54] Others, for the time, remained convinced that any collaboration with capitalist and imperialist governments, Britain among them, would be self-defeating. But the influence of the trade union movement—a trade unionism that was increasingly troubled by the growing threat of the Nazi rulers of Germany—began to undermine the reluctance of labour to confront the realities of the contemporary situation. Slowly, some of the more discerning leaders forced Labour to realize that the movement could no longer stand aside while the enemies of the international order made gain after gain. Tentatively, Labour began to accept that, in the world that existed, rearmament was a painful necessity upon which survival itself might rest.

8

The Triple Crisis

As the international situation became more ominous, Labour continued to struggle over its stance on rearmament, collective security, and international collaboration through the League of Nations.[1] Hitler's remilitarization of the Rhineland, Mussolini's triumph in Abyssinia, and the outbreak of the Spanish Civil War formed the backdrop for the continuing differences within the party over policy, differences that were hardly masked by official statements implying unity. In every instance, Labour's opposition to the actions of the National Government was a unifying factor in its internal discussions. Aside from that, much of the labour movement's earlier reluctance to deal with the realities of world affairs continued. Slowly, however, some leaders were won over by the dire warnings of those within their ranks who were certain that the overwhelming threat of the European dictatorships required, in particular, the abandonment of Labour's rejection of rearmament. The corollary was the general acceptance of the government's program of preparedness, despite the fact that Labour looked upon many other government policies with suspicion.

On the issue of rearmament, there was what the Parliamentary Party's earlier minutes delicately had called a diversity of views.[2] When the government prepared to present its White Paper on Defence on the morrow of the Rhineland reoccupation, it precipitated an extensive debate in Labour circles. At a meeting of the Parliamentary Labour Party, Sir Walter Citrine spoke on behalf of the General Council of the TUC. As early as May 1934, the General Council had passed a resolution indicating that its members were in favor of mobilizing public opinion against war of any kind except one undertaken in defense of the collective peace system under the auspices of the League of Nations Covenant.[3] Citrine suggested that an effort be made to have the government pledge that armed forces would only be used in support of League of Nations policy, making clear the view that the League was not a substitute for military power, but rather required to be supported by arms if it were to be effective. He went on to propose that the League be requested to call a conference to determine the armed forces necessary to uphold the principle of collective security, that it be asked whether further efforts would be made to develop non-aggression and mutual assistance pacts open to all states wishing to join, and finally that it be urged to renew efforts to secure a Disarmament Convention. He noted that the General Council was anxious that nothing should be said in the forthcoming Commons debate which could be interpreted as a desire to make concessions to Hitler. In response, Arthur Greenwood, speaking for the majority of the political leadership of Labour, insisted that, in view of the government's record, the party could not go into the lobby in support of the White Paper, which outlined the government's plan for substantial rearmament.[4]

Despite the General Council's emphasis on the use of armed strength only in support of the League, Citrine himself, like Ernest Bevin and Hugh Dalton, by now had come round to the view that rearmament, even by the National Government, was imperative. Dalton had hoped that the trade unionists' lead in fostering a more realistic approach to national defence would lead to a change in policy. To his despair, both the Parliamentary Labour Party and even the National Council of Labour persisted in supporting the policy of opposing rearmament in the hands of the National Government.[5] As in the past, Attlee, speaking for Labour in the House of Commons, insisted that the present level of armaments was sufficient to fulfill Britain's obligations under the League of Nations Covenant. He drew no conclusions about the hollowness of that contention in light of the contemporary ineffectiveness of the League in the Italo-Abyssinian affair.[6] Nevertheless, as yet only a handful of MPs expressed their disagreement with the position of the leadership by quietly abstaining when their colleagues went into the "no" lobby during a vote on supplementary armament estimates.[7]

Both Bevin and Dalton by now were convinced that rejection of the arms estimates, however much the action was merely symbolic, was disastrous. Bevin warned the TUC annual meeting that what was called collective security was in danger of becoming a shibboleth rather than a practical operative fact. "We are…satisfied," he insisted, "that we are not going to meet the Fascist menace by mere resolutions. We are not going to meet it by pure pacifism….If in certain respects it means uprooting some of our cherished ideals and facing the issue fairly in the light of the developments of Fascism, we must do it for the Movement and for the sake of posterity."[8] Dalton, for his part, confided to his diary that the Labour Party still would not face up to reality. "There is still much more anti-armament sentiment," he wrote, "and many are more agin' our own Government than agin' Hitler."[9]

Labour continued to indict the Italian rape of Abyssinia. It urged maintenance of the boycott of Germany to protest the persecutions there no less than Germany's unilateral repudiation of the Versailles settlement. But it still shied away from support of an arms program carried out by a mistrusted government. The emphasis continued to be placed not on support of the government's rearmament program, but on the organization of collective security by the

League of Nations, without Germany if she refused to participate in a general agreement.

The position of Attlee and of the majority of Labour's political leaders postulated an inclusive League of substantially disarmed states in which coercion—moral, economic, financial, even perhaps military—would be in the control of the international body. As for the argument that arms were necessary to protect British interests, the *Herald* outlined the rationale of the official Labour Party line when it proclaimed that there had been no serious effort to determine what "British interests" were, nor had there been any serious attempt to assess to what extent the system of collective security could be relied upon to protect those interests. Instead, the government's request for armed forces sufficient to enable them to "exercise authority in international affairs" revealed that under all its talk of the League and the Covenant it still held to the idea that the Great Powers could exercise their authority by the threat of armed national force. "Arms are Policy," intoned the *Herald,* and the National Government's demand for increased arms must be resisted at all costs. [10]

Similarly, the *New Statesman,* from its "moderate" left position, trumpeted that the government was putting its trust in competitive armaments, which always ended in war. The White Paper, in its view, was the preface to a colossal enterprise, which stretched vaguely into the alarming future, without limit of time or of cost. The journal assured its readers that there were currently plenty of League armaments. The forces of Great Britain, France, the USSR, the Little Entente, and other League Powers were already large enough to cope with any aggression—"if they hold together."[11] Throughout 1936, the Labour press reflected a view that was still dominant in Labour circles, however much the triumphs of Italy and Germany may have altered the assumptions upon which that view was based. As yet, that position insisted that armaments must serve international law, that they should be made into the instruments of world justice, or that they should be treated as a demonstration that all nations (including Britain) must renounce the claim to define their own sovereign right and accept third-party judgment in all their disputes with their neighbors.[12]

For most members of the Socialist League, the policy of supporting a democratic international system based on the League of Nations was self-deluding. A few agreed with the ex- communist J. T. Murphy, who sponsored a resolution at the League's annual conference backing collective security along with an alliance of Britain, France, and Soviet Russia. Others were willing to consider economic but not military sanctions. But Stafford Cripps undoubtedly spoke for a majority of the Socialist League's members when he argued that the sanctions accepted by the powers were deliberately chosen to have no effect.[13] Cripps was opposed to any and every encouragement of war or arming by a capitalist government. What was needed for security was an alliance with the USSR and other socialist states. "If we are to continue with capitalism and imperialism," he wrote in a little book published in 1936, " it is certainly better that we should leave them to be controlled and operated by those who believe in these systems."[14]

The disappearance of capitalism, postulated by Cripps and his followers as a requirement for an effective international system, was hardly in the realm of realistic expectation. Neither was the creation of a system of collective security based upon an alliance of progressive forces operating through the League of Nations. Even before the debate on the White Paper, when Hitler moved his troops into the demilitarized Rhineland, Bevin persuaded the TUC's National Council of Labour to invite the Bureau of the Labour and Socialist International and the Executive of the International Federation of Trade Unions (IFTU) to London. The result, aired a few months later, was an IFTU statement that condemned Hitler's action and agreed that aggression could not be restrained by moral force alone but required the show of collective force. The international body proposed that a convention for collective security by means of mutual aid and disarmament be the basis upon which the League of Nations should invite Germany to negotiate on an equal footing for the conclusion of a general agreement. A refusal would indicate Germany's persistent intention to disturb European peace and order. It would then be the duty of governments and peoples to organize peace without Hitlerite Germany and to take all measures of security necessary for maintaining that peace. For the most part, there was little follow up, even in the Labour Party. [15]

It was too much to expect that Germany would contentedly accept a system which left her richest and most vital industrial areas absolutely undefended and forbade her to mount a single anti-aircraft gun for their protection. The German move was a fact and had to be recognized as such.[16] Even Hugh Dalton, despite his conviction that rearmament was essential in the face of the Nazi threat, supported the National Government when it asked only for a formal condemnation of Germany by the League. Like many in all sections of the labour movement, he found it difficult, after the years of deploring the "unjust" treatment of Germany, to speak out against Hitler moving into Germany's own territory. Indeed, he confided to his diary his conviction that no military and probably no economic sanctions could be justified. Neither would be supported by public opinion and in particular by the Labour Party unless Germany actually attacked anyone. Instead he urged the party to press for an All-European Pact of Mutual Assistance against any aggression along with a conference to discuss colonies, markets, and other such issues of contention.[17]

During the summer of 1936 the need for such a discussion was explored by an Advisory Committee at the request of the National Executive. Dealing with the problem of equality of economic opportunity and access to raw materials, it placed special emphasis on the demand for colonial territory by Germany and Italy. The fact of discrimination, warned the committee, must not delude Labour into thinking that the colonies were quantitatively important, nor should they be deluded into thinking that economic discrimination was even a substantial cause of the economic difficulties of Germany and Italy. General tariff policy was more important than colonial policy and monetary policy more important than tariff policy.

The committee concluded that colonies were of some, but not great, economic importance and that non-possession of them was only really injurious if the "possessors" adopted discriminatory practices. Further, the abolition of such discriminatory practices would not remedy the dissatisfied powers' principal economic troubles. Nevertheless, while the remedy for those troubles was in their own hands, the removal of discrimination, both for its modest economic and general moral importance, should be undertaken. More important, however, was as much return to multilateral trade as was possible in present circumstances. While the National Executive Committee made clear that it was not bound by all the recommendations of the report, it continued to explore ways to appease the supposedly "have not" powers within the framework of the obviously crumbling international system.[18]

The result was the pamphlet, "The Demand for Colonial Territories and Equality of Economic Opportunity," prepared by a committee from the international and imperial advisory groups and issued as an official statement of the Labour Party.[19]

In the meantime, Mussolini's conquest of Abyssinia proceeded relentlessly. It has been argued, as Dalton argued in the House of Commons to which he had returned after the October election, that if only Britain and France, acting through the League of Nations, had imposed oil sanctions, Mussolini's armored vehicles and tanks would have soon ground to a halt. Instead, Clement Attlee charged, the British government had permitted companies under its control to supply the needs of Mussolini while hindering the Abyssinians from obtaining arms.[20]

Attlee's argument failed to take into account the actions of suppliers outside the influence of the League. American exports of oil to Italy grew dramatically during the months of Italian action in Abyssinia and then dropped precipitously as the campaign was completed. The implication was clear. Despite sanctions by the League powers, oil would nevertheless have been available to fuel the Fascist war machine.[21]

However much oil sanctions may have been frustrated by the absence of American cooperation, Labour spokesman continued bitterly to castigate both the British and French governments for skillfully avoiding every form of preventive sanctions and for endeavoring to keep the Abyssinian issue away from the Council of the League.[22] By early May, Emperor Haile Selassie had fled and total defeat was only a matter of time. After the collapse of resistance, the National Council of Labour issued a declaration denouncing the aggression and insisting that it was more than ever the duty of all loyal members of the League of Nations to maintain and intensify the measures adopted against

Fascist Italy until the authority of the League was vindicated. When the National Government decided to abandon sanctions, a mass meeting sponsored by Labour protested the move as a betrayal of Abyssinia and as destructive of the effectiveness of the League of Nations.[23] Nevertheless, the Italian triumph was a fait accompli and Labour's opposition, despite the temporary blocking of the Hoare-Laval policy, had had little if any effect on the policy of the National Government.

In the final reckoning, Labour's responses to the tangled issues of the civil war that broke out in Spain in July of 1936 were much more significant in determining the movement's policy towards the collapse of the European order than the question of how to deal with the rape of Abyssinia. The creation of the second Spanish Republic in 1931 seemed to some observers to promise the resolution of some of the conflict that had plagued Spain from at least the middle of the nineteenth century. As the new government strove to implement a series of reforms of the old regime, its actions had strengthened the opposition of the army, the church, and the landowners of the old regime. When out of the complex turmoil of the next five years a Popular Front government supported by a split Socialist Party, communists, anarcho-syndicalists, and middle-class liberals emerged, the Fascist Falange movement gained adherents and the forces of the right were poised to overthrow the Republic. The murder of a prominent right-wing politician provided the precipitating factor for a revolt that had been in the planning for some time. By the middle of July, Spain had been plunged into a brutal civil war that was to last for three years and cost the country over a million lives.[24]

Labour's first reaction to the Spanish conflict was perhaps best reflected in the editorial columns of the *Daily Herald*, which argued that the Spanish government was defending nothing more nor less than the democratic principle, the right of the Spanish people to elect the rulers of its choice and to be master of its future. Thus the paper, alluding to the "facts" as outlined in a manifesto of the International Federation of Trade Unions and the Labour and Socialist International, called upon every state to permit the legal government of Spain to secure all the necessary means of defence.[25] When Clement Attlee proposed, to a conference of Labour Party and Co-operative delegates gathered for another purpose, a resolution pledging all practicable support to the Spanish comrades struggling against reactionary Fascist forces, it was accepted evidently without much question. Similarly, both the National Council of Labour and the Parliamentary Labour Party urged that the Spanish government be given every legal support that international law provided for. At the same time, they were careful to make clear that they were not asking the British government to intervene in the conflict.[26]

Nevertheless, leaders of both the Trades Union Congress and the Labour Party had more than a little suspicion of the Spanish Popular Front, whose internal differences seemed to make strong government next to impossible, and whose allies, the anarchists and communists, were regarded as adversaries of the international socialist labour movement. When Léon Blum, the socialist leader of the new French Popular Front government, after first authorizing the shipment of arms to the Spanish Republicans, proposed an agreement by outside powers not to intervene in the Spanish struggle, Labour's spokesmen were quick to go along. The tenuous position of Blum, abhorred by the French right and suspected by the Radicals with whom he shared power, was clearly a major factor in Labour's decision to support the non-intervention agreement that emerged from the deliberations of the major European powers. [27]

While Hugh Dalton's comment that his Labour colleagues knew little of the Spanish leaders may be taken with a grain of salt, it appears clear that many of them shared his fear that armed support for Spain might precipitate either a right-wing overthrow of the Blum Government or its internal disintegration in the opposition of the Radicals in the shaky Popular Front. [28] For him, the fate of the French democracy was more important to Britain than that of the Spanish Republic. Much more to the point, Dalton, as has been noted, by 1936 had come to see dealing with Nazi Germany's threat to peace and security as the overwhelming priority for Britain in foreign affairs. Unlike Noel Baker, for example, who argued for rearmament yet continued to posit the League of Nations as the instrument for its use, Dalton was convinced not only that such rearmament was imperative but that it must be supported even in the hands of a National Government. While he continued occasionally to make ritualistic public obeisance to the League of Nations, he was prepared to accept that even his political opponents were concerned for the national safety of their country.

Dalton's position was shared by Ernest Bevin and Walter Citrine, the odd couple who dominated the trade union movement in the nineteen-thirties. In a situation where the Labour Party was still recovering from the debacle of 1931, the trade union influence on decision making—through the National Council of Labour, for example—became crucial. The motives of some of the trade union leaders were complex. Many were, *inter alia*, defending the status quo of a labour movement not at all united—*vide* British Catholic workers' support for Franco—behind the Spanish Republicans.[29]

But to emphasize the bureaucratic necessities of a domestic labour movement would be a mistake. Beyond assigning priority to confronting the Nazi menace, Labour shared with virtually all of British society a quite evident fear of future war. The result was the reluctant acceptance of a policy that in the long run meant the demise of the Spanish Republic.[30]

When the National Council of Labour met on August 25, the decision had already been taken by the major European powers to implement the French call for non-intervention, including an embargo on the supply of arms and munitions of war to Spain. The National Council called for an urgent meeting of the Parliamentary Labour Party, the General Council of the TUC, and the National Executive Committee of the Labour Party. That meeting, which was held on August 28, issued a statement which denounced the rebellion against the legitimate Spanish government and the immediate support for the rebels from Italy and Germany, while deploring the repudiation of international law under which that government should have been able to buy arms. The group expressed regret that it should have been thought expedient, on the ground of the danger of war, to conclude agreements among the European powers which put rebels and legitimate government on an equal footing. At the same time, its statement essentially accepted the reasoning behind the policy of non-intervention. Admitting that its commitments might lessen international tensions if applied immediately, loyally observed, and effectively coordinated and supervised, the conference called for the utmost vigilance to prevent the agreements from being utilized to injure the Spanish government. Several weeks later, essentially the same resolution was presented to the Trades Union Congress after an explanation by Citrine of the reasoning of the National Council in supporting, albeit reluctantly, the non-intervention policy. [31]

In a short matter of months, indications began to pile up of the flouting of the non-intervention agreement by Germany and Italy in support of the rebellion led by General Franco. Nevertheless, both the TUC and the Labour Party continued for a time to support non-intervention as the best of a bad situation. At the TUC's annual conference in September, Walter Citrine explained in some detail why the leadership had acted as it did. The General Council, he noted, had to consider whether the risk of war—by sending munitions to the Spanish government—was real or not. The first reaction was to take the risk by publishing a manifesto declaring unmistakably the right of the Spanish government to be supplied with the arms it needed. Then it became clear that Italy was mobilizing its forces to support the rebels and the French government took the initiative to promote not supplying either side with arms. When a Labour delegation put the case for supplying arms, the French Government made clear its intention to support non-intervention as essential to avoid war between two rival blocs of powers. Labour's leaders were aware of evasions of the agreement from the start, for example through Portugal, yet given the situation in France, the General Council believed that the non-intervention policy, distasteful as it was, was the only practical policy to follow. Although there was dissent from the action of the leadership, the conference then accepted a resolution, moved by Ernest Bevin, endorsing the position of the General Council, but keeping open the possibility of reviewing the situation if the agreement was not loyally observed by all the governments involved. [32]

By early October, when the Labour Party met in conference, it seemed clear that the leadership would follow the trade union lead, although some, not necessarily on the left, disagreed. Philip Noel Baker, for example, outlined his opposition to endorsing non-intervention in a letter to Clement Attlee. He conceded that there was probably a good deal of public support and realized the risk of going against a pretty strong tide. But he warned of the real dangers of a policy of solidarity with the National Government, the danger, as he put it, of winding up "in a sort of national union with the Tories [on] armaments and foreign policy generally."[33]

At the Edinburgh conference, the views of those who shared the concerns of Noel Baker were rejected by the National Executive. By then, Fascist intervention was hardly a secret, while relatively substantial Soviet aid to the Republicans had emerged, presumably as a response. Arthur Greenwood almost apologetically presented to the delegates the resolution endorsing the National Council of Labour's support for non-intervention. Admitting that such a policy was "a very, very bad second best," he argued that the labour movement was faced with the fact that non-intervention was generally accepted and that the initiative for it had come from the left-of-center Government of Léon Blum in France. In the circumstances, there had seemed to be no alternative than to go along with non-intervention as long as it was really effective. The National Council would keep a constant watch over the situation and would take necessary action if it was found that non-intervention was not being honorably carried out.

Sir Charles Trevelyan, who had at an earlier conference discounted the effectiveness of the League of Nations, now insisted that the League could at least have done something against the fascist states that were destroying the democratic government of Spain. "I do not ask for war," he insisted. Instead he urged international consultation of all the socialist and democratic countries of the world to see if aggression could not be stopped, rather than a policy of sympathy "accompanied by bandages and cigarettes."

Ernest Bevin's reply to Trevelyan was blunt and personal. Recalling that he had taken an unpopular line on war and peace for the last four years, he insisted that the National Council had not departed "one inch or one tithe" from the claim that international law should be observed. But what was the situation? International law as described by Trevelyan was dead. Fascist governments had emerged that would respect neither treaties nor international law. Unless the democratic countries, in conjunction with Russia, and, he hoped, the United States, would come together and assert international law, then the price for its re-establishment was going to be bitter indeed. Blum's fear, he declared, had been that the insistence upon international law would lead to Fascist recognition of the rebel government, with dire consequences not only for Spain but for France as well. Clearly uneasy about the rationale for the National Council's position, Bevin urged the conference not to give its vote as if the National Council report confirmed non-intervention, but "confirms the active work that the National Council is trying to do, and back it in its effort to assist Spain to the best of its ability."

Aneurin Bevan, the fiery Welshman who had become a major voice of the Labour left, supported the Trevelyan position in a passionate speech which asked the conference to consider the consequences in Europe if the present situation was allowed to proceed to its logical conclusion. Was it not obvious to everyone that, if arms continued to pour into the rebels in Spain, their Spanish comrades would be slaughtered by the hundreds of thousands? Had Bevin, who had spoken before him, considered the fate of the Blum government in France if a fascist government was established in Spain? How long would French democracy stand against fascism in Germany, fascism in Italy, fascism in Spain, and fascism in Portugal? And if the Popular Front and democracy in France were destroyed, the Franco-Soviet pact would soon be denounced, and democracy in Europe would shortly be in ruins. That would be the consequence of the non-intervention policy.

The uneasiness of a considerable number of the conference delegates was reflected in the vote that was taken on the National Executive's Spanish policy at the end of the debate. Although the bloc votes of most of the trade unions ensured a victory for the Labour Party's National Executive, the Parliamentary Party, and the TUC, the actual count—1,836,000 in favor, 519,000 against—made clear how disunited Labour remained as the threats to the European order continued to grow.[34]

That disunity was further reflected the next day when Hugh Dalton introduced a long resolution damning the National Government for betraying the League and Abyssinia and breaking its pledges to the electorate. The Executive's resolution at the same time reaffirmed Labour's policy of maintaining such defence forces as were consistent with the country's responsibilities "as a Member of the League of Nations, the preservation of the people's rights and liberties, the continuance of democratic institutions, and the observance of international law." Though Dalton himself was convinced that British rearmament was essential regardless of distrust of the government, he supported the decision of the majority of the Executive in refusing to accept responsibility for a "purely competitive" arms policy, but rather to reserve full liberty to criticize the rearmament program of the government. Deploring the deterioration of the international scene since the optimistic days of 1931 when Arthur Henderson was foreign secretary, he pleaded for support of the resolution, while reiterating Labour's belief that the Baldwin government must go. Ironically, even as he argued for a policy which papered over the differences in the labour movement, he warned that Labour "must get rid of the fog of mushy generalities and come down to a clear-cut policy and until we do that, we shall never clear out this gang of incompetents who are misgoverning this country."[35]

The ensuing debate offered little beyond the familiar staking out of positions. As Herbert Morrison put it, "the Party continues, to be willing, as before, to provide arms for the collective organisation of peace, but, as before, it declines to be a party to the Government's policy of competitive national armaments and complete absence of any intelligible foreign policy."[36]

Despite the first day's vote in support of non-intervention in Spain, Edinburgh was so electrified by the speeches of the two Spanish fraternal delegates who addressed the conference that the conference agreed that Attlee and Greenwood would go to London to discuss the Spanish situation with Neville Chamberlain, the acting prime minister. The result was a resolution which tempered the action of the first day, committing Labour to investigate breaches of non-intervention and supporting, in that event, the right of the Spanish government to buy arms. While there was officially no shift in Labour's posture towards non-intervention, it was clear that policy was already beginning to change. [37]

As yet, however, the danger of a general war precipitated by the Spanish conflict loomed larger for many in the labour movement than the possible shift in the European balance of power resulting from German and Italian involvement in Spain. There, Italy's action, in the first instance, was motivated by a desire to weaken France as much as by the wish to defeat any possible revolution in Spain.[38]

Collaboration with Hitler, who was content to let Italy play the leading role in Spain, transformed a local struggle into a European-wide issue. Though to a certain extent the French and, by late 1936, increasingly the Soviets, evaded the agreements not to supply arms to either side in Spain, the fate of the Spanish Republic was largely decided in the first few months of the Civil War.[39] At the same time, non-intervention ensured the weakening of ties between the Soviet Union and both France and Britain. Concern over the fragile tenure of the Popular Front in France, lack of confidence in the disparate coalition that made up the Spanish Republican government, and the putative ineffectiveness of any possible alternative, all coupled with the fear of a European conflagration, continued to persuade a majority in the National Council of Labour that there was no present alternative to non-intervention. That view was reflected in the *Daily Herald*, whose first reaction in support of supplying arms to the Spanish Republicans gave way to arguments to back the cause of non-intervention, albeit with less than eager enthusiasm.[40] Yet, almost on the morrow of the Edinburgh conference, in the face of evident violations of the agreement, even the *Herald* admitted that unless the position suddenly improved to an extent that could no longer be hopefully expected, non-intervention in Spain had better be candidly written off as a failure.[41]

Reaction to the Spanish war added to the dissatisfaction of the Socialist League with the direction of Labour policy. In early 1937, Sir Stafford Cripps assumed the lead in a Unity Campaign, which called for an alliance of the Labour Party, the ILP, and the Communist Party to drive the National Government out of office. The campaign, promoted by *Tribune*, a new left-wing newspaper largely subsidized by Cripps and George Strauss, was a direct challenge to the Labour Party's Executive, which had consistently rejected collaboration with the communists as a backdoor maneuver towards subversion of the labour movement. The National Executive decided on the disaffiliation of the Socialist League from the Labour Party. Subsequently Socialist League members were banned from individual membership in the Labour Party. As a result, in a matter of months, the group disbanded, although criticism of official policy, not the least in *Tribune,* continued.[42] Meanwhile, both trade union and Labour Party leaders were shifting their ground, both in regard to Spain and about the international situation in general. In relatively short order, any optimism about the success of non-intervention was eroded by the continuing evidence of substantial violations by Italy and Germany. In the House of Commons, Attlee and Arthur Henderson, son of the former foreign minister, found it abundantly clear that non-intervention had not removed international tension, nor had it done anything effective to shorten the conflict in Spain. With hindsight, Attlee now found it easy to affirm that firmness at the start would have prevented the intervention by the fascist powers from extending.[43] Outside Westminster, both the *Daily Herald*, as was to be expected, and the *New Statesman*, now increased their condemnation of non-intervention, with the latter seeing it as a delusion that served to render British and French weakness respectable.[44] While Hugh Dalton in particular had been unsuccessful in persuading the majority of the National Executive and the Parliamentary Labour Party to abandon what he regarded as a self defeating opposition to the service estimates, he persisted, with strong support from the trade union side of the labour movement, in his efforts to reverse the policy. He was aided by an important Advisory Committee memorandum which bluntly affirmed that the prevention of war in the next few years would depend not upon the League of Nations or collective security, but on inducing the fascist powers to believe that war would not benefit them. The idea that this could be achieved by some kind of common front among a large number of pacific or democratic or socialist states was illusory. The destruction of the League system showed that the basis for such a "front" did not exist. Even the grounds for a firm Franco-Soviet-British alliance did not exist, but must be approached "tentatively" in the next several years by close cooperation between France and Britain, who then might gradually move towards a more comprehensive security system. In the present state of Europe, the memorandum concluded, a mere negative opposition to a rearmament policy was sterile and ineffective. Fear of attack and of war and loss of confidence in the League had made the vast majority of people everywhere turn to armaments as the only possible hope to ward off an attack or successfully resist one. Labour should continue to denounce the policy that had led to such a situation, but should at the same time base its policy on supporting a close accord with France backed by a scale of arms related to the common defence and the obligations assumed in attempting to recreate a security system for Europe.[45] In effect, the committee was trying to reconcile Labour's defense policy—a reluctance to support the "unilateral" rearmament program of the mistrusted National Government—and its foreign policy, hitherto resting upon support of the League of Nations but coming around to a definition of "collective security" whether through the

League or a more traditional form of defensive alliance. Dalton paralleled the Advisory Committee argument in the preparation of a paper on International Policy and Defence which, despite the opposition led by Arthur Greenwood, Deputy Leader of the Labour Party, was adopted by the National Council of Labour.[46]

As if to emphasize the ambiguity in the party's policy, Greenwood's position was similar to that of the Labour left whose pressure for a United Front of "progressive" groups had been emphatically rejected by the leadership, but whose suspicion of the National Government was essentially an exaggerated version of the posture of many in the majority section of the labour movement.

At its annual meeting in early September, 1937, the TUC heard Bevin in his presidential address and Citrine, more fully, introduce the composite resolution on international policy and defence which made the case for a change in policy. Bevin outlined the very black outlook overhanging the nations— Italian and German bombs on children and women in Spain; Japan's war in China; widespread arming and the limitation of freedom. On Spain, he was particularly defensive. A year ago, the labour movement had reluctantly followed the lead of French premier Léon Blum, a policy which gave an opportunity to consolidate the democratic forces in France, hold Fascism in check there, and probably avoid a world war at that time. Now it was recognized that non-intervention had become a complete farce and "one can only hope that the democratic forces in Spain will emerge victorious." [47]

The report of the General Council alluded to the fact that a manifesto had already been issued, drew attention to the violation of the Non-Intervention Agreement by the fascist powers, and called upon the League of Nations to assist the Spanish people to recover their independence, both by providing for withdrawal of foreign troops from Spain and giving the Republicans full liberty to purchase arms, while not granting belligerent rights to the rebels.[48]

For his part, Citrine, like the authors of the Advisory Committee memorandum, gave little weight to the view that the League of Nations could now be used to promote European security. To be sure, collective security should be fostered: "In the meantime it may be that the primary responsibility for the maintenance of peace will fall upon one or two countries who are adequately prepared, and ready to shoulder their responsibility. How, in these circumstances, can we escape the conclusion that some measure of rearmament is indispensable if this country is to face its obligations?" To Aneurin Bevan's demurrer resting on Labour's long-standing suspicion of the motives of a capitalist British government, Citrine was caustic: "I frankly ask those who put the argument, do they really believe that any British Government would dare to pledge the forces of this country behind the Fascist Powers. Do you really believe that?" In the event, the resolution denouncing non-intervention and supporting rearmament was passed by a show of hands after a motion to refer it back was overwhelmingly defeated by 3,544,000 bloc votes to 224,000.[49]

Given the determining number of trade union votes at the Labour Party conference, acceptance of "International Policy and Defence" at Labour's Bournemouth conference in October was a foregone conclusion when it was presented by the veteran J. R. Clynes on behalf of the National Executive. The pacifist contingent, among others George Lansbury and Arthur Ponsonby, challenged the document. Ponsonby professed to be amazed that after the failure of the attempt to support collective security in the Italo-Abyssinian war the party should still adhere to it. For his part, Aneurin Bevin discounted the pacifist argument, but insisted that if the immediate international situation were used as an excuse to get Labour to drop its opposition to the rearmament program of the National Government, then the next phase must be to desist from any industrial or political action that might disturb national unity in the face of fascist aggression. "Along that line," he warned, "is endless retreat, and at the end of it a voluntary totalitarian State with ourselves erecting the barbed wire around." Not all supporters of what may be called the Dalton-Bevin-Citrine doctrine of abandonment of token opposition to the government's rearmament program were ready to jettison their hopes for a reconstitution of the League of Nations system. Noel Baker argued that the resolution presented the possibility to do "nine-tenths of everything that Mr. George Lansbury wants," including the rebuilding of the League and an attack on the roots of war. And Richard Crossman argued that support for rearmament must be tied in with the collaboration of England, France, and Russia if it were to lead to a real policy for world peace and the revivifying of the League of Nations. Even Dalton, in his chairman's address, warned that arms, however powerful and however necessary, were not enough. Paying lip service to long-standing Labour positions, he argued that they must be linked to a foreign policy that would breathe new life into the League of Nations and recreate respect for international law.

Whatever the motivation for the change in tactics, at the end of the debate the conference rejected a substitute resolution and an attempt to have the matter referred back. The NEC resolution was then accepted by a vote of about 8 to 1. While its supporters made clear that neither the constitutional procedures of Parliament or the rules of the Labour Party permitted the conference to direct Labour MPs on how to vote, it was equally clear that the "advice" in the leadership's resolution—that Labour MPs abstain in votes for war credits rather than divide against the estimates—would determine the stance of the Parliamentary delegation.[50] However much aspects of earlier, traditional Labour attitudes still persisted, particularly on the left, the message of the party had become so clear as to leave no room for misinterpretation.[51]

The change in regard to rearmament by no means meant that Labour was about to soften its criticism, however much ambivalence there might be as to what precisely government policy should be. In the debate on the Defence White Paper, it was Morrison, using the same language as that employed by his

more radical colleagues, who had branded the government as foes of governments of the left and foes of democracy, animated by class considerations as
well as by concern for the national interest.[52] Once the change in tactics had
been decided, the theme continued to animate much of the discussion in the
House of Commons. Attlee, who was closer to Noel Baker than to Dalton in his
emphasis, charged that Anthony Eden, who had earlier upheld the ideal of the
League of Nations in former speeches to the House, now stressed only the
interests of British imperialism.[53] Dalton, for his part, quoting the military
writer Basil Liddell Hart, suggested that some members of the government
desired a Franco victory in Spain because of class prejudice and concern for
property rights. Recurring to his constant charge of retreat from the "strong,
well-prepared and easily defensible positions" which the government inher-
ited in 1931, he traced the retreat from what he descried as a strong League of
Nations and a relatively peaceful general situation, starting with Sir John
Simon's policy in the case of Japan in China and outlining each subsequent
concession culminating in the "farce" of non-intervention.[54] Yet, despite its
differences, Labour was now officially committed to the view that Britain
must be powerfully armed in order to face what was at best a dangerous international situation.

9

The Chamberlain Factor

The appointment of Neville Chamberlain as prime minister in June of 1937 slowed the Labour Party's reluctant acceptance of the need for rearmament. Chamberlain's determination to play a greater role in shaping foreign policy than his predecessor made many factions of Labour uneasy, particularly since the prime minister's cold demeanor left little room for debate. Rigidly righteous, Chamberlain seemed to signal certainty about the correctness of his initiatives that appeared to discourage discussion.

Meanwhile, Japanese ambitions on the Asiatic continent again came to the fore. From the time of the seizure of Manchuria, sporadic incidents of conflict continued as the Japanese military tightened its grip over sections of the Chinese mainland. Finally, in the summer of 1937, one such incident at the Marco Polo Bridge provided the excuse for a full-scale assault by heavily reinforced Japanese troops. In short order, both Tientsin and Peking fell as Japanese troops took over control of substantial parts of Chinese territory. By the end of the year, both British and American ships on the Yangtze River had been attacked. It seemed apparent to Anthony Eden and others in the government that cooperation with the United States was essential if any attempt to control Japan was to be successful. But neither the United States nor the British prime minister was ready to take significant action. Chamberlain was implacably opposed to any form of sanctions and, in the end, Japan, rather than Britain or the United States, determined when, and under what circumstances, the Anglo-American position in the Far East was finally challenged by force.

Labour reacted to the acceleration of Japan's aggression substantially by repeating the stance taken in 1931 and 1932. The Advisory Committee on International Questions, for example, sent to the National Executive a memorandum proposing support for an embargo on Japanese imports and exports by a combination of nations including, "at a minimum," the USSR, the USA, Great Britain, the Dominions, France, and the Netherlands. The committee warned that an explicit guarantee of mutual aid from the governments of all of these countries was essential in the event of a Japanese attack upon the armed forces or territories of any of the participants. It should be accompanied by a commitment to address Japanese claims in the Pacific area and in the sphere of commercial relations with the rest of the world.[1] In the House of Commons, Attlee on several occasions called in more general terms for the intervention of the League of Nations to support the victim of aggression, essentially by resort to economic pressure. At the same time, he commented hopefully on American participation in discussions of the 1922 Nine-Power Treaty which had pledged respect for China's independence and territorial integrity. At no time in the Parliamentary debates did the Labour spokesmen meet head-on the charge that economic measures might have to be backed by arms in order to be effective.[2]

In calling upon the government to resort to the League of Nations, Attlee was carrying out the policy of the National Council of Labour, just as his hopes for American cooperation mirrored the suggestions of that body.[3] But neither the National Council nor the Parliamentary Labourites mounted as sustained a criticism of the British government along with the Japanese as appeared in the *Daily Herald,* official Labour's almost only popular organ of opinion. There assessments such as W. N. Ewer's "Japan Gets a Free Hand" set the tone for a series of articles castigating the "isolationist" policy that gave Japan her way because the Sino-Japanese war did not menace British interests.[4] Now the government was discovering, as in the occupation of the International Settlements in Shanghai, that its policy had been endangering Britain all the time. The whole world now recognized Japanese action as a case of flagrant and unprovoked aggression against China, yet the British government had done nothing, made no proposals, and showed no signs of making any. Even when the government sent a "stiff" note to Japan, the *Herald* labeled it useless because it was based on "the old pre-League diplomacy of trying to do a deal." The plain truth, charged the paper, was that ever since the government rejected a League policy in the Far East in 1931, British efforts to stem the tide of lawlessness had been unreal and ineffective. [5]

On the Labour left, *Tribune,* while it devoted relatively little space to the Far Eastern conflict, professed to see a government paralyzed by indecision in regard to both Spain and the Far East. In the latter case, a victory for Japan, it concluded, would mean the destruction of British interests in China, while a Chinese triumph might involve the extension of Russia's influence in that country. Between these two unpleasant possibilities, the National Government wavered and hesitated.[6] On balance, *Tribune* devoted almost as much attention to an American journalist's highly positive picture of the communists in North Western China as to the Japanese aggression in that country.[7]

All of Labour's discussion of how to stop Japan in the Far East was built upon a conception of League of Nations cooperation that was hardly realistic. As a result, it paid no attention, except as a means of criticizing the government, to the fact that British naval power in the area was stretched so thin as hardly to be a deterrent to Japanese ambitions. In any case, in 1937 and well into the next year, the war in Spain loomed much larger in Labour's attack on the National Government than the conflict in the Far East. Whereas talk of sanctions of any kind, even economic pressure, left a minority in the labour movement quite uneasy, calls for an end to the non-intervention policy in the Spanish conflict served as a unifying cry, if only for a brief period. As early as June, 1937, a joint meeting of Labour's National Executive Committee, the General Council of the Trades Union Congress, and the Executive Committee of the Parliamentary Labour Party had endorsed a statement submitted by representatives of the Spanish labour movement to the Labour and Socialist International and the International Federation of Trade Unions. The statement called upon all League of Nations members to assist the Spanish government in recovering its political and territorial independence and in particular to return to commercial liberty so that the legitimate government might acquire the arms for the defence of its territory and its rights.[8]

The attack by disguised Italian submarines on British and French merchant ships attempting to supply the Republicans led to a conference of Mediterranean powers at Nyon. The Italians refused to attend, but the British and French set up an anti-submarine patrol and the attacks stopped. Even earlier, Ellen Wilkinson, "Red Ellen," the feisty left-wing MP who had been a co-founder of *Tribune,* was asking for the logic which justified putting the ships of Italy and Germany in charge of the government coast of Spain, where they were interfering overwhelmingly on the side of Franco.[9] A few weeks later, *Tribune* branded the Nyon agreement as a partial and timid effort to deal with piracy in the Mediterranean. It gave Franco a free hand in Spanish territorial waters against ships of all nations, while at the same time the land blockade of "non-intervention" remained in place.[10]

Instead, Arthur Henderson, son of the former foreign minister, suggested in the House of Commons that non-intervention should be the responsibility of the League of Nations—all the nations of the League. Then, if Germany or Italy or any other country sought to commit aggression League members must be prepared to face up to their obligations under the Covenant.[11] Both Attlee and Dalton, as has already been noted, now saw policy towards the civil war as one stage in a long retreat started by Sir John Simon, the foreign secretary in 1931, in the case of Japan in China.[12] Dalton, who had earlier not been enthusiastic in support of the Spanish Republic, confided to his diary that even Leon Blum had admitted that he would no longer be embarrassed by British Labour's denunciation of the non-intervention agreement.[13]

Chamberlain's hope that it might be possible to appease Hitler by African concessions, mainly at the expense of Portugal and Belgium, but also involving British strategic interests in Tanganyika, was only one of a number of issues that revealed the gulf between his thinking and that of his foreign secretary. In particular, the prime minister and a majority of his cabinet, for a period, sought to separate Britain's two potential enemies, Germany and Italy, by negotiations with the latter. In the face of Italy's resignation from the League of Nations, and despite Eden's skepticism, Chamberlain believed that it might be possible to detach Italy, which had interests similar to those of Britain in a free Mediterranean and Red Sea, and an independent Austria, from collaboration with the Nazis. Eden's resignation and the appointment of Lord Halifax as his successor simply strengthened the determination of the prime minister to press on with his search for a formula to circumscribe Germany by buying off Italy. [14]

In the House of Commons, although Attlee complimented Eden for taking a principled line in foreign affairs, the latter's somewhat tepid explanation of his resignation was a disappointment. As for Chamberlain's initiative, Attlee in particular was caustic in his complaint that the prime minister believed that everything was going to be wonderful because he had a promise from Mussolini that some time he would come to an agreement that some time he might carry out. [15]

Greenwood emphasized the promises made by government representatives during the election campaign of 1935 to follow a League of Nations policy. [16] The prime minister agreed that the policy had been changed, but attributed its demise to the inadequacies of the League and not the failure of the government.

The position of Labour's Parliamentary spokesmen was paralleled by the National Council of Labour which met on February 22 and endorsed the action of the Parliamentary Party in deciding to move a vote of censure in the House. An emergency meeting of the labour movement's three Executives, held the next day, decided to press for an immediate election and agreed upon a declaration to issue to the press. In calling for an election, Labour pointed to the government's disregard of its pledges made during the last campaign and denounced the decision to enter into negotiations with the Italian Fascists, a decision which implied the sacrifice of the Spanish people in their struggle to preserve their freedom and independence. During the past year alone, the document charged, Italy had again and again broken faith with Britain, while Hitler had violated one treaty after another. Yet the British government was willing to accept a mere verbal promise from Mussolini—another worthless formula—for the withdrawal of foreign troops from Spain. To negotiate unconditionally with either Hitler or Mussolini was to court disaster. Instead, what was needed was a clear declaration that Britain stood for the enforcement of treaties against lawless force and against aggressive interference in the internal affairs of independent states: "Czechoslovakia in particular should be assured at once that Great Britain and the other League Powers will fulfil their obligations to maintain her integrity and independence." [17]

Before the Italian discussions could be carried to fruition, Hitler had carried out his coup in Austria and accomplished his long-standing ambition for its

Anschluss, unification, with Germany. Although both Britain and France protested, it was clear that no further steps would be taken. In the Commons, Attlee, who was later to deplore Chamberlain's "amazing credulity," pointed out that the Nazi action took place at the very time the British government was pursuing friendly conversations with the German government. "Each successive instance of bad faith," he warned, "each successful act of aggression leads to another. The whirlwind which the government is reaping to-day springs from the wind sown by the present Chancellor of the Exchequer. Manchuria, Rhineland, Abyssinia, Spain, China, Austria—what next?" What to do? Attlee repeated the customary Labour mantra: "Back to League principles; back to the support of the rule of law."[18]

Similarly, a full conference of the labour movement's three executive bodies, called by the National Council, unanimously demanded that the League Assembly be called at once in order to thrash out collective measures to check aggression in Spain and Central Europe. The conferees did not outline what those collective measures should specifically be. When a number of national unions called for a special conference of the Trades Union Congress to discuss the international situation, the leadership noted that while the proposals had been made as a result of the aggressive action of Germany towards Austria, the general menace of the European situation, and the serious danger to Republican Spain, the petitioners had made no specific proposal as to the policy which should be followed. In the circumstances, the TUC's General Council was unable to see what action it could suggest which would be more effective and more likely to cause the government to change its policy than the action already taken by the General Council, the National Executive of the Labour Party, and the Parliamentary Labour Party, all of which had maintained the closest collaboration on the whole international situation with the National Council of Labour. The General Council's decision not to call a special conference of the trade union movement was in effect a realistic recognition of the limits of labour's influence on the policy of the government.[19]

Although they differed from the leadership on how to deal with that policy, many on the left were even more aggressive in their condemnation than the official spokesmen. To be sure, pacifists like Lansbury and Ponsonby or advocates of further appeasement such as C. R. Buxton demurred from criticizing efforts at accommodation.[20] But Stafford Cripps, for example, spoke of the prime minister as "without policy or direction, without philosophy or morality, being pushed from pillar to post by the dictators of Europe." Chamberlain was being forced by the logic of his own past policy to become one of the Fascist International, to seek, by alliance with them, the safety he could not get in opposition to them.[21]

And Kingsley Martin, editor of the *New Statesman*, was even more outspoken. Historians would find it hard to explain," he predicted, "the part played by the British ruling class in the collapse of European civilization in the twentieth century." It was time, he wrote, that the people of England told Mr. Chamberlain in unmistakable language that for a policy of connivance and encouragement of Fascism the British nation was not prepared for more taxation, for more conscription or for more discipline. On the other hand, there was no sacrifice it was not prepared to undergo for a government which really intended to throw its weight on the side of democracy and against aggression.[22]

Despite the evident firmness of Martin's argument, the uncertainties still troubling many of the opinion makers in the ranks of Labour were nowhere better illustrated than in the journal he edited. He argued that if only Germany and Italy would halt their "war policies" and cooperate peacefully with their neighbors, the latter could offer reasonable political and economic concessions. "We would do this," the *New Statesman* assured its readers, "even if Germany and Italy continued under their odious internal political regimes. Countries' internal government must be reckoned their own affair, and so long as they do not menace others, their domestic barbarities ought not to prevent us from collaborating with them on economic matters." Nothing was acceptable that did not check the armaments race and lessen the threat of war, but for those two ends almost anything was worth doing.[23] In effect, even the editor of the *New Statesman* still hoped, against what others saw as overwhelming evidence to the contrary, that some form of appeasement could temper the aggressive ambitions of the fascist powers.

Despite the evidence of Hitler's intransigence, Chamberlain was persuaded that, if a violent coup in the case of Czechoslovakia could be avoided, it might be possible for Europe to settle down and undertake peaceful discussions once again with Germany. For the moment, he continued the search for a rapprochement with Italy. The Anglo-Italian agreement which resulted provided for the British recognition of the Italian conquest of Abyssinia in return for Mussolini's promise to withdraw his troops from Spain—where the success of Franco seemed to promise a quick victory for the rebel cause. When Chamberlain presented the agreement to Parliament, Herbert Morrison, who led the debate for Labour, denounced it point by point. He claimed that the pro-fascist bias of the government was made visible when Eden resigned and the only new member to go into the government was an openly proclaimed partisan of Franco. The agreement proved, he asserted, that the government's foreign policy was motivated by "the international interests of the capitalists of the world," taking the country back to the power politics of prewar days and building up the circumstances that had brought about the Great War of 1914.[24] Attlee repeated Morrison's assessment in winding up for Labour.[25] In subsequent sessions, MPs such as Noel Baker and Aneurin Bevan seconded him. Each of them put his own particular gloss on the argument, Noel Baker emphasizing the bypassing of the League of Nations,[26] Bevan blasting Italian bombing of British ships and declaring that one of the government's conditions for peace with Italy appeared to be that Italy should be allowed to murder British seamen.[27]

In the days and weeks that followed, the few voices of the Labour press joined in the chorus of accusation. For the *Herald,* it was bad enough that the British government, for reasons of political expediency, was determined to break its pledge and to violate the law of the League to which it still professed allegiance. Worse was the casuistry and evasion of the fantastic claim that the final betrayal of Abyssinia and the Covenant was a "practical victory for peace."[28]

The *New Statesman* warned that if British and French policy did not change and the fascist powers were permitted to conquer the Iberian peninsula, the British and French empires would be in mortal danger: "Their defence will be incalculably weakened, and we doubt if the people of England will think it worth while to fight a war to defend them. As an Empire we shall perish and we shall deserve to."[29] And farther to the left, *Tribune* insisted, on the second anniversary of the outbreak of war in Spain, that Labour still had the power to end "two years of Fascist blackmail" by Germany and Italy which had played with Great Britain and France as a cat played with a mouse.[30]

Meanwhile, now that Labour had abandoned its self-defeating policy of voting against the service estimates as a protest against the policies of the government, the inadequacy of that government's rearmament efforts became a focus of criticism. Dalton, in particular, as the shadow foreign secretary, pressed the government to rearm more quickly while at the same time damning the imprudence of pacifying Hitler by the making of concessions. Much of Labour's criticism, for example in its public press, was based on a scant foundation of technical knowledge, but Dalton was well briefed by, among others, Sir Robert Vansittart and a secret Air Ministry informant. Dalton was especially concerned about the obvious inferiority of Britain's air strength to that of Germany, as well as about its provision for air raid precautions.[31]

When Chamberlain discounted Labour's criticism of rearmament by noting that Labour had voted against the arms estimates in the past, Attlee pointed out that various members of the present government, as early as 1928, had voted against the entire army, navy, and air force estimates. It was well known that Labour's earlier votes had been a criticism of policy, not a demand that there should be no provision. Admitting that it was hard to have an open debate, because members of Parliament did not know how much possible enemies might know, Attlee suggested that there might be a private inquiry instead. Decrying the "rosy picture" of great achievements to come in 1940 unless the Air Ministry was going to correct mistakes already made, he commented, "I see no sign that the Air Ministry have yet learned the lesson of the past."[32]

Once the *Anschluss* with Austria had been effected, Hitler turned his attention to Czechoslovakia. It appeared apparent to all quarters of the labour movement that the demands for political autonomy of the Sudeten Germans who inhabited the borderlands of the Czech state were designed to destabilize its government and facilitate an eventual German domination. Yet the cry of self-determination—for the German inhabitants of Czechoslovakia—was a powerful argument for many who had seen it, in the years after World War I, as a major remedy for many of the nationalistic ills of Europe.

In April, the Advisory Committee on International Questions prepared a long memorandum for the NEC. Entitled "Guarantees to Czechoslovakia: in relation to Spain," the long document outlined a patchwork of existing pledges, which the committee viewed as an attempt to find substitutes for the League's "open alliance against aggression." Indeed, it charged, the Chamberlain government, having in effect withdrawn from the organized society of nations, now found itself making the worst of two worlds—the world of commitments and the world of isolation. Nevertheless, under the circumstances, a prior guarantee might prevent German aggression, but only if it were "in a form guaranteed by reference to the League of Nations," not a blank subscription to the Franco-Czech or Soviet-Czech Pacts. Even so, the Advisory Committee noted a "fearful doubt" about Russia's real strength or loyalty to the League in the face of Stalin's purging of the higher command of the army, navy, and civil government. And without Russian power, "the League's sum won't come out." This important memorandum suggested that the government might be calculating the risks of calling a halt to aggression now as compared with those anticipated from doing so in 1940. Lacking some of the material necessary for judgment, the committee warned that the risks were evidently so great that the Labour Party's spokesmen ought to be extremely chary of pressing for more explicit prior guarantees to Czechoslovakia than the government felt able to give.

Still, tying in the conflict in Spain with the general European situation, the document turned to the risk involved in the present British policy of "everlasting retreat." Noting the strategic importance of Spain, particularly for the position of France, it conceded that any resolute stand against the German-Italian invasion in Spain was almost too late. Indeed, if it was now made, one effect might be to speed whatever blow Hitler might contemplate in Czechoslovakia. And if Spain was conquered for Fascism, the defence of Czechoslovakia would become very much more difficult and dangerous than at present.[33]

By now, Labour's public pronouncements began to take on a note of virtual desperation. Calls for measures to avoid war joined messages such as that issued by the National Council and directed to the German people. "Why Kill Each Other?," the message asked, while at the same time warning the Germans, "We know your difficulties. We know that in your country and in Italy the dictators are so afraid of their peoples that they will not let them speak, they will not permit free discussion. You are not allowed to know the thoughts of other peoples nor what is happening in other countries. You are not told of the vast preponderance of arms and economic power which your country would have to face in the event of war."[34]

Such warnings may well have had as much to do with bolstering domestic morale as with the hope of influencing the thinking or actions of the German people, as more and more attention came to focus on what was necessary to avoid defeat in a war increasingly seen as virtually inevitable. Stafford Cripps, despite his earlier certainty of the futility of any cooperation with a "capitalist" government, now saw the opportunity to exploit the evident cracks in Conservative support for Chamberlain's reading of the international situation. Some of those who supported the strategy of a Popular Front were unwilling to work with "imperialists" such as Churchill or even Eden. As Cripps now saw it, however, the difference between Chamberlain and Churchill was that the latter was more concerned with the safety of the British Empire than with the danger of working class power. Accordingly, he reasoned, it would be possible to join forces with such liberal imperialists in rallying all opponents of the National Government in order to replace it. Departing from his earlier intransigence about collaborating with non-socialists, he now called for an emergency conference on Spain of all those to the left of Neville Chamberlain. In *Tribune* he admitted that "any idea of real Socialism would have to be put aside for the present."[35] He was supported particularly in the House of Commons by George Strauss and Aneurin Bevan, but somewhat surprisingly *Tribune* played a minor role in the initiative. At that journal, its editor, William Mellor, who was out of sympathy with the attempt more or less to emulate the French and Spanish Popular Fronts, was forced out, but the dispute ensured that *Tribune*'s influence was minimized in the campaign for a change in Labour Party policy.[36]

Over 1,800 delegates, representing trade unions, Labour Party, Left Book Club, Communist, Liberal, and various branch organizations attended the emergency conference on Spain. Ellen Wilkinson, H.N. Brailsford, and Cripps from the Labour Party, as well as by Harry Pollitt and Tom Mann of the Communist Party, and a number of Liberal MPs and Parliamentary candidates addressed the meeting chaired by the Liberal Gilbert Murray. Conservatives were conspicuous by their scarcity. Although the meeting had been called to discuss policy regarding Spain, it was Sir Charles Trevelyan's call for a "Popular Front" that triggered a flood of oratory urging collaboration not only to aid Spain, but also to remove the Chamberlain government.[37]

Because a change in rules at Bournemouth provided that the next Labour Party conference would not meet until late spring of 1938, Labour's Executive Committee was able to avert a party meeting to discuss the Front proposals. Instead, it moved quickly to publish a long statement which justified its opposition to the Popular Front. Arguing that the formation of a such a coalition would not lead to a crisis in the Conservative Party or to an early election, the document pointed instead to Labour victories in by-elections as proof that the public was beginning to be aware that in matters of foreign policy the Labour Party had consistently been right and it opponents wrong. Refuting the arithmetic of Front advocates, which purported to show that a collaborative effort

would lead to the early breakup and electoral defeat of the national government, the Executive Committee questioned whether the Liberal electorate
could be relied upon to follow the advice of the Liberal leaders. More importantly, "The Labour Party and the Popular Front" repeated the conviction of
the majority of the NEC that communist participation would be an electoral
liability rather than an asset. The Communist Party was subject to political
directions from abroad, and both the Liberal Party and Labour would be dis-
tracted from the main purpose of the Popular Front by the need to protect
themselves against communist maneuvers. Without effective Conservative
support, the proposed alliance of Labour with the Liberals and the communists would have less electoral appeal than a united and independent Labour
Party. It would take the heart out of large numbers of the Labour Party's most
loyal supporters, who deeply valued the party's unity and independence and
considered them an asset to the nation. Instead, the Labour Party invited all
men and women who desired Great Britain to take the lead for democracy and
peace—whatever their political attachment—to join Labour in its effort, as-
serting "The policy at the next Election is between the policy of Labour and
the policy of Mr. Chamberlain."[38]

The *Daily Herald* put the view of the leadership succinctly. For those who
sought an effective conqueror of the National Government, it suggested that
the point to grasp was "that nothing is so likely to provoke dissension and
quarreling in the Labour Party as the attempt to tie up its independence in a
bargain with those who do not share, in the one case, its belief in Socialism, in
the other, its belief in Democracy."[39]

How could repeated declarations that Labour alone was too weak to defeat
the government, "despite its crimes," be other than dispiriting to a rank and
file which had been slaving and hoping for fifty years for an independent
Labour government with power?[40] During the summer months, Popular Front
agitation was muted, in part because Cripps was taking a long family holiday
in Jamaica, in part because attention was centered on the escalating Czech
crisis.[41]

In May, shortly after a purported Nazi move resulted in Czech mobilization
and a show of Anglo-French solidarity, Dalton noted in his diary that while the
moves had, for the moment, stopped Germany, the British public continued to
be divided, confused, and uncertain. He rejected the position that Labour
should declare for no concessions by the Czechs to Nazi Germany. "This
would be a most stupid public declaration. If British opinion is to be held, C.S.
[Czechoslovakia] must at any rate appear to be conciliatory." A few months
later, on the eve of Chamberlain's first meeting with Hitler, he noted a discussion with Robert Vansittart in which he asked whether the latter thought that
the time had now come privately to urge the Czechs to give way rather than
make a hopeless and heroic fight against overwhelming odds if they were to be
deserted by all the great powers. Dalton's private admission was somewhat less

firm than that of the Labour Party or his own public statements attacking the policies of the national government. Nevertheless, he still believed that collective security was a practical possibility if only enough states would face up to it.[42]

During the summer and early fall, Chamberlain and his Foreign Secretary were negotiating with Hitler not from strength but from weakness. In the 1930s, the government had held fast to a strategic policy of limited liability. In the face of a difficult economic situation, the electorate's presumed reluctance to support rearmament, and the reality of three possible enemies in widely separated areas, wishful military thinking had all but ruled out the preparation of even a small but modernized expeditionary force for the support of Britain's undoubted vital interests on the European continent.[43] Appeasement depended on Britain possessing a military capacity large enough and threatening enough to deter Hitler. In 1938, the British did not believe they yet possessed a credible deterrent and thus could not afford to call Hitler's bluff. Still, there is some evidence to suggest that the British would have avoided confrontational diplomacy even if they had believed the balance of forces to have been more favorable. The Chamberlain government, like some on the Labour left such as C. R. Buxton, considered the Sudeten issue to be one of the anomalies created by Versailles whose removal could be part of a general European settlement.[44]

For its part, the Labour Party, now that it had abandoned its symbolic vote against the government's defence plans, continued to hammer away at the country's lack of preparation. Most official pronouncements for a time solved the dilemma of how to deal with Nazi aggression if British defences were as inadequate as Labour contended by holding on to the League of Nations and collective security. The leadership played down even that attempt to maintain some continuity with past positions as the Czech crisis deepened despite the Runciman mission to Prague. The Parliamentary Labour Party and the General Council met jointly in Blackpool, prior to the TUC's annual gathering. The result was a document that, this time, gave little emphasis to the role of the League of Nations except to condemn the National Government for having helped to undermine its authority and prestige. Instead, "Labour and the International Situation" bluntly called for a warning to the German government that the British would unite with the French and Soviet governments to resist any attack upon Czechoslovakia. France and Russia were bound by treaty to support Czechoslovakia if attacked and they had announced that they would at once honor their engagements. British interests were too closely involved, as declarations of the British government had affirmed, for Britain to be able to stand aside. Calling for an immediate summoning of Parliament, the Labour manifesto concluded, "Whatever the risks involved, Great Britain must make its stand against aggression. There is now no room for doubt or hesitation."[45]

Some members of the Labour leadership still clung to a hope that a firm stand would modify German policy. In a letter that Noel Baker wrote to Attlee in mid-September, he suggested that if the government would say it would resist aggression because it was a violation of international law, "then the power of the moderate Germans would be enormously increased, and they might be able to defeat the Himmler and Goebbels extremists."[46]

By the time "Labour and the International Situation" appeared, President Beneš of Czechoslovakia had agreed to concessions that appeared to accept almost all of the demands of the Sudeten German Party, which acted as Hitler's surrogate. As border incidents and other pressures on the Czechs continued, Chamberlain, not yet ready to call Parliament into session, determined to reach out to Hitler in a dramatic turn to personal diplomacy. The almost inexorable retreat—hailed by the government as a triumph—from Berchtesgaden to Godesberg to the final capitulation at Munich has been studied again and again. Here it is useful to note Chamberlain's meeting, after Berchtesgaden, with Citrine, Morrison, and Dalton representing the National Council of Labour. All three agreed that he had reported Hitler's insistence that everything depended on whether the British government would accept the principle of self-determination for the Sudetenland. Chamberlain had replied to the Führer that he would have to consult his colleagues. To the three Labour representatives, he had pointed to the crumbling of French resolution as a problem. Dalton warned Chamberlain that this would not be the last of Hitler's demands, while Citrine, although he reported that the preponderance of opinion in the National Council was that the prime minister had done the right thing in going to see Hitler, asked whether Chamberlain believed Hitler wanted a peaceful settlement.[47] Chamberlain's somewhat equivocal answer was hardly satisfactory and a few days later the full National Council condemned the possible dismemberment of Czechoslovakia as a shameful betrayal of a peaceful and democratic people.[48]

The Labour press mirrored Citrine's comment that most of the National Council thought that Chamberlain had done the right thing in going to see Hitler. The *New Statesman* observed that apart from the *News Chronicle* and the *Manchester Guardian* the press seemed to have given Chamberlain something like a doctor's mandate. Even the *Herald,* the journal noted, wished him luck, confident that he could not commit the British people.[49] Another exception was *Tribune,* which carried a constant stream of criticism as Chamberlain pursued his policy of conciliating Hitler. When the Runciman mission to serve as a mediator in Czechoslovakia was announced, *Tribune* branded him an "envoy of war" and a few days before the Munich agreement essentially confirmed the surrenders at Berchtesgaden and Godesberg *Tribune* charged, "Chamberlain Has Sold You" and "The Czech Betrayal Means World War—on Installment Plan."[50]

The escalation of Hitler's demands—for the immediate occupation of areas to be ceded to Germany—made Chamberlain's explanation in the House of Commons appear like the grim portent of war. Accordingly, Labour joined with the great majority of MPs who expressed relief and indeed gratitude when Chamberlain announced that he, along with Daladier of France and Mussolini, had been invited to come to Munich by Hitler. At the same time, the Parliamentary Executive decided that Attlee and Greenwood, the deputy leader, should seek an interview with Lord Halifax, the foreign secretary, to make it clearly understood that while the labour movement attached the utmost importance to the Munich visit, in the opinion of Labour (a) the limits of concession to Hitler had been reached; (b) the gravest view was taken of the fact that no Czech representative would apparently participate in the discussions; and (c) that it would be a great blunder if any action were taken which would alienate the Soviet government. At the same meeting of the Parliamentary Executive, Dalton informed the group that similar pressure was brought to bear upon Daladier, the French premier, and that Attlee and Greenwood had established contact with Maisky, the Soviet ambassador, and Masaryk, the Czech minister in London. In the event, Labour later charged, all three caveats had been ignored. [51]

When Parliament considered the Munich Agreement, which did little to change the import of Godesberg, in a long, emotion-charged, four-day debate, the tortured requirements of decision-making were evident on the Labour benches. Chamberlain's justification of his policy of détente evidenced a confidence in Hitler's good faith that was challenged in an impressive resignation speech by Duff Cooper, one of the few members of the government who felt that appeasement had gone too far. Subsequently, Attlee's lead for Labour was reflective of the mixed emotions with which Labour received the news of Munich. "We all feel relief that war has not come at this time," he admitted in what may have been the most eloquent speech of his career. "Every one of us has been passing through days of anxiety; we cannot, however, feel that peace has been established, but that we have nothing but an armistice in a state of war." Munich, he went on, had been a victory for brute force, the terms not negotiated but laid down as ultimata. The cause of the crisis was that Hitler had decided that the time was ripe for another step forward in his design to dominate Europe: "The real question that faces us in this Debate is not just a review of the past, not just our apprehensions of the present; it is, What can we do for the future of the human race?"[52]

Dalton and Morrison, among others, supported Attlee's lead. The former painted a bleak picture of the future: "Our fear is that if British foreign policy continues along the lines which it has recently followed, we shall continue to sacrifice more friends, more allies, at every stage, and that we shall be faced with the military and economic might of Germany which would be utterly overpowering, and in the end this country, with or without a hesitant and intimidated France, will be left to face its fate alone."[53] Morrison seconded Dalton's prescient vision. After a corrosive condemnation of the course of the national government's policy, he concluded, "If and when, unhappily, our country should be attacked and forced into war, the prospects for the triumph of the principles that we hold dear are doubtful in the circumstances with which we are now faced." [54]

During the course of the debate, the somewhat different views of both Cripps and Lansbury accompanied the strictures of the official leaders of the Labour Party. The former, too, damned the government for abandoning collective security and the rule of law, going on to call for an alliance of the nations that still believed in the principles of law and justice in international affairs in order to get a breathing space to deal with issues of economic justice. "The greatest contribution they can now make," he insisted, "is not by piling up armaments, but by taking the lead in working out a better policy for the co-operative economic development of world resources." [55] And Lansbury, holding firm to his pacifist creed, announced, "I hear all this denunciation of Herr Hitler and Signor Mussolini. I have met both of them and can only say that they are very much like any other politician or diplomat one meets." Suggesting, equally unrealistically, that the government could try to persuade the Dominions, which had hundreds of miles of open space, to take in refugees from Europe, "who want to make a better life for themselves," he insisted that the only way to combat evil was "to set something better against it." [56] His undoubted sincerity was singularly unpersuasive in the light of what was the reality on the European continent.

The first reactions of the labour press reflected the mixture of relief and apprehension that characterized the words of Labour's Parliamentary spokesmen. Only *Tribune,* convinced that Chamberlain was more interested in waging class war and defending British colonies than in the preservation of democratic security, displayed little relief at the presumed respite from the threat of war. In that connection, the journal asserted that, indeed for weeks, the German people had feared war and the limitation of their possible breathing space. But they felt chagrin and mortification as the Führer had made clear his determination to go ahead with his conquest plans. Once again, as in 1918, the unwillingness of the politicians to make common cause with the Russian Bolsheviks underlined the class hatred that was at the foundation of their policy. Meanwhile, the world was beginning to add up the results of the betrayal of Czechoslovakia—not the least in the transfer of workers and arms to the Reich. Not relief but bitterness at a surrender to fascism was the recurring theme in *Tribune* in the days following Munich. [57] By way of contrast, the *New Statesman,* so frequently critical of the tactics of the leadership, repeated much of the argument made by Attlee, Dalton, and Morrison when its editor noted that neither Czechoslovakia nor Russia was represented at the Munich conference. He feared that the cause of Spanish democracy might be bartered away in the course of any bargain reached at Munich, and even before the exact terms of any agreement became public, he remained deeply anxious for the safety and independence of the Czech people. The best that could be hoped for was a check on Hitler's most extreme ambitions and a respite from war. The test of success at Munich would be whether or not the vast German mobilization would be ended and with it a mobilization of the French army and the British navy: "As long as vast armed forces remain ready for action, peace will hang on a straw."[58]

Within a few weeks, however, the *New Statesman* had become as pessimistic as *Tribune* and other spokesmen of the left. With the League destroyed, it asserted, Europe had either to return to the ancient system of balance of power or to give Hitler a predominance such as Europe had not known except in the days of Napoleon. The Munich settlement freed Germany in the East and opened the way to the Balkans and the USSR. In the West, where *Mein Kampf* decreed the destruction of France, there was still a chance for democracy to survive if Britain and France were true to the Spanish Republic. But the victory of Franco meant a France beleagured on three sides, with her communications to Africa highly precarious; it meant that neither the British nor French empires would be defensible. And the journal now clearly envisaged the fascist triumph in Spain.[59]

In a long manifesto issued to the public, the National Executive of the Labour Party, for its part, paralleled the arguments of the Parliamentary Party's leadership in calling upon the people of Great Britain to support and demand a supreme national effort for peace. "In October 1938, " the manifesto warned, "we are back in 1914." Indicting the responsibility of the National Government, it charged that the whole standing of Great Britain in the world had been gravely damaged:

> British ships are bombed and British seamen killed and mutilated with impunity; British interests in Europe, the Mediterranean and the Far East, are being sacrificed without heed to the consequences; British diplomacy has suffered a series of shattering defeats in Manchuria, Spain, China, Austria, Czechoslovakia; Great Britain has abandoned her historic position as the champion of freedom and of the rights of small nations, and thereby has thrown away the support and respect of many nations and peoples.

As early as 1935, the document claimed, the Labour Party had declared that it would unhesitatingly provide whatever arms were necessary in order to defend the country and to fulfil its obligations under the Covenant of the League of Nations. The manifesto was essentially a campaign document. It said nothing about support for the existing government's arms policy and insisted that it must be replaced by a government which could inspire and lead the British people in a crusade to mobilize its strength in the service of its ideals—"that peace, justice, and liberty shall be preserved."[60] In effect, Labour was preparing for the next election as much as it was confronting the immediate crisis attributed to Chamberlain's censured policy.

When the prime minister took the next step in his approach and introduced a motion for approval of the Anglo-Italian agreement in the Commons, Greenwood warned that the issue was not the agreement but the price that would have to be paid for it. Outlining all the reasons for opposition, he charged that it abandoned the Spanish republic, for an unspecified period, to the untrammeled power of and of Italy. Ellen Wilkinson seconded him, caustically noting, to cries of "Shame," that if the prime minister believed Signor Mussolini, he was the only man in the world who did. And Noel Baker made the Labour case by posing a question. "We are sacrificing the Abyssinian people," he declared. "We are giving our consent to Mussolini's continued aggression in Spain. We may be allowing him to establish a domination which some day may prove a serious danger to us in the Empire which we rule. We are condoning the violation of a number of international engagements. We are thereby striking to-night still another blow at international law. Why are we doing this and what are we getting in return?" [61]

The Munich capitulation signaled to many that the crisis had not abated and that war was most likely. In Labour's mainstream, Dalton stepped up his exploration of collaboration with the dissident Tories, while Cripps made clear his readiness to postpone socialist purity. As the prime minister pressed ahead with the appeasement of the dictators, Labour's opposition to his policy balanced somewhat uneasily two related themes: the urgency of replacing his government at the next election and preparation for a war that increasingly appeared inevitable. In the process, Labour increasingly shared the views of others outside its ranks—Liberals and dissident Tories—for whom Chamberlain's price of peace was also too high.

10

Prelude to War

In the foreign policy debates that took place in the labour movement early in 1939, leaders who had long disagreed about so much came to agree on the proper response to the looming international crisis. Chamberlain was wrong, Labour insisted, in assuming that Nazism was simply an expression of frustrated nationalism.[1] Its far broader international ambitions meant that war was coming. In calling for multiparty cooperation to oppose the policy of appeasement and to meet the Nazi challenge, some of Labour's leaders were consciously taking a significant step away from Labour's long-standing doctrine of disarmament and non-violence in international affairs.

The major sticking point, not for the first time, was the inclusion by Sir Stafford Cripps of the Communist Party in the coalition he envisaged. Hugh Dalton, like most leaders of the Party, had been opposed to cooperation with members of other political parties. Labour's long-standing opposition to collaboration not only with the communists but with most non-socialist groups in general made the project of building a centrist front against Chamberlain's foreign policy a difficult one.[2] Now, however, the Munich disaster impelled Dalton to respond favorably to a Tory initiative for a meeting arranged by Harold Macmillan with Churchill, Eden, Brendan Bracken, and others. Both sides were cautious in their proposals, and seem to have agreed only that if the dissident Tories were penalized by their Party, presumably in the run-up to the next election, the group would talk again. Nevertheless, when Labour tabled an unfriendly amendment in the Commons, between thirty and forty supporters of the government abstained, an action which implied the possibility of further joint action.

Meanwhile, Cripps, on the morrow of Munich, had reconciled long-standing differences with Dalton and urged the latter to seek an alliance with any of the dissident Tories who might be interested. Quickly, however, when discussions with the Tory dissidents appeared to be going nowhere, he abandoned his brief flirtation with the notion of a centrist coalition against the National Government and renewed his support for a Popular Front. This time, in a memorandum presented to the National Executive Committee early in January, he called for an alliance of all parties to the left of the Tories, once again excluding even the Churchill group from his proposals. As before, the inclusion of the Communist Party marked the gulf between Cripps and his fellow Labourites. Already his backing of the Popular Front candidate Vernon Bartlett in a by-election had been in defiance of the NEC and it was inevitable that the "Cripps Memorandum" be voted down by that body. The NEC made its case in a long document entitled "Notes on the Memorandum of Sir Stafford Cripps." Going back to the Campbell case of 1924 to demonstrate that a minority Labour government could not count on the support even of the Liberal Party, the analysis produced instance after instance to cast serious doubt on the fact that a Labour government, without a majority and dependent upon allies, could be assured of full support in implementing an agreed program. It then went on, almost using a hammer to slay a gnat, to compare the Labour Party's "Immediate Programme" with the proposals of Cripps, reasonably accurately in the case of the contents of the Cripps memorandum, but clearly to the advantage of the Party leadership.[3]

When his memorandum was rejected by a vote of 17 to 3, Cripps immediately sent copies to a wide circle of Parliamentary candidates and affiliated organizations. When he refused to recant, even after Dalton had pleaded with him to observe party discipline, the Executive expelled him, along with Aneurin Bevan and George Strauss, from the Labour Party, with only Ellen Wilkinson dissenting.[4]

Cripps did not go quietly. His expulsion was followed by a highly emotional and bitter left-wing campaign in support of the Popular Front movement and countered by an equally bitter response from the leaders of the Labour Party. While the Popular Front advocates managed to mount a moderately widespread campaign of support, the Party leadership was able to keep it contained. A manifesto, "Unity—True or Sham?," was issued outlining the reasons Labour rejected the Popular Front and those for believing that Labour could win the next election. Calling upon all members to pull together to help throw the Tories out of office, the statement insisted that no member of the Labour Party, least of all a member of the National Executive, could be permitted to conduct an organized and privately financed campaign in support of a program of his own making.[5]

The firmness of the Labour leaders was bolstered by the uncertainties among its critics, foremost among them Cripps. Under the pressure of the evident crisis in the international situation, by the end of January he was once again advocating joining hands with Liberals and dissentient Conservatives with a moderate program in a government dominated by the Labour Party.[6] His National Petition Campaign confused many of his supporters, so that he lost such left-wing members of the NEC as D. N. Pritt and Ellen Wilkinson, while respected figures such as Richard Tawney, the Webbs, Christopher Addison,

Leonard Woolf, and J.A. Hobson, although they questioned the Petition tactics, nevertheless called upon the National Executive to reach a compromise with Cripps.[7] Perhaps more predictably, consistent critics of the Executive such as Richard Crossman and G.D.H. Cole joined a number of others in deploring Cripps' expulsion and faulting the Executive for failing to mobilize the opposition to the National Government they believed existed among members of all parties and among those who belonged to no party. For them, the position of the leadership was a prescription for political impotence.[8] By the time the Labour Party conference met in late May and early June, however, the campaign had pretty much played itself out. At the conference, Cripps made a somewhat dull and dry defense of his policy and the conference endorsed the decision to expel him by a 5 to 1 majority. During the course of the next few years, it is possible that his status as an independent gave him the opportunity to play a greater role than otherwise might have been the case, but in any event he was not readmitted to the Labour Party until late in the war.[9]

The struggle over the Cripps initiative emphasized Labour leadership's view that success in the next election—due to take place no later than the fall of 1940—was essential to any significant change in British foreign policy. Having twice experienced the limitations of minority government, most of them had little faith in a collaboration with representatives of other political views, whether of the left or the right. They held to their insistence on independence despite the critical nature of the international emergency and continued to believe—or at least professed to believe—that only a Labour victory could turn around the international outlook of the British government. Even Dalton's tentative discussions with the Tory dissidents, though they perhaps prepared the way for future collaboration once war had come, for the moment were barren of concrete results.

One of the features of Labour policy almost from the moment of the formation of the Party early in the century was its opposition to conscription except in the case of the direst of emergencies. That opposition continued well into 1939 in both the industrial and the political wings of the movement. In the spring of 1938, when it appeared that the government might be making plans for the introduction of conscription, the Parliamentary Labour Party made clear that it demurred, as did Aneurin Bevan, who infrequently found himself so solidly on the side of his fellow MPs in the PLP.[10] Trade unionists of every political complexion likewise agreed, looking upon manpower conscription without a parallel conscription of wealth as designed to destroy the trade union movement under the guise of national necessity. As one of the Labour Publication Department's flyers put it: "Britain needs conscription of wealth not man-power." Even Ernest Bevin, who more than most understood the manpower needs of preparation for conflict, agreed with the many union and constituency branches whose opposition was recorded in the many letters that flowed into TUC and Party headquarters. The depth of the feeling may be gauged in a letter to Bevin from Morgan Phillips, in no way an extremist, who agreed with the opposition to conscription because he saw Chamberlain as the tool of international capitalism, and the enemy of the common people in every country of the world.[11]

At the same time, when the government introduced a plan for National Voluntary Service in the fall of 1938, Bevin, more realistic than many of his correspondents, supported the scheme as a way of avoiding the more drastic method of compulsion. As he later explained to a correspondent, the trade unions did not want industrial or military conscription, but Hitler must be defended against, so that it was imperative to make the voluntary effort work.[12] His assessment was accepted by the National Council of Labour, which issued a manifesto in March of 1939 on "The Labour Movement and National Voluntary Service." Although it insisted upon various guarantees in the application of voluntary service, the statement essentially made at some length the same argument made succinctly by Bevin.[13] Basically, Labour was motivated to resist compulsion until the last moment by mistrust of the government much more than by the theoretical view that a democratic society did not require forced service in order to defend itself.[14]

The Nazi seizure of Czechoslovakia precipitated a shift in British policy signalized by guarantees to Poland and subsequently to Greece, Rumania, and Denmark. Perhaps even more indicative of the change in temper was the introduction of conscription, which the Chamberlain government had hitherto resisted, at the end of April. Characteristically, Labour continued to oppose the move in the House of Commons, charging the government with a breach of faith in turning to compulsion while still at peace. Despite Chamberlain's somewhat tardy recognition in his retort that changed circumstances required a reluctant change of policy, his repudiation of his promise was looked upon with misgivings by more than his political foes. Hostility among the trade unions was especially bitter. Bevin, for example, accurately reflected the views of his union colleagues when he refused to accept military necessity as an excuse for compulsion. The voluntary response of free men, he argued, could be counted on to defend the values of a democratic society.[15] Labour's opposition, in any case, persisted until the outbreak of war a few months later, when criticism of the administration of the system substantially replaced opposition to compulsion itself.[16]

The government's apparent sincerity in finally standing up to Hitler continued to be regarded with suspicion in Labour circles. Above all, the failure to reach out for an alliance with the Soviet Union was assailed. On this issue, there was little difference in the public pronouncements of the left-wing from those of the more representative middle-of-the-road spokesmen for Labour, however much the former criticized the tactics of Labour's own leadership. The New Statesman, for example, charged that the government, "which now dictates the policy of France," refused to take the one step which could make sense of the policy it pretended to follow. There was still no alliance with the Soviet Union. When Chamberlain underwent his sudden conversion to collective security "we prophesied that the public would soon be disillusioned. There has been no real change in the government's policy." But then the journal went on to complain that the Labour Party always advocated the right policy, but then tended to accept the government's statements. It urged the leaders to stop wasting time expelling "the keenest advocates of the peace bloc" and make the country understand that talk of collective security was dangerous and fraudulent if Russia was excluded.[17] Similarly, in *Tribune*, both Konni Zilliacus, often regarded as a fellow-traveler but more accurately at this stage a single-minded believer in the League of Nations, and Cripps agreed that there could be no peace without the Soviet Union. "Our safety," wrote Cripps, quite simply, "depends on alliance with Russia." [18]

Virtually all of Labour's public spokesmen took it for granted that the Soviet Union was eager for an agreement with the Western powers. Privately, Dalton was not so sure. "It is all very well that optimistic rumours should flow week after week from the Soviet Embassy and the F.O. about the Anglo-Soviet pact negotiations," he confided to his diary. "I am less and less inclined to believe them...." That his doubts were about Soviet intentions as well as about the reluctance of the British government seems clear from his subsequent arrangement once again to see Maisky, the Soviet ambassador to Britain.[19] Dalton was puzzled about the stance Labour should take: "Either we press the Government or not. In the first case, we may encourage the Russians to be more difficult and be represented by Ministers here as impeding the negotiations...; in the other case we are taken to be acquiescing in H.M.G.'s conduct of the negotiations and make our supporters in the country impatient." [20] His concerns were shared by the Parliamentary Party's Executive Committee, where it was suggested by some that the Russians were becoming "pernickety" now, just as the British side had been in the past.[21]

As negotiations for a possible grouping against aggression dragged themselves out in the spring and early summer, Chamberlain appeared anxious to avoid as much Parliamentary discussion as possible. For the most part, for a number of weeks he was successful. When Dalton suggested, during question period on May 10, that Halifax should proceed to Moscow and have a "straightforward" discussion with Vyacheslav Molotov, the prime minister simply replied: "I think we had better await the reply of the Soviet Government and then we shall see what further steps are required."[22] The one exception was a fairly extensive exploration on May 19, triggered by Lloyd George's corrosive overview of the international situation. Seconding Lloyd George's description, Attlee complained that the House did not know what the government's policy was. There had been a policy of appeasement, but that had failed, in the aftermath of Czechoslovakia and the recent Italian invasion of Albania, because it had no real basis. "Without a firm policy of resistance to aggression, and without a bold policy for removing the causes of war," he warned, "this country and the British empire will drift into disaster, a disaster which will overthrow something even greater than the British Empire and this country, that is, the free spirit of human beings." In his reply, Chamberlain understandably offered no additional information about his government's policy, but did comment that Lloyd George had painted a "somewhat over-gloomy picture."[23] Shortly thereafter, Parliament adjourned for the summer recess, arrangements being made to recall it if the international situation worsened.

Before the Labour Party conference met in late May, the Advisory Committee prepared a long and important memorandum on Labour's international policy, pointing out that over the past eighteen months it had forwarded various memoranda dealing with the subject of appeasement and peaceful change, recommending that "appeasement through international justice" which had always been a part of Labour policy should be more fully stressed than had recently been the case.

The memorandum commended the soundness of the broad outlines of Labour policy over the past twenty years. The Party had opposed the punitive and unjust clauses of the Versailles Treaty and foretold the rise of a militant Germany if they were insisted upon—as they had been insisted upon by the "national government" of that time, only to become an important cause of Hitlerism. In the years immediately following the treaty, Labour had stood for just and generous treatment of the German people, for their inclusion in the League of Nations, and for carrying out the Covenant provisions for the reduction of armaments. It had foretold the impossibility of keeping Germany weak and disarmed and the certainty that any attempt to do so would lead to a more militant Germany and the threat of war. Instead the Party had based its policy on the League of Nations, urging its use for four purposes: establishing an international system based on law and order instead of force and armaments in Europe; promoting political and economic appeasement by removing justified national grievances and economic barriers by reasonable revision of treaties by compromise and peaceful change; stabilizing peaceful relations between the states of Europe by building up a system of peaceful settlement of international disputes and collective security; and relieving Europe of the universal fear of armed attack by beginning at once the process of disarmament.

During the two decades, the Advisory Committee's assessment continued, the need for such a policy had become ever more imperative and remained the only sane long-term policy which gave the chance of establishing a stable peace. But instead the National Government had rejected such a long-term policy and had contributed to the state of international anarchy in which the democracies were threatened by militant and aggressive dictators. This in turn had increased the imminent danger of war. The National Government had met the situation by rearming but continually still giving way, at the expense of the smaller democratic states, to Germany and Italy, whose internal and external policies stood for everything Labour abhorred. The short-term situation put Labour in a false position. Because of the crisis caused by the National Government, it had no present choice but to support the government's main policy of rearmament. In the circumstances, Labour's "real and fundamental policy of law, justice, collective security, peaceful change and disarmament" sank into the background, making it easy to misrepresent to less thoughtful electors.

What to do? The Advisory Committee urged that the long range policy of the Party be brought more prominently into the picture and be put before the electorate in a concrete and practical form. The destruction of Czechoslovakia had opened many eyes. Real appeasement must rest on the willingness of the democracies to consider political and economic concessions to the dictatorships in return for the latter's acceptance of the reconstruction of law, order, and peace in Europe. Britain, in particular, could no longer buy peace at the expense of others; it must be willing to consider what concessions it might make in return for the concessions of others. In the light of what had more and more become a prewar end game, the Advisory Committee document was a curious amalgam of realism and fantasy, resting on positions which unfortunately had been disregarded after World War I but had long since lost much of their relevance in dealing with the new fascist regimes.[24]

When the Labour Party conference met at Southport, the debate over the expulsion of Cripps, despite its virtually preordained outcome, took precedence over a thorough discussion of foreign policy. The recommendations of the Advisory Committee were to a large degree disregarded, not because they were not given consideration, but because the major leaders of the NEC, like those of the TUC and the Parliamentary Party, had by now come to the conclusion that, however Labour's long-term policy of genuine redress of grievances and the reconstitution of the international law of Europe was preferable to the "power politics" of the National Government, the immediate crisis, and the defence of Britain itself, required a rethinking of long-held convictions. Labour's leaders did not abandon their criticism of the manner in which the government pursued its presumed change of policy, but, having abandoned their symbolic opposition to the funding of rearmament in 1937, they were coming increasingly closer to conventional formulas for the protection of national interests. The resolution presented to the conference and overwhelmingly adopted placed emphasis on the government's delay in coming to some agreement with the Russians.[25] No longer was the insistence on doing so only under the aegis of the League of Nations. Instead, Labour was speaking in traditional tones which mirrored those of Churchill, the major Tory critic of the Chamberlain policy.[26]

Meanwhile, the government pursued what Labour saw as a desultory approach to a military arrangement with the Russians. The dispatch of William Strang rather than a higher-level figure, delays in the appointing of a military mission to engage in talks with the Soviets, even the use of a slow boat instead of air as the means of transportation to meet the Russians, all heightened the suspicions of the purposes of Chamberlain's tactics. Neither he nor Halifax, it was taken for granted, really favored a Russian alliance, and indeed appeared not fully to accept the urgency of the international situation. Proof of this was the way in which the government was implementing its rearmament program. There had been a long delay in appointing a minister of supply after the government had announced its intention to create such an office and even the hated conscription system, applied to future age groups only as they reached twenty, appeared to indicate that there was little sense of an immediate danger of war.[27]

Once again, Dalton's diary, however much designed in part to put its author in the best possible light, offers a clue to the approach of Labour's leaders to the actions of the government. When the National Council of Labour deputed Citrine, Morrison, and Dalton to see the prime minister on the international situation, Dalton reported that while Citrine was a reasonable and excellent team man, he nevertheless was so anti-Russian that he saw more clearly than was necessary the difficulties of the government over the Russian pact. For himself, Dalton warned Chamberlain that the delay in reaching an accord with Moscow was rapidly robbing the arrangement of much of its significance. All of them should understand and be prepared to make large concessions to the Soviet point of view regarding the Baltic states. They were as vital a concern to the Russian as the Low Countries were to Britain. If Hitler was to be effectively warned—and the air was full of talk about another German aggression within a few weeks—the conclusion of the Russian pact must be an essential part of the warning. To his diary Dalton confided that he thought the prime minister realized the danger of letting the negotiations break down. Nevertheless, when pressed for his view of the consequences of such a breakdown, he said, in what Dalton described as his flat, obstinate way, "Well I don't think that would be the end of the world."[28]

Dalton attempted to put pressure on the government at question time in the House of Commons without trying to force a debate, in part because some of his colleagues, such as Morrison and Greenwood, saw some merit in the government's case. He remained concerned, even at this stage, that the government might make a real "peace offer" to Germany. "If Chamberlain makes this sort of proposal in the autumn, just before an election, the Labour Party will be in a hole, for if we oppose we are warmongers, and if we support we agree with the Government."[29]

Dalton's concern that Chamberlain might still make a "peace offer" to Germany was not shared by some of those on Labour's left, although there was little unanimity of judgment in those quarters. To be sure, the *New Statesman* warned, Hitler must be assured that aggression either in East or West would mean European war. But at the same time, if he was not to be given the ability to portray the forces against him as an aggressive encirclement of Germany, the peace front as a whole must put forward a joint peace policy, outlining the conditions for a stable peace in Europe. The journal was no more specific, but, referring to suggestions of Ernest Bevin and Sir Arthur Salter, judged that even at such a late moment, a challenging proposal, authoritatively made, would alter the atmosphere of Europe and, above all in Germany, might even avert war.[30]

Tribune would have none of this easy optimism. Chamberlain planned for a new Berlin-Rome-Tokyo deal, it thundered in a front page article, warning its readers not to take too seriously stories about the early completion of Anglo-Soviet negotiations. The Anglo-Japanese agreement, "recognizing …the right of the Japanese Army to do as it likes in Northern China, providing it leaves British interests alone"; discussions of economic assistance to Germany; and the breakdown of Anglo-Polish loan negotiations, all pointed to "appeasement," the readiness to do a deal with the aggressor at someone else's expense. All of this, to *Tribune,* helped explain the delays in the approach to the Russians, as it spun out its criticism of the optimism of the "capitalist press."[31]

Within a little more than a month the need to make such a decision as Dalton feared was wiped out by the actions of the Nazi and Soviet governments. The Nazi-Soviet Pact, the public terms of which provided for a non-aggression agreement between the two dictatorships-came as a bombshell, even for those, like Dalton, who had some misgivings about the eagerness of the Russians for an agreement with the West. His own earlier uneasiness about Russian intentions notwithstanding, he was soon realistically advising Rab Butler, Halifax's second at the Foreign Office, that the government not treat Russia with high pique, while at the same time warning against spreading British commitments too thin. Britain should abandon the concessions in China, in which its citizens had extra-territorial rights, at the earliest possible moment. It did not want war with the Japanese and really could not go on taking risks on behalf of China, particularly in view of the Russian attitude both in Europe and Asia. He made clear that this was his personal view, with which not all his colleagues would agree.[32]

Labour's political and trade union leaders, like Dalton, were also clear that the government must honor its commitment to Poland and stand firm against this latest attack upon the international system they had once hoped was coming into existence. On August 25, the National Council of Labour called a meeting of the three Labour executive bodies, at which it was decided to renew the appeal to the German people to realize the danger that war would result from the policy followed by their government. At the same time, the meeting declared its satisfaction that the British government was doing its utmost to find a peaceful solution to the dispute between Germany and Poland, which of course had been intensifying throughout the summer under

German pressure upon the Poles. The joint meeting agreed that Labour's spokesmen in Parliament should make a clear declaration of the nation's solidarity in the crisis and gave the National Council of Labour authority to act for the labour movement during the period of emergency according to the lines of policy already laid down.[33]

Reaction in the Labour press was more mixed. The *Daily Herald,* as was almost always the case, gave voice to the position taken by the leadership. Whatever may have been its criticism in the past, in the event of war, the nation would be united behind a government which had expressed the nation's determination admirably. Once war came and forces poured into Poland from two sides, the *Herald* bitterly reported that Russian Communism now joined with German Nazism in the scramble for plunder. Yet, while the prosecution of the war would be made more difficult for France and Britain, there need be no fear that the ultimate outcome would be altered. The confident tone of the *Herald,* despite warnings such as those of Churchill over the past several years, reflected perhaps wishful thinking rather than hard-headed knowledge of German preparations. Only a few weeks earlier, Harold Laski, in one of his least prescient assessments, had written in the same paper of "The Myth of Germany's War Strength." His view was widely shared until events in 1940 turned myth into reality.[34]

The *New Statesman* was considerably less sanguine. In an article entitled "Peace in the Balance," it branded the Nazi-Soviet Pact the direct result of Britain's failure to form the full Anglo-Soviet alliance when it was honestly offered. The journal argued that Stalin was so convinced he was being double-crossed and that there was to be another Munich over Poland that he decided himself to double-cross the Western powers. But the crisis did not mean that those who had criticized the National Government should now meekly line up behind Chamberlain. Never was the need for an independent Opposition greater. Whether for peace or war, a coalition of all parties under the present leadership would be a national disaster.[35]

Even less accommodating was *Tribune.* Its first reaction to the Nazi-Soviet Pact was to headline, "Soviet Peace Move Exposes Chamberlain" and to contend that the fact the British people would not allow the prime minister to break his pledges only made matters worse, bringing war nearer rather than postponing it. A few days later *Tribune* assured its readers that Russia had not given Hitler a free hand, but rather that the non-aggression pact signed by Stalin with Hitler had strongly reinforced the power for peace in Europe. Only on September 8, when war had come, was this self-delusion modified. Then, Cripps and Aneurin Bevan jointly prepared an article, "Our Duty!," which called for no compromise in the war against Nazi aggression and fascism, but reminded readers that the struggle against capitalism and for socialism must at all costs be continued.[36]

Despite such differences, Labour's leaders faced the second great conflict of the twentieth century with a clearer view of their purposes than had been the

case in the First World War. In a sense, four decades of controversy had culminated, if not in consensus, then in a governing view of foreign policy issues
that shared numerous elements with Conservative and Liberal criticisms of the
national government's positions. Whatever may have been meant in the past
by a socialist foreign policy, by the outbreak of war it had a great deal in
common with the outlook of many of Labour's opponents. The implications
were to affect policy for years to come.

Epilogue

In the first four decades of its existence the Labour Party, and indeed the entire labour movement, progressed from an almost total lack of attention to foreign affairs to a relatively responsible policy that accepted the need to accommodate ideologies and slogans to the existing realities of the international world. Even at the beginning there were exceptions—Keir Hardie, Ramsay MacDonald, Philip Snowden—to the picture of indifference, but on balance it was some time before the views of these key figures took hold within the struggling and not very cohesive environment of early "working-class" political independence.

From the beginning of the period under discussion—and well into subsequent years—a variety of strands of thought persisted, in one form or another. One such strand took its view of international relations from the nineteenth-century Liberal world in which most of the pioneers of independent Labour had learned their political lessons. Peace, to this way of thinking, often meant a kind of isolation from the complex issues of the outer-world. The notion that free trade throughout the developed world and equal access to the raw materials of the rest were a key to a peaceful and prosperous world remained for a long time a standard feature of its rhetoric.

Another small but often quite vocal minority was made up of pacifists, some of whose rejection of the use of force in world affairs stemmed from deeply felt religious convictions, while others, quite secular in their approach, appealed to reason and simple good sense as the sanction for opposing armaments and all forms of militarism. The outlook of a substantial cadre stemmed from its ideological opposition to capitalism and imperialism. To them the present economic organization of society meant not only the exploitation of the working classes but inevitably led to bitter rivalries and eventual war. They often assumed that only when a significant number of major governments had turned to socialism—"people's governments," in their formulation—would there be the possibility of a peaceful and productive world.

As time went on, particularly during the course of the First World War, various groups within the labour movement were among the leading advocates of a new form of international organization to take the place of what they regarded as the deadly and outdated competitive "power politics" that had led, they believed, to the disastrous conflict. Some viewed such an instrument as a substitute for a final recourse to arms in the settlement of international disputes; others envisaged a much more extensive role for the proposed body in such matters as access to raw materials, worldwide—or at least European-wide—labour standards, even the international administration of underdeveloped areas of the world.

When the war was over, most of Labour was deeply disappointed by the peace settlement. In the absence of Germany, the Soviet Union, and the United States, even the League of Nations which came into existence was regarded by many as simply an instrument of the hegemony that France, in particular, but also Britain, was determined to maintain over a defeated Germany.

Slowly, in the years immediately after the war, a small group on Labour's moderate right took the lead in trying to wean the movement from the bitter rejectionism that stemmed from disillusion with Versailles and the other settlements reached in the various Paris arrangements. Men such as Arthur Henderson and J.R.Clynes argued that the League Covenant itself could be used to remedy some of the deficiencies of Versailles and that in addition, if the Covenant itself was imperfect, it contained the means by which it could be amended and improved.

These various views did not disappear as Labour moved closer to its somewhat surprising assumption of minority office after the December general election of 1923. On the whole, that tenure of office was modestly successful. MacDonald shepherded the Dawes Plan through to a successful conclusion and Henderson at Geneva reached a meeting of the minds with some of his continental colleagues in shaping the so-called Geneva Protocol. That aborted document attempted to provide a means for defining the aggression which League powers were, in theory at least, pledged to resist.

Once Labour was out of office, and as the Baldwin government moved towards development of the Locarno Agreements, Labour engaged in what may have been the crucial rethinking of its foreign policy positions in the inter-war years. A small group of young men—Hugh Dalton, Philip Noel Baker, Will Arnold Forster—all of them close to Henderson, became the major advocates of what they called collective security through the unconditional use of the League of Nations and its machinery. Tackling the issue about which there was quite patently the most disagreement in labour circles, they more or less uncompromisingly argued that just as domestic life required the use of police forces to sustain social tranquility, so did international life require the sanction of force behind the operations of an international organization. Their contention was not accepted readily by pacifists such as George Lansbury or Arthur Ponsonby, both key figures in the inter-war annals of the labour movement. Nor was it congenial to those who have been called pacificists, not out-and-out pacifists, but those reluctant to accept the use of force as s substitute, as they saw it, for reason and discussion.

Nevertheless, when Labour again took office, once more as a minority government, Henderson as foreign secretary attempted with some success to implement this "League of Nations" policy as he moved to sign such provisions as the Optional Clause and the General Act of the League Covenant. Again, Labour seemed to have achieved some superficial gains both at Geneva and in relations, conducted by MacDonald himself, with the United States. But the onset of the Great Depression destroyed not only the Labour government in its struggle over dealing with the economy, but also a foreign affairs policy which rested on assumptions of rationality and good will that were rapidly being abandoned in the Europe of the thirties.

For Labour, the early thirties were years of the locust. Decimated in the election of October 1931, Labour was hardly in a position to make its weight felt as Japanese militarists, German Nazis, and Italian Fascists in a variety of ways challenged the stability of the international order. Labour's less than robust reaction to the Japanese aggression in North China, for example, must be seen in the light of the disarray, not to say impotence, of the political wing of the movement. And while the trade unions, in these circumstances, came to have a greater influence than ever on Labour policies, the impact of the Depression inexorably siphoned off much of the industrial wing's attention to urgent matters of domestic concern.

As the thirties progressed, Labour's symbolic opposition to the Service estimates to protest against government policies was increasingly self-defeating. Both Ernest Bevin and Hugh Dalton fought for some years to persuade the Parliamentary Party to abandon the tactic. By the mid-thirties they were convinced that Nazi and Fascist aggression was only likely to be halted by force. Not until 1937 were they able to obtain a reversal of the negative policy and a decision for Labour MPs to abstain on votes for the Service estimates. In effect, in the face of Japanese aggression in China, the Italian rape of Abyssinia, and the long horror of the Spanish Civil War with its attendant German, Russian, and especially Italian intervention, this meant that Labour was finally accepting the need to rearm—even if it meant supporting (although criticizing the administration of) rearmament by the National Government. By the outbreak of Hitler's war, the major leaders of Labour have given up their illusions about the effectiveness of the League of Nations in the new and frightening world that had emerged. They supported Britain's resort to arms finally to halt the march of aggression and while refusing to serve under Chamberlain, whose policies and person they mistrusted, they had come to a definition of national need—and of national interest—that enabled them to serve fully in the Churchill coalition when it was formed in 1940.

Aside from George Lansbury, whose deeply felt religious pacifism did not falter with the onset of war, and a score or so MPs who continued to press for a negotiated peace, Labour's representatives supported the war fully and responsibly. To be sure, in its early stages many Labour MPs, like Neville Chamberlain himself, hoped "that it would go away without the necessity of having to fight it."[1] As before, and even after the formation of Churchill's coalition in which the major Labour leaders played a prominent part, criticism of how the war was conducted, in the field but especially at home, was a constant theme in the Labour press and at such conferences and meetings as continued to be held during the course of the conflict.

Nevertheless, over the preceding forty years, the labour movement—both political and industrial—had by the beginning of the Second World War gradually hammered out an approach to foreign policy that was viable in the dramatically changed environment of the post-1945 world. While in a sense the exigencies of war took precedence over systematic consideration of post-war foreign policy issues, planning for the future did, of course, take place. For the most part, despite the persistence of differences which had characterized the labour movement throughout its first four decades, its mainstream leaders, by the time they took office after the Second World War, had come a very long way from the essentially negative slogans of the early days of the movement.

In the early months of the war, the Labour party moved slowly to make its position clear. Transmitting a declaration on "Labour and the War" to the National Executive Committee on January 25, 1940, J.S. Middleton, the Party's secretary, pointed out that the Party had not yet issued any statement of its attitude since the outbreak of hostilities. He warned that the continued silence might lead to misunderstanding and misrepresentations. The draft declaration, interestingly, reflected the continued hope that something short of all-out war would be sufficient in the days ahead. "Victory for democracy must be achieved," it read, "either by arms or economic pressure, or—better still—a victory of the German people over the Hitler regime, resulting in the birth of a new Germany." "Labour, the War and the Peace," as it was retitled, condemned any attempt from outside to break up Germany and warned that any effort, after the war, to keep Germany as an outcast, must fail.[2]

Even after the creation of the Churchill coalition and the fall of France, a small group within the Party hoped for a negotiated settlement. Its chief spokesman was R.R. Stokes of the Ipswich Divisional Labour Party. At the Party conference in the fall of 1941, he referred to earlier statements by Clement Attlee to validate his opposition to a dictated peace. But Stokes was supported by fewer than a handful of delegates and was able to muster only a meager 19,000 votes, out of some two and a half million, in opposition to the official policy of the Party, which by now had become clearer and much firmer.[3]

As the war progressed, differences did develop between the public posture of the labour movement and the views of its chief leaders in the coalition. In August 1943, when a draft circular by William Gillies took a hard line on Germany and condemned the German people as a whole, it was overwhelmingly rejected. Not only figures on the left—Aneurin Bevan and Harold Laski are cases in point—but such a mainstream politician as Noel Baker challenged the Gillies formulation. A resolution in support of the latter's position was roundly defeated at the TUC annual conference where an amendment was accepted distinguishing between the German people and the Nazis.[4]

But this view had its skeptics in high places. All sections of the labour movement looked forward to some kind of democratic revolution in Germany, but neither Attlee nor Bevin nor Dalton agreed with the "soft" formulation of the left. Attlee and Bevin aimed at a permanent reduction of German power. The former now believed that Germany had been treated too tenderly the last time and Bevin went so far as to speak of a return to the days of Bismarck. Dalton, for his part, was so convinced of the need to control Germany that he was prepared to continue the coalition after the war if it was necessary to do so. His first draft of Labour's policy statement, "International Post-War Settlement," emphasized German not Nazi responsibility for Axis crimes. Although it was not accepted by the NEC, it highlighted the differences that continued to be felt within the ranks of Labour.[5]

Relations with the Soviet Union also revealed disagreements among the critics of government policies. After a root and branch denunciation of the Nazi-Soviet Pact by the leadership and especially of the attack upon Finland, Labour was more than relieved when Hitler launched his attack of Russia in the summer of 1941. Support for the Soviet Union, however, had its various nuances. On the left, while all were grateful for the Soviet war effort, Laski and the *New Statesman,* where his views were often aired, were optimistic about postwar collaboration. Aneurin Bevan and *Tribune*, on the other hand, were not nearly so positive about such cooperation. Already the latter's uneasiness about a postwar world dominated by Great Britain, the United States, and the Soviet Union was evident. For the most part, however, most Labour Party activists gave somewhat perfunctory attention to the international post-war planning initiatives of the Party's leadership.[6]

Altogether, the Labour Party came to power after the war with what most of its leaders considered a more realistic view of foreign policy possibilities than those of the socialist theorists of an earlier day. For the most part that view prevailed. Usually the critics of the policies pursued by Labour's leaders were a small minority. But their disapproval often influenced the tactics of those leaders, who were struggling, often almost desperately, to construct responsible foreign policy positions while at the same time retaining the support of a divided group of followers. For the first time, in 1945, those leaders found themselves not only in power, but with an overwhelming Parliamentary majority that seemed to promise considerable freedom of action. Almost immediately, the realities of the international situation provoked changes in Bevin's outlook as foreign secretary and shifts in the attitudes of both Attlee and Dalton. They easily carried their government colleagues with them, but once again a Labour Party minority demurred from policies regarded as uncomfortably similar to those of the politicians whom Labour had supplanted. Even though the criticisms of what has been called "Labour's conscience" were largely stilled by the end of 1947, they were not completely erased.[7] Questions about atomic energy, Britain's role in the Middle East and the Korean War, relations with Communist China, the affordability of Labour's defence program, all testified to the continuation of doubt and concern within the ranks of Labour as Britain, reluctantly perhaps, faced up to the tensions and the dangers of what was to become a half-century of an onerous Cold War.

Notes

Introduction

1. A few of the outstanding biographies are D. Marquand, *Ramsay MacDonald* (1977); B. Pimlott, *Hugh Dalton* (1985); F. M. Leventhal, *The Last Dissenter. H. N. Brailsford and his World* (1985); K. O. Morgan, *Keir Hardie* (1967); P. Clarke, *The Cripps Version: The Life of Sir Stafford Cripps, 1889-1952* (2002). Valuable period studies are D. Carlton, *MacDonald versus Henderson. The Foreign Policy of the Second Labour government* (1970); J. Naylor, *Labour's International Policy: The Labour Party in the 1930's* (1969); my own *Paths Not Taken: British Labour and International Policy in the 1920s* (1994) and *The League of Nations Movement in Great Britain, 1914-1919* (1952). See also M. R. Gordon, *Conflict and Consensus in Labour's Foreign Policy* (1969) and K. Miller, *Socialism and Foreign Policy: Theory and Practice in Britain to 1931* (1967). A largely straightforward account of official positions is E. Windrich, *British Labour's Foreign Policy* (1952).
2. Some have questioned whether the attention to Labour's foreign policy views was not excessive, given that it had so little experience of political power before 1940. See D. C. Watt, *Personalities andPolicies: Studies in the Formation of British Foreign Policy in the Twentieth Century* (1965), p. 19.
3. D. Burridge, *British Labour and Hitler's War* (1976), pp. 13-4.

Chapter 1

1. It is instructive that when the maverick journal Robert Blatchford published a little pamphlet entitled *What Is Socialism?* [n.d.] early in the century he did not feel it necessary to mention foreign affairs at all. The closest approximation was his rhetorical question, "If the Government can manage a fleet of war vessels, why not fleets of liners and traders?" p. 10.
2. Colin Cross's comment, in his *Philip Snowden* (1966) that Ramsay MacDonald was the only leading socialist before 1914 to devote sustained attention to foreign affairs seems singularly off base. On the other hand, much of the specialized literature tends to exaggerate the consideration of such matters by the various elements of the labour movement.
3. K. Morgan, *Keir Hardie* (1967), pp. 2-3.
4. Ibid., pp. 2-3 and *Labour People* (1987), pp. 26-7, 33; C. Benn, *Keir Hardie* (1992), pp. 316-7, 323-8. See also D. J. Newton, *British Labour, European Socialism and the Struggle for Peace* (Oxford, 1985), pp. 292-3 and A. J. A. Morris, "Labour and Foreign Affairs. A Search for Identity and Policy," in K. D. Brown, ed., *The First Labour Party 1906-1914* ([1985], pp. 268-91; 27 HC Deb., 4s., July 17, 1901, cols. 755-6.
5. 97 HC Deb., 4s., July 17, 1901, cols. 758-9; H. Pelling, *The Origins of the Labour Party 1880-1900* (1954), pp. 189-90; P. Ward, *Red Flag and Union Jack: English-*

men, Patriotism and the British Left, 1881-1924 (Woodbridge, Suffolk, 1998), pp. 67-8.

6. S. Howe, *"Labour and International Affairs"* in D. Tanner, P. Thane, N. Tiratsoo, eds., *Labour's First Century* (2000), p. 128; L. Thompson, *The Enthusiasts: A Biography of John and Katherine Bruce Glasier* (1971), p. 115; D. Marquand, *Ramsay MacDonald* (1977), p. 65; P. Poirier, *The Advent of the British Labour Party* (New York, 1958), p. 112.

7. *Clarion*, July 13, November 23, December 7, 20, 27, 1901; Ward, *Red Flag*, pp. 60-4.

8. Benn, *Keir Hardie,* p. 159.

9. *Labour Representation Committee Conference Report*, 1901, p. 44; Benn, *Hardie*, pp. 159-60.

10. A. Davey, *The British Pro-Boers 1877-1902* (Capetown, 1978), pp. 124-5; A. M. McBriar, *Fabian Socialism and English Politics 1884-1918* (1962), pp. 30 5 - 6 ; R. Price, *An Imperial War and the British Working Class: Working-Class Attitudes and Reactions to the Boer War 1899-1902* (1972), pp. 234-5; D. Howell, *British Workers and the Independent Labour Party 1888-1906* (Manchester, 1981), pp. 345-7. Recently Paul Readman has questioned Price's analysis, suggesting that even the working classes seemed receptive to the "abstractions" of patriotic appeals divorced from immediate and material concerns. But in turn Readman's own use of electoral statistics in making his argument at the very least also raises questions. See P. Readman, "The Conservative Party, Patriotism, and British Politics: The C a s e of the General Election of 1900," in *Journal of British Studies*, 40 (January 2001), 107-45.

11. See *Labour Leader*, December 17, 1909; January 14, May 27, September 30, October 7, 14, 1910; July 7, December 8, 1911. Also Newton, *British Labour*, pp. 314-5. Jowett also made the argument against secret diplomacy in *Clarion*, where he wrote a weekly parliamentary column until his differences with Blatchford on the latter's attitude towards Germany made it impossible for him to continue. *Clarion*, July 31, 1908.

12. Resolutions are in *Labour Party Conference Reports (LPCR)*, 1907, 1908, 1909, 1910. See also, as an illustration, the resolution proposed in the minutes of the Labour Party's National Executive Committee, January 28, 1914.

13. McBriar, *Fabian Socialism*, p. 337.

14. Robbins, *The Abolition of War,* p. 11.

15. *J.S. Middleton Papers*, JSM/PE/38.

16. *Socialist Review*, vol. 2, no. 7 (September, 1908), p. 487.

17. *Labour Leader*, October 9, 1908; Morris, *Radicalism*, p. 175.

18. *Clarion,* June 10, 1904. See also issues of June 17 and July 8, 1904.

19. Ibid., July 31, 1908.

20. Blatchford's anti-German campaign gathered momentum from the summer of 1908. See, for example, *Clarion* articles of August 7 and 21, 1908; March 12, April 2, 1909.

21. *Socialist Review*, vol. 2, no. 8 (October, 1908), pp. 562-3.

22. Ibid., vol. 3, no. 13 (March, 1909), p.5.

23. Morris, *Radicalism*, pp. 210-11.

24. *Labour Leader*, December 17, 1909; Thompson, *Enthusiasts, pp. 190-1.*

25. *Socialist Review*, vol. 1, no. 2 (April, 1908), pp. 90-2.

26. Ibid., vol. 1, no. 5 (July, 1908), including Dilke's "The International Aspect," pp. 330-5, Brailsford's "Liberalism and the Russian Government," pp. 335-403, and Nevinson's "What I Saw," pp. 340-2. Also A. J. P. Taylor, *The Trouble Makers: Dissent over Foreign Policy 1792-1939* (1957), p. 113.

27. 190 HC Deb., 4s., June 4, 1908, cols. 252-61.
28. *Socialist Review*, vol. 3, no. 17 (July, 1901), pp.325-7; vol. 3, no. 18 (August, 1909), p. 405; *Labour Leader*, July 16, 1909, quoted in Morris, *Radicalism*, p. 188; A.J. Williams, *Labour and Russia. The Attitude of the Labour Party to the USSR, 1924-34* (Manchester, 1989), p. 6.
29. Morris, *Radicalism*, p. 205.
30. *Socialist Review*, vol. 3, no. 14 (April, 1909), pp. 81-3 and vol. 5, no. 26 (April, 1910), pp. 89-90; *Labour Leader*, October 14, 1910.
31. Anderson. "Labour's War against War." in *Labour Leader*, October 14, 1910; Hardie in 22 HC Deb., 5s., March 13, 1911, cols. 1923-29; G. H. Perris, "The Cost of Provocation" in *Clarion*, March 18, 1910.
32. 50 HC Deb., 5s., March 27, 1913, cols. 1908-11; 53 (May 20, 1913), cols. 407-10, 457; 55 (June 17, 1913), col. 1504.
33. *Labour Leader*, December 11, 1913, quoted in Morris, *Radicalism*, p. 336.
34. R.J.Q.Adams and P. Poirier, *The Conscription Controversy in Great Britain, 1900-18* (Columbus, Ohio, 1987), p. 21; *Labour Leader*, November 13, 1913.
35. Report of Special Conference on Disarmament and the International Situation. Held on Tuesday, January 31st. 1911, in the Temperance Hall, Leicester, Appendix I, *LPCR*, 1911, pp. 111-20.
36. Newton, *British Labour*, pp. 292-3.
37. *Socialist Review*, vol. 7, no. 37 (March, 1911), p. 4; Morris in Brown, ed., *T h e First Labour Party*, p. 274; K. E. Miller, *Socialism and Foreign Policy: Theory and Practice in Britain to 1931* (The Hague, 1967), p. 41. It is interesting that as late as February 22, 1911 the Report from the Head office of the ILP carried clause e (the general strike clause) in its copy of the resolution circulated to membership. *ILP National Administrative Council Minutes*, February 22, 1911.
38. Ibid., October 24, 1911; Robbins, *Abolition*, p. 22.
39. Report of the Executive Committee, *LPCR*, 1912, pp. 10-11.
40. Benn, *Hardie*, p.239; *Labour Leader*, December 8, 1911; *Socialist Review*, v, 4, no. 24 (February, 1910), pp. 420-21.
41. *Labour Leader*, July 28, 1911.
42. *Socialist Review*, vol. 8, no. 43 (Sept. 1911), pp. 8-10 and no. 44 (October, 1911), pp. 92-3; 28 HC Deb. 5s., July 27, 1911, col 1880-1.
43. *Labour Leader*, December 8, 1911 and Angell, "Capitalism and War," *Labour Leader*, September 29, October 4, 1911.
44. Ibid., March 6, 1913.
45. Ibid., July 30, 1914.
46. Morris, *Radicalism*, p. 215.
47. *ILP National Administrative Council Minutes*, September 9, 30, 1910.
48. *LPCR*, 1914, p. 197.
49. Ibid., 1913, p. 27.
50. Morris, "Labour and Foreign Affairs," in Brown, ed., *First Labour Party*, pp. 272-3.

Chapter 2

1. For the middle classes in the ILP see K. Laybourn, "Recent Writing on the History of the I.L.P., 1893-1932," in D. James, T. Jowitt, and K. Laybourn, *The Centennial History of the Independent Labour Party* (Halifax, 1992), pp. 129-30, citing also C. Levy, "Education and Self-Education: Staffing the early I.L.P.," in C. Levy, *Socialism and the Intelligentsia 1880-1914* (1987). Robbins, *Abolition*, p. 27.
2. "Socialism and European War," *Labour Leader*, July 30, 1914.

3. *Labour Leader*, August 6, 1914. In urging its readers to attend the anti-war rally organized by the *Daily Herald* League, the paper headlined its July 31, 1914 story, "Workers Must Stop the War! The Greatest Crime of the Century." See J. Shepherd, *George Lansbury. At the Heart of Old Labour* (Oxford, 2002), pp. 158-60.
4. *Parliamentary Labour Party (PLP) Minutes,* July 30, 1914.
5. *MacDonald*, pp. 167-8; Robbins, *Abolition*, pp. 33-4; 65 HC Deb., 5s, August 3, 1914, cols. 1829-31.
6. Martin Ceadel's discussion of the phases through which the wartime peace movement went provides a useful framework for the more general assessment of the labour movement's responses. M. Ceadel, *Semi-Detached Idealists: The British Peace Movement and International Relations, 1854-1945* (New York, 2000), p. 187.
7. *The War in Europe. Manifesto of the Independent Labour Party* (August, 1914). Also published in *Labour Leader*, August 13, 1914.
8. *Labour Leader* August 6, 13, 1914. Morris, *Radicalism*, p. 420 quotes Hardie in *Labour Leader*. August 6, 1914.
9. *Clarion,* August 7, 1914; Robbins, *Abolition*, p. 44; *Labour Leader*, August 20, 1914.
10. Thompson, *The Enthusiasts*. p. 207.
11. Clynes, James Parker, and G. N. Barnes, all Labour M.P.s, disagreed sharply with the National Administrative Council's position against aiding in the recruiting drive. *ILP National Administrative Council Minutes,* October 5, 1914.
12. K Laybourn and J. Reynolds, *Liberalism and the Rise of Labour 1890-1918* (1984), p. 191.
13. J. Turner, *British Politics and the Great War: Coalition and Conflict 1915-1918* (New Haven, 1992), p. 118-9, 441.
14. T. Jowitt and K. Laybourn, "War and Socialism: the Experience of the Bradford IL.P. .1914-18," in Laybourn, Jowitt, and James, *Centennial History,* pp. 163-78; McBriar, *Fabian Socialism*, p. 141.
15. The Anderson-Henderson letter is in Labour Party, *National Executive Committee Minutes and Papers;* Miller, *Socialism*, pp. 48-9.
16. MacDonald's motives have been variously interpreted. For Bruce Glasier's biographer, he "wobbled alarmingly on his intellectual tight-rope," while Keith Robbins suggests that he used the occasion of the war to step down from an office which had become distasteful. Brock Millman is perhaps nearest the mark when he quotes an early MacDonald biographer in describing him as a "practical pacifist." He was so opposed to war in principle that he could scarcely identify a single case which would justify it. See Thompson, *Enthusiasts*, p. 206; Robbins, *Abolition*, p. 34; B. Millman, *Managing Domestic Dissent in First World War Britain* (2000), pp.8-9.
17. F. Williams, *A Pattern of Rulers* (1965), P. 68; T. Lloyd, "James Ramsay MacDonald," in J. Mackintosh, ed., *British Prime Ministers in the Twentieth Century*, Vol. I, *Balfour to Chamberlain* (New York, 1977), p. 159; K. Morgan, *Labour People. Leaders and Lieutenants, Hardie to Kinnock* (Oxford, 1987), p. 43.
18. Marquand, *MacDonald*, p. 189. When the editor, Horratio Bottomley, later repeated his charge that MacDonald was a traitor and a coward, Seymour Cocks wrote to Charles Trevelyan that the only reply was to give Bottomley a public horse-whipping when he was met on the street. "I wish I had the strength,": he declared, "to do it myself." Cocks to Trevelyan, Sept. 1, 1915, *Trevelyan Papers*, 76/138.
19. *Clarion,* November 13, 1914; *Herald,* August 19, 1914. George Lansbury, editor of the *Herald*, shared MacDonald's horror of the war, but felt he must support the men who did the fighting, as did trade unionists like Ben Tillett, because most of them were workers. J. Schneer, *Ben Tillett. Portrait of a Labour Leader* (Urbana, 1982),

p. 164. See also F. L. Carsten, *War against War. British and German Radical Movements in the First World War* (Berkeley, 1982), pp. 176-7.

20. *Labour Leader*, September 10, 17, 24, October 1, 22, November 5, 1914. 66*NAC Minutes*, April 2, 1915.

21. *NAC Minutes*, April 2, 1915.

22. Angell, "The Case for the Statement of Principles" (March 25, 1915); Ponsonby, "The Case for a United Europe (April 1, 1915); Trevelyan, "The Rights of Nationalities" (April 8, 1915); Jowett, "The Case against Secret Diplomacy" (April 15); Newbold, "The Nationalisation of the Armaments Industry" (April 22, 1915; Glasier, "The Case for Disarmament" (May 20, 1915; all in "Towards a Permanent Peace" and Morel, "An Appeal to Sanity" (August 26, 1915) in "Towards a New Europe." When it was suggested to Brockway that Morel's various articles be republished in book form, Brockway wrote to Morel indicating his view that because Morel's articles were so concentrated on explaining Germany's position they would add to the prejudice against the Union of Democratic Control, whose secretary Morel had become. Brockway hoped that the emphasis on Germany would be balanced by "a different note" in a second publication. Brockway to Morel, December 5, 1915 in *Morel Papers*, F6/4.

23. Philip Kerr (later Lord Lothian) of the *Round Table* wrote to Morel that in his view a committee for foreign affairs would increase the very evil that the UDC sought to destroy. He did not believe that the American democracy had any real control over its foreign policy. In times of crisis the president was in a despotic position even greater than that of Sir Edward Grey. Kerr to Morel, July 29, 1915 in *Morel Papers*, F6/4. The standard account is M. Swartz, *The Union of Democratic Control in British Politics during the First World War* (Oxford, 1971).

24. Ceadel, *Semi-Detached Idealists*. p. 199.

25. P. Brock and N. Young, *Pacifism in the Twentieth Century* (Syracuse, 1999), p. 24. 71

26. S. Harris, *Out of Control. British Foreign Policy and the Union of Democratic Control, 1914-1918* (1996), p. 68; J. R.MacDonald, *War and the Workers. A Plea for Democratic Control*, n.d., pp. 1-14.

27. Taylor, *The Trouble Makers*. pp. 135-6; Morris, *Radicalism*, p. 420; Miller, *Socialism*, p. 55.

28. Herbert Bryan, Secretary of City of London Branch of the I.L.P., to Morel, July 6, 1915, in *Morel Papers,* F6/4.

29. Morel to Trevelyan, July 9, 1915, in *Morel Papers,* F6/4. It is worth remembering, however, that the *Labour Leader* and the *Herald*, to say nothing of the No-Conscription Fellowship's *Tribunal*, continued to be published during the war and to provide an outlet for the opponents of the war and its conduct. See Carsten, *War against War.*

30. *Minutes of UDC General Council*, June 22, 1915 quoted in Harris, *Out of Control,* p. 67.

31. Morel to Trevelyan, June 9, 1915 in *Morel Papers*, F6/4. It is worth remembering, however, that the *Labour Leader* and the *Herald*, to say nothing of the No-Conscription Fellowship's Tribunal, continued to be published during the war and to provide an outlet for the opponents of the war and its conduct. See, Carsten, *War against War.*

32. Ceadel, *Semi-Detached Idealists*, esp. Pp. 210-26; Brock and Young, *Pacifism*, pp. 25-29; N. Young, "War Resistance and the British Peace Movement since 1914," in R. Taylor and N. Young, eds., *Campaigns for Peace: British Peace Movements in the Twentieth Century* (Manchester, 1987), pp. 28-37.

33. *LPCR,* 1916, pp. 95, 116-24.
34. *LPCR*, 1917, p. 140.
35. For what follows on the League idea, Winkler, *The League of Nations Movement in Great Britain 1914-1919.*
36. N. Mackenzie, ed., *The Letters of Sidney and Beatrice Webb.* Vol. III. *Pilgimmage 1912-1947* (1978), p. 45.
37. Goldsworthy Lowes Dickinson, who was a key activist in the League of Nations Society, complained to Arthur Ponsonby that "our worst enemies are really men like Brailsford and Hobson, who go for federation. They won't get that, but they may easily prevent our getting what we ask for." Nevertheless, Brailsford, like Hobson, collaborated with Dickinson and others in speaking for the League of Nations Society and popularizing the concept of a League. F. Leventhal, *The Last Dissenter: H. N. Brailsford and the World* (Oxford, 1985), quoting Dickinson to Ponsonby, April 2, 1915, in E. M. Forster, *Goldsworthy Lowes Dickinson* (1934), p. 165.
38. Advisory Committee on International Questions (ACIQ), *Minutes*, May 30, 1918. Present at the first meeting were Sidney Webb, Leonard Woolf, G. Lowes Dickinson, H. Duncan Hall, G. D. H. Cole, Major Gillespie, C, Delisle Burns, and Arnold Toynbee.
39. Ibid., p. 141; *NEC Minutes,* September 27, 1917, February 25, April 10, 1918; L. Woolf, *Downhill All the Way: An Autobiography of the Years 1919-1939* (1968), p. 239.
40. 93 HC Deb., 5s., May 16, 1917, cols. 1625-37, 1657-64, 1707-16, 1725-31.
41. J. M. Winter, "Arthur Henderson, the Russian Revolution, and the reconstruction of the Labour Party," *The Historical Journal*, XV, 4 (1972), 765-71; F. M. Leventhal, *Arthur Henderson* (Manchester, 1989), pp. 64-8. Henderson's explanation of his resignation is in 97 HC Deb., 5s., August 12, 1917, cols. 909-26.
42. *Labour Leader, December 4, 20, 1917.*
43. Swartz, *UDC*, pp. 168-9. Marquand, *MacDonald,* pp. 221-2 also notes the influence of the Fabian Society.
44. Harris, *Out of Control*, p. 164 comments on most UDC members' lack of r e a l interest in a League.
45. Inter-Allied Labour and Socialist Conference, *Memorandum on War Aims Agreed upon at Central Hall, Westminster, London, S.W., on February 20th to 24th, 1918,* pp. 3-13. A few months later the newly formed Advisory Committee on International Questions made a strong case against any attempt to create a league of allied nations without giving the Central Powers an opportunity to participate. *NEC Minutes,* June 12, 1918.
46. "Thoughts on a League to Enforce Peace," *Labour Leader*, December 14, 1916; *National Defence. A Study in Militarism* (1917), pp. 56-64; "Peace Guarantees," *Socialist Review*, XIV (1917), 29-30; *Labour and International Relations* (1917), pp.5-7, all by MacDonald. See K. Robbins, "Labour's Foreign Policy and International Socialism: MacDonald and the League of Nations." in his *Politicians, Diplomacy and War in Modern British History* (1994), pp. 247-9.
47. Snowden, "Review of the Week" in *Labour Leader*, June 27, August 8, 1918; Brailsford, "Maximum or Minimum'?" *Herald*, March 2, 1918.
48. *Report of I.L.P. Conference,* 1917, p. 72.
49. N. Buxton, "Labour's War Aims," *Labour Leader*, February 14, 1918; A. Henderson, *Labour's Peace Terms (1918).*
50. 41. Ibid., 1918, p. 94.
51. *LPCR,*1918, pp. 105-6.
52. *New Statesman,* vol. IX, no. 224 (July 21,1918), 365-6.

Chapter 3

1. C. F. Brand, *British Labour's Rise to Power* (Stanford, 1941), pp. 129-41; A. Van Der Slice, *International Labour, Diplomacy, and Peace1914-1919* (1941), pp. 218-31.

2. A few of the unnumbered party leaflets were entitled "Why Labour Supports a League of Nations," "Why Women Should Join the Labour Party" and, of course, "Why I Shall Vote Labour."

3. Mimeographed memoranda in 1918 were "A League of Nations," "The Freedom of the Seas," "Colonies," "The Reform of the Civil Service," "Intervention in Russia."

4. *Herald*, January 4, 1919; *Forward,* October 5, 1918; *Labour Leader,* January 9, 1919.

5. *Herald,* January 11, 1919; *Labour Leader,* January 9, 1919.

6. Van Der Slice, *International Labour*, pp. 303-41; *LPCR*, 1919, pp. 14, 196-8; Labour Party, *International Labour and Peace* (1919), p. 4; Independent Labour Party, *International Socialism and World Peace*, new ser., no. 1 (1919), pp. 1-2.

7. Beatrice Webb *Manuscript Diary* 35 (May 10, 1919), 3694-5.

8. Henderson, *The Peace Terms* (1919), pp. 18-9.

9. 118 HC Deb., 5s., July 21, 1919, cols. 959-64.

10. S. Howe, "Labour and Foreign Affairs," in Tanner, Thane and Tiratsoo, eds. *Labour's First Century*, pp. 119-20.

11. The attitude of some of the ex-Liberals was perhaps best summed up by Arthur Ponsonby who wrote to Charles Trevelyan on March 30, 1918 about the "hopeless complexity of labour organization and the prevalent suspicion & jealousy which I see more & more as I get to close quarters with it has had the effect of putting me off a good deal." But he then added, "I always remember Internationalism" and by November 28, 1918 he was writing that there could be no doubt that he would join the I.L.P. *Trevelyan Papers*, 79/5.

12. A.J. Williams, *Labour and Russia. The Attitude of the Labour Party to the USSR, 1924-34* (Manchester, 1989), pp. 8-9; Ward, *Red Flag,* pp.156-7.

13. Ceadel, *Pacifism,* pp. 54-5; Ward, *Red Flag*, p. 158. See also *Labour Leader,* August 12, November 18, 1920.

14. *Herald,* January 22, February 28, March 17, May 11, 1920.

15. *PLP* Minutes, August 9, 1920, pp. 79-80; *Labour Leader,* August 19, 1920.

16. An example is H. N. Brailsford, who took over the editorship of the *New Leader* (which succeeded the *Labour Leader)* in 1922. Somewhat less hyperbolically he viewed the actions of Foreign Secretary Curzon as an incitement to war. See "The Plot against Russia," *New Leader,* May 4, 1923. See also *Foreign Affairs*, 2 (January 1921), 105 and (February 1921), 120.

17. Arthur Greenwood (Secretary to the Joint Research and Information Department of the TUC and Labour Party) to J. S. Middleton, March 21, 1922, in *Middleton Papers, JSM/INT/70,* Labour Party Archives; *New Leader,* June 8, 1923; *LPCR,* 1923, p. 193.

18. 17. *Herald*, January 1, 1920.

19. For example, H. N. Brailsford, "The Peace of Strangulation," *Labour Leader,* January 1, 1920.

20. See, as one example, the resolution on the peace treaties and reparations, introduced in 1921 by J. H. Hudson of the ILP and passed unanimously. *LPCR,* 1921, pp. 200-1.

21. R. Dell, "What France Seeks. European Civilisation in Danger," *Forward,* March 3, 1922; Leventhal, *Henderson,* 157-8.

22. Ibid., p. 201.
23. Brailsford to Henderson, *Middleton Papers, JSM/INT/29* (September, 1920).
24. D. Morel, *The Horror on the Rhine* (1920), pp. 8-20; Ponsonby to Morel, n . d . {spring, 1923}. *Morel Papers,* F8/123.
25. E. D. Morel, "The Disruption of Germany," *Labour Magazine* (November, 1923), pp. 300-1.
26. *Herald,* April 8, 10, 17, 1920.
27. C. R. Buxton, "France and Her Ruins," *Socialist Review,* 20, no. 107 (August, 1922), 82-92 and "Opinion in France: the Root of the Trouble," *Labour Magazine,* 1 (September, 1922), 201-2.
28. *Foreign Affairs,* (July, 1922), p. 12.
29. Ibid., (February, 1923), p. 161.
30. H. N. Brailsford, "The Invasion of the Ruhr," *Labour Magazine* (February, 1923), pp. 436-8; C. R. Buxton, *Labour Magazine* (December, 1923), pp. 346-7; F. W. Pethick Lawrence. *Labour Magazine* (July, 1922), pp. 128-9; A. Henderson, "War against War," *Labour Magazine* (January, 1923), pp. 391-3.
31. N, Angell, "The Danger from France," *New Leader,* February 2, 1923.
32. Interestingly, Arthur Henderson was shrewd enough to perceive that the agreement reached among the Pacific powers about the political and economic rivalries in that area was more important than the modest limitation of naval armaments. "War against War," p. 391.
33. W. Arnold Forster, "France, Ourselves and the Future" (1923), pp. 2-17.
34. Advisory Committee on International Questions (ACIQ), "Memorandum on Ruhr Situation," 1923; "Draft Manifesto," 1923.
35. Examples: *Forward,* January 27, February 17, 1923; *Bradford Pioneer*, February 23, October 5, 1923; *Herald,* January 22, 1923; *New Statesman*, vol. XX, no. 514 (February 17, 1923), 560-1 and no. 515 (February 24, 1923), 588-9. Also vol. XXI, no. 522 (April 14), 1; no. 524 (April 28), 65; no. 526 (May 12), 132-3; no. 527 (May 19), 157, all in 1923; and *New Leader,* almost every issue throughout the year.
36. *Foreign Affairs,* 4 (March, 1923), 185-6, 191-4; (May, 1923), 223; 5 (September, 1923), 45-6; (October, 1923), 70-2.
37. *ILP Conference Report,* 1923, pp. 24-5, 44-7, 86-97.
38. *LPCR*, 1923, pp. 221-4.
39. Ibid., pp. 176-7.
40. PLP *Minutes,* May 3, 1923; NEC *Minutes,* April 25, 1923.
41. 160 HC Deb., 5s., February 15, 1923, col. 363; February 16, 1923, cols. 496-510, 520-8, 543-54; February 19, 1923, cols. 709-14.
42. J. R. MacDonald, *National Defence. A Study in Militarism* (1917), pp. 114- 7.

Chapter 4

1. Webb's memorandum on the Labour government of 1924, "Working of Government," is in Webb Papers, 4, item 18, pp. 20-47.
2. Marquand, *MacDonald,* p. 245.
3. 141 *New Statesman,* vol. XXII, no. 564 (February 9, 1924), 500-1.
4. See, for example, "I.L.P. Weekly Notes for Speakers," no. 253, April 24, 1924.
5. *New Leader,* January 25, February 15, 22, 1924.
6. *Herald,* January 3, 29, February 11, 1924. See Sidney Webb's criticism of the "sentimental weakness" of George Lansbury and the real disloyalty and communist sympathies of others on the staff. Webb Papers, 4, item 18, p. 30.
7. *Foreign Affairs,* 5 (March 1924), 167 and (May 1924), 193-4.
8. E. Y. O'Riordan, *Britain and the Ruhr Crisis* (2001), pp. 145-6, 171-2.

9. E. Maisel, *The Foreign Office and Foreign Policy, 1919-1926* (Brighton, 1994), p. 135, quoting memorandum of May 15, 1924 in FO371/9802, C7879/737/18.
10. The first memo of January, 1924 was sent to MacDonald by Arthur Greenwood, Secretary of the Joint Research and Information Department of the T.U.C. and the Labour Party. It is in PRO/FO371/9807. "Labour, the League and Reparations" was drafted by a League sub-committee of the Advisory Committee and accepted by the full committee. With follow-up reports it was transmitted and noted by MacDonald's private secretary, C. W. Orde (in W 2855/338/98) and called to the attention of officials in the Foreign Office. See FO371/10573/81-2.
11. D.C. Watt, *Succeeding John Bull: America in Britain's Place 1900-1975* (Cambridge, 1984), p. 54; F. Williams, *A Pattern of Rulers* (1965), p. 84.
12. W. A. McDougall, *France's Rhineland Diplomacy, 1914-1924: The Last Bid for a Balance of Power in Europe* (Princeton, 1978), pp. 366-8.
13. *Foreign Affairs*, 5 (May 1924), 217-8; (June 1924), 243. Norman Angell hardly concealed his impatience with Morel. On May 20 he wrote to Morel, "I am not clear what it is you propose. Do you suggest that the U.D.C. should oppose the Dawes Report? One may well doubt whether that would be wise just now. I do not think there is anything dishonest in the Report. No one can tell absolutely just what a nation like Germany could or could not pay, if this, if that, and if the other thing...." In a long letter on July 3, he added, "As to the arguments summarised in document A which you send me, they are almost completely fallacious. They do not represent at all the real case for Britain maintaining her share of the Reparations claim. The actual payment of large Reparation sums by Germany will not cripple her as a competitor at all. They might quite conceivably render her competition in foreign trade much more severe." Angell to Morel, Morel Papers, F7/3. And MacDonald commented to Morel that "What Germany is now suffering is not the result of anything we are doing, as its own complete collapse of leadership." MacDonald to Morel, *Morel Papers*, F6/11.
14. *New Leader*, August 15, 22, 1924.
15. Lansbury to Beatrice Webb, March 14, 1924. *Webb Papers*, 2, 4(h).
16. P. Snowden, *An Autobiography,* 2 vol. (1934), pp. 673-9; Beatrice Webb Manuscript Diary, 38 (August 30, 1924), 4303-4; MacDonald Diary, August 13, 1924 in PRO30/69/1753; R. Lyman, *The First Labour Government* (1957), p. 167.
17. *TUC Annual Meeting Report,* 1924, pp. 69, 72-3, 256-9. Lyman, p. 165, notes the Miners' Federation of Great Britain's anger over proposed reparations payments in coal.
18. *LPCR*, 1924, pp. 143-4.
19. 171 HC Deb., 5s., April 1, 1924, cols. 2003-5.
20. *TUC Annual Meeting Report*, 1924, p. 259; *LPCR*, 1924, p. 56.
21. Ponsonby to Morel, May 1, 1924, Morel Papers, F8/123; *Bradford Pioneer*, July 25, 1924; *Herald*, September 11, 1924.
22. *PLP Minutes,,* June 4, 1924.
23. P. Hennessey, *The Prime Minister: The Office and its Holders since 1945* (2000), p. 90.
24. Lyman, p. 157; R. A. Jones, *Arthur Ponsonby: The Politics of Life* (1989), p p . 143-4.
25. *Bradford Pioneer,* July 18, 1924.
26. *Foreign Affairs*, 6 (September, 1924), 62. The signatories included C. R. Buxton, Mary Hamilton, E. D. Morel, Bertrand Russell, Helena Swanwick, and Leonard Woolf, among others.
27. ACIQ, "Alternative Policy for a British Labour Government," 1924.

28. "Memorandum on the League and Disarmament by Professor Shotwell." 1924.
29. Cover note in Advisory Committee's "Draft Treaty of Mutual Assistance." 1924.
30. See also "Draft Memoranda Prepared by the special Sub-Committee," 1924.
31. Minutes by MacDonald in FO371/9818, C11164/2048/18 on July 17 and February 6, 1924, cited in Maisel, *The Foreign Office and Foreign Policy,* p. 137. See also 169 HC Deb. 5s., February 12, 1924, cols. 772-4.
32. CP 309 (24) and CP 311 (34) in CAB 24/167.
33. L. Lloyd, *Peace Through Law. Britain and the International Court in the 1920s* (Woodbridge, Suffolk, 1997), pp. 34-51.
34. Cecil, *All the Way* (1949), p. 166. Lloyd, *Peace Through Law,* p. 35 cites the memoirs of Salvador de Madariaga for the comment that MacDonald's style was inappropriate to the occasion.
35. The text of the British rejection of the Draft Treaty (July 5, 1924) is in *League of Nations. Reduction of Armaments. Treaty of Mutual Assistance, Replies of Governments,* League of Nations Documents A.35.1924.9. MacDonald's speech was published in a Labour Party pamphlet, "War and Peace" (1924) and the general argument for rejection was in "Labour's Great Record" (1924), pp. 5-6. See Marquand, *Ramsay MacDonald,* pp. 351-4 and Maisel, *The Foreign Office,* pp. 145-6.
36. *New Leader,* September 12, 19, 1924; *New Statesman,* vol. XXIII, no. 597 (September 27, 1924), 694-5.
37. See my "Arthur Henderson" in G. Craig and F. Gilbert, eds., *The Diplomats 1919-1939* (Princeton, 1953), pp. 314-6.
38. A. Orde, *Great Britain and International Security 1920-1926* (1978), p. 69.
39. *League of Nations. Fifth Assembly. Verbatim Record,* 26th and 27th Meetings, October 1, 1924.
40. CAB24/168/CP456, September 27, 1924 and CAB24/168/CP478, October 17, 1924.
41. Leventhal, *Arthur Henderson,* pp. 128-30.
42. Lyman, *First Labour government*, pp. 179-80; Marquand, *Ramsay MacDonald,* pp.355-6.
43. Buxton's defense of the Protocol began before the general election of October and continued after the seating of the new government. Buxton, "Labour's Work for Peace at Geneva," *New Leader,* October 23, 1924, pp. 7-8.
44. *New Leader,*December 19, 1924.
45. Ibid., September 26, 1924.
46. *Foreign Affairs,* January, 1925.
47. Maisel, *The Foreign Office,* p. 133.
48. Morel to Ponsonby, July 31, 1924, Morel Papers, f8/123. For a discussion of the Russian issue see Williams, *Labour and Russia,* pp. 15-19.
49. Jones, *Arthur Ponsonby*, pp. 144-51.
50. "Anglo-Russian Treaties" (1924), pp. 4-9; J. R. Clynes, *Memoirs* (2 vols., 1937), vol. 2, p. 252.

Chapter 5

1.   A. Bullock, *Life and Times of Ernest Bevin*, vol. II (1967), pp. 100-1.
2.   D. Howell, *MacDonald's Party: Labour Identities and Crisis 1922-1931* Oxford, 2002), p. 68. Howell notes Bevin's continuing suspicion of MacDonald, heightened by the latter's role during the General Strike of 1926, quoting a letter from Bevin to Henderson on June 4, 1926: "I am not prepared to go on a platform in support of the leader whom I regard as having been wantonly guilty of stabbing us in the back at the moment when we had the whole force of capital unleashed against us." Ernest Bevin Papers MS 126/EB/GS/7/44 cited in Howell, p. 187.

3. M. Cole, ed., *Beatrice Webb's Diaries, 1924-1932* (1948), August 8, 1925, pp. 62-3; Bullock, *Bevin*, vol. I (1960), pp. 258-60; *LPCR*, 1925, pp. 244-51.
4. B. Pimlott, *Hugh Dalton* (1985), pp. 182, 639.
5. R. E. Dowse, *Left in the Centre: The Independent Labour Party, 1893-1940* (Evanston, 1966), pp. 124-6.
6. *New Leader*, March 6, 29, June 6, 1925.
7. Ibid., January 30, February 23, March 6, 1925.
8. *Forward*, January 17, 31, March 28, 1925.
9. *Bradford Pioneer*, May 22, June 12, October 9, 1925; *Socialist Review*, 25, No. 135 (January 1925), 4.
10. *Lansbury's Labour Weekly*, February 28, March 21, 28, September 26, 1925.
11. *LPCR*, 1925, p. 94; PLP *Minutes,* March 17, 1925.
12. *Clarion*, January 16, 30, July 3, 1925; *New Statesman*, 24 (January 3, 1925), 355, and 24 (March 14, 1925), 645.
13. Joint Meeting of General Council and National Executive Committee, *Minutes,* February 25, 1925.
14. 182 HC Deb., 52 (March 24, 1925), 291-301, 367-72. Henderson's speech was later published as a pamphlet, "Labour and the Geneva Protocol" (1925).
15. ACIQ, "Memorandum on Security Pact" and "Report of Sub-Committee on the Security Pact," both 1925. Noel Baker also privately advised MacDonald not to attack the government's negotiations, but to insist that military commitments be made contingent upon the acceptance of a plan for general disarmament. Noel Baker to MacDonald, July 3, 1925 in *MacDonald Papers*, PRO 30/69/1170, files 45-8.
16. PLP *Minutes, November 17, 1925.*
17. MacDonald, "Protocol and Pact," (April 1925), pp. 531-4; Noel Baker, "The Protocol and the Status Quo," (March 1925), pp. 497-500; Barnes, "The Geneva Protocol," (January 1925), pp. 391-3; all in *Labour Magazine.*
18. *Forward*, November 7, 1925.
19. 188 HC Deb., 5s., November 18, 1925, cols. 434-46.
20. Labour and Socialist International. Resolutions and Manifestos. Executive Committee, London, November 4-5, 1925 in *LPCR*, 1925, p. 121.
21. *Why We Will Not Fight!*, MacDonald Papers, PRO 30/69/1833. The clearest example of Ponsonby's position is in an article he wrote, "Disarmament by Example," in the *Journal of the Royal Institute of International Affairs*, 7, no. 4 (July 1928), 228-40. Miller, *Socialism and Foreign Policy* also cites Ponsonby's "Now is the Time: Disarmament by Example" in *Contemporary Review*, 132, no. 6 (December 1927), 687-93 and his speech at the 1929 ILP conference.
22. Ponsonby to UDC Executive, June 14, 1928, in *UDC Papers*, DDC 4/10; Hobson to Ponsonby, June 27, 1928, *Ponsonby Papers*, fol. 114.
23. Correspondence with B. Rawson [1928], Ponsonby Papers, fol. 58-9.
24. Lansbury was fairly consistent in pointing out that his pacifism differed from the official policy of the Labour Party. On a number of occasions he offered to resign the leadership of the party, only to have both the National Executive Committee and the Parliamentary Party reject his initiative. Shepherd, ch. 16.
25. MacDonald to Ponsonby, November 16, 1927, Ponsonby Papers, fol. 50.
26. Noel Baker, *The Geneva Protocol for the Pacific Settlement of International Disputes* (1925) and *Disarmament* (1926).
27. *Disarmament,* p. 327.
28. Arnold Forster, "The Victory of Reason. A Pamphlet on Arbitration" (Women's International League, 1926); Dalton, *Towards the Peace of Nations* (1928).
29. Buxton, "Sanctions in the Covenant," ACIQ, 1927, pp. 1-3.

30. *LPCR,* 1926, pp. 233, 331.
31. Mitrany, "A Labour Policy on Sanctions," ACIQ, 1927, pp. 1-9.
32. Arnold Forster, "Sanctions (commentary on Mr. Buxton's Paper)," ACIQ, 1927, pp. 1-9.
33. Henderson, "Principles of the Protocol," *Labour Magazine,* 6 (Novemberr 1927), 298-300.
34. *LPCR*, 1927, pp. 235-6, 334.
35. 203 HC Deb., 5s., March 10, 1927, cols. 1407-31, 1454-74, 1488-93 and March 17, 1927, cols. 2227-40, 2283-85, 2311-15.
36. Woolf, "Proposals for the Outlawry of War," ACIQ, 1927. See also J. M. Kenworthy, "Memorandum on Outlawry of War" and revised memoranda, 1928. Memoranda are in Noel Baker Papers, NBKR 2/9. See also Arnold Forster, "The American Offer," *Labour Magazine*, 7, no. 2 (June 1928), 65-6.
37. 217 HC Deb., 5s., May 10, 1928, cols. 431-58.
38. *Daily Herald,* December 1, '1927, February 24, 1928; *New Leader*, January 11, 13, 1926; *Clarion*, January, May 1928.
39. Examples are in *Bradford Pioneer*, April 20, May 25, 1928; *New Leader*, May 25, August 10, 1928; *Forward,* September 1, 1928; *Daily Herald,* November 7, December 1, 1928 and January 17, 1929; *Foreign Affairs*, 10 (September 1928).
40. "British Reply to Mr. Kellogg," ACIQ, 1928; "American Peace Pact and the British Reply," ACIQ, 1928; 220 HC Deb., 5s. (July 30, 1928), 1803-61 and 222 HC Deb., 5s. (November 6, 1928), 18-47.
41. *LPCR,* 1928, pp. 183-94.
42. "Labour and the Nation" (1928), pp. 41-2, 49.

Chapter 6

1. This chapter rests heavily upon David Carlton's solid monograph *MacDonald versus Henderson: The Foreign Policy of the Second Labour Government* (New York, 1970). As will be evident, I agree with Carlton except to give substantially greater importance to the "League of Nations" policy of Henderson and his political team, which, despite the weaknesses and ambivalences of Labour Party policy in the thirties, helped prepare the Labour movement for its leaders' participation in the Churchill coalition of 1940-1945 and provided the background for Labour's outlook when it assumed real political power in 1945.
2. Winkler, "Arthur Henderson," in Craig and Gilbert, *The Diplomats*, p. 321.
3. M. Cole, "The Labour Movement between the Wars," in D. Martin and D. Rubinstein, eds., *Ideology and the Labour Movement. Essays Presented to John Saville* (Totowa, 1979), p. 213.
4. 230 HC Deb., 5s., July 26, 1929, cols. 1301-1635-52.
5. For their respective attitudes see especially MacDonald-Henderson correspondence, 27 and 30, July, 1929, in FO 800/280 cited by Carlton, p.169, who summarizes the negotiations succinctly, pp. 168-73. It has even been suggested that MacDonald inspircd articles in the press hostile to Henderson's Egyptian policy. See F. Leventhal, *Arthur Henderson*, p. 140, citing Emanuel Shinwell, *The Labour Story* (1963), pp. 135-6.
6. See, for example, *Daily Herald,* May 9, 1930.
7. Carlton, p. 173.
8. 229 HC Deb., 5s., July 5, 1929, cols. 457-8.
9. J. Kent, *British Imperial Strategy and the Origins of the Cold War 1944-49* (Leicester, 1993), p. 251.

10. An American scholar has commented that this threat aroused widespread apprehension in France that Britain was downgrading its commitment to continental affairs, particularly when seen in the light of MacDonald's trip to Washington in the fall of 1929. See M. Leffler, *The Elusive Quest. America's Pursuit of European Stability and French Security, 1919-1933* (Chapel Hill, 1979), pp. 219-21.

11. *Towards a European Settlement. Reparations. An Exposition of the Dawes Report and the London Agreement* (Can Labour Rule, No. 7), (1930), p. 15.

12. Henderson memo, June [n.d.], 1929, FO 800/280/29-37.

13. *LPCR,* 1929, p. 208, pp. 111-66; W. M. Jordan, *Great Britain, France and the German Problem* (1943), p. 207.

14. A. J. Toynbee, et al., *Survey of International Affairs, 1929* (1930), pp. 102-29; *Documents on British Foreign Policy (BD),* second series, I, 475-8.

15. Henderson to Rumbold, November 11, 1930, FO800/282/192-3.

16. Carlton, p. 148.

17. *LPCR,* 1929, p. 207; 229 HCDeb., 5s., July 5, 1929, cols. 418, 466; 231, November 5, 1929, cols. 900-2, 920-1; 233, December 18, 1929, cols. 1447-98; and 239, cols. 2581-2633; H. Dalton, "British Foreign Policy, 1929-1931," *Political Quarterly,* II (1931), 499-500.

18. It has recently been argued that the gulf between Labour and the Tories on the matter of the Optional Clause was not as wide as often depicted. See L. Lloyd, *Peace Through Law: Britain and the International Court in the 1920s* (1997), pp. 196, 249-52. The difference between the views of Chamberlain and those of Henderson is well summarized in a letter from the former to the latter on April 13, 1930. "I have more faith in the League as a prevention of war," he wrote, " than as an avenger of aggression and dread Article 16 [the sanctions article] because I do not believe that we could or should act up to it except in a case where we felt our own safety or interests to be menaced." In FO800/28/199.

19. *Survey of International Affairs,* 1929, p. 75; Dalton in *Political Quarterly,* II, 496.

20. *Record of the Tenth Assembly of the League of Nations,* third plenary session, September 3, 1929, pp. 2-5 and seventh plenary session, September 6, 1929, pp. 5-6.

21. *LPCR,* 1929, pp. 215-16. A good example of the disarmament by example argument is in the Commons speech of A. W. Haycock, an ILP member of the Labour Party, 236 HC Deb., 5s., March 17, 1930, cols. 1796-1801.

22. *Official Journal of the League of Nations,* Special Supplement, no. 75, p. 52.

23. *BD, 2nd series, I, 313, 324-6, 330-1, 336-47.* Henderson's coolness was shared widely in Labour circles. See, for example, "Mr. Briand Hatches His Egg," *New Statesman,* vol. XXXV, no. 891 (May 24, 1930), pp.204-5. French reaction may be sampled in J. Bardoux, *L'Isle et l'Europe, la politique anglaise, 1930-1932* (1933), pp. 294-9 and J.-F. Charvet, *L'Influence britannique dans la S.D.N. (Des origines de la S.D.N. jusqu'a nos jours)* (1938), pp. 134-5.

24. *Times,* February 20 and 27, 1930, cited in Carlton, pp. 28-9. The "kindergarten" was the group of young men who served with Milner in South Africa before the war.

25. Carlton, pp. 88-91.

26. *New Statesman,* vol. XXXIV, no. 881(March 15, 1930), 728. Nevertheless, as in 1924, when Labour was in office, the *New Statesman,* like most of the few organs of both the center and left of the party, continued to support the foreign secretary's handling of the French and to affirm that he did indeed speak for his party as well as for the country. *New Statesman,* vol. XXXV, no. 908 (September 20, 1930), 724.

27. Brailsford, "The Fable of Security. What the French Really Mean," *New Leader, March 21, 1930.*

28. Woolf, *Downhill All the Way*, pp. 241-2 claimed that MacDonald opposed Henderson's ratification of the General Act and that Noel Baker had confirmed that fact.
29. *Daily Herald,* March 9, 1931.
30. See, for example, Sisley Huddleston, "Mr. MacDonald in America," *New Statesman*, vol. XXXIV, no. 860 (October 26, 1929), 77-89.
31. B.J.C. McKercher, *Transition of Power. Britain's Loss of Global Pre-eminence to the United States, 1930-1945* (Cambridge, 1999); pp. 40-1; Marquand, *MacDonald*, pp. 301-2; Watt, *Succeeding John Bull*, pp. 60-1; Carlton, pp. 108-18; "The Risks of Arbitration," *New Statesman,* vol. XXXIV, no. 869 (December 21, 1929), 356-8. Hankey later wrote to Henderson pointing out that the exercise of belligerent rights and economic pressure on Germany had proved one of the decisive factors in the last war and arguing against giving them up. Henderson replied disagreeing on most points. Sankey to Henderson, October 21, 1930 and Henderson to Hankey October 26, 1930, in FO800/282/103-12.
32. The phrase was attributed to the "newspapermen of the world" by Sisley Huddleston in the *New Statesman*, vol. XXXIV, no. 876 (February 8, 1930), 561.
33. See ibid., vol. XXXIV, no. 881 (March 15, 1930), 725.
34. Carlton, pp. 118-43 has an excellent account of the naval conference. See also, McKercher, *Transition*, pp. 101, 114-6.
35. Dalton, *Call Back Yesterday*, p. 254, cited in Carlton, p. 94. See also *Daily Herald,* "Navies of Peace," March 2, 1931.
36. McKercher, pp. 100-1.
37. *BD,* second series, I, p. 510, note 5 and pp. 598-603.
38. Ibid., pp. 536-8. With regard to the possible German request for a moratorium in the working of the Young Plan he wrote to Rumbold: "I can imagine no action more calculated to sow suspicion of Germany than any such development, and I sincerely trust that in the interests of the policy on which we are now engaged we may hear no more of the proposal." FO800/282/192-3.
39. Carlton, pp. 197-217 is a useful summary based on the British and League of Nations documents. See also comments by McKercher, pp. 100-2, 113-6.

Chapter 7

1. R. Pearce, *Attlee* (1997), p. 78. Cripps, for his part, continued well into 1933 to call for a revision to "undo the iniquitous provisions of the postwar Treaties, especially with regard to frontiers." 322 HC Deb., 5s. (March 23, 1933), cols. 607-13.
2. R. Bassett, *Democracy and Foreign Policy: The Sino-Japanese Dispute, 1931-33* (1952), *passim*. C. Thorne, *The Limits of Foreign Policy: The West, the League and the Far Eastern Crisis of 1931-1933* (1972) p. 383 notes Noel Baker's contention in a summary on September 15, 1971 that if Henderson had remained as foreign secretary he could have removed the Japanese from Manchuria "by the pressure of world opinion." Thorne effectively destroys that argument in terms, among other factors, of what the public opinion of the major Western powers would have accepted in the way of possible military sanctions. See pp. 407-8.
3. 260 HC Deb. 5s., November 25, 1931, cols. 461-4.
4. J. Naylor, *Labour's International Policy: The Labour Party in the 1930's* (Boston, 1969), p. 29.
5. "Far Eastern Situation. British Labour's Declaration" (published on February 23 by the central organs of the British Labour Movement), NJC *Minutes*, February 23, 1932.
6. *New Statesman,* v. II, no.36 n.s. (October 31, 1931), 537; no. 38, n.s. (November 14, 1931), 599; vol. III, no. 51 n.s. (February 13, 1932), 188-9; no. 53 n.s. (Febru-

ary 27, 1932), 252-3; no. 54 n.s. (March 5, 1932), 282; vol. IV, no. 92 n.s. (November 26,1932), 648-9.

7. *Daily Herald,* October 3, 1932.
8. "The League is Dead," *New Leader,* February 19, 1932. See also issues of November 13 and 25, 1931.
9. Clarke, *The Cripps Version,* pp. 39-44.
10. B. Pimlott, *Labour and the Left in the 1930s* (Cambridge, 1977), pp. 41-2; E. Estorick, *Stafford Cripps: A Biography* (1949), pp. 115, 120-1.
11. *LPCR,* 1932, p. 204. Naylor, p. 26, citing Dalton's *The Fateful Years, Memoirs 1931-1945* (1957), p. 31.
12. The National Joint Council, representing the Trades Union Congress, the Labour Party, and the Parliamentary Labour Party, published in 1933 "Democracy v. Dictatorship," which repudiated both Fascist and Communist dictatorships and argued the case for democratic socialism. The text is Appendix IX of *LPCR,* 1933, pp. 277-8
13. *LPCR,* 1933, pp. 185-6.
14. Ibid., p. 186.
15. ACIQ No. 413A, March, 1935.
16. Dalton, *The Fateful Years,* pp, 45-6, cited by Ceadel, *Semi-Detached Idealists,* p. 303.
17. *LPCR,* 1933, p. 188.
18. "Labour's Foreign Policy" (1933).
19. *LPCR,* 1933, pp. 192-4.
20. Noted in R.A.C.Parker, "Alternatives to Appeasement," in P. Finney, ed., *The Origins of the Second World War* (1997), p. 207.
21. B. Pimlott, *Hugh Dalton* (1985), pp. 224-5. Ponsonby summed up the differences in the party in a letter to Lansbury on October 22, 1933. "Some are pro-League and would favour more or less the Henderson attitude. Others are strongly anti-League and after Japan's move and Germany's move regard it as hopelessly futile. All condemn Hitlerism but some would carry this so far as to pay no attention to Germany now. Many would refuse to allow Germany to rearm although they could not say how they would prevent her. Some say if we do not disarm Germany must be allowed to arm up to our level. Some want to repudiate Locarno *now* so that we may not be involved in a Franco-German conflict. Others regard Locarno as a means of moderating any possible outbreak of excitement in France. The party as a whole supported Locarno in 1935, but many have changed their minds since." Hopefully, if unrealistically, he commented that "The principle of antiwar in all circumstances has grown very strongly even to the extent of Disarmament by Example." *Lansbury Papers,* 13/90.
22. H. Dalton, "The World Disarmament Conference. A Challenge to the Sanity of Mankind," *Labour Magazine,* vol. X, no. 7 (December, 1931), 444-7.
23. W. Arnold Forster, "Equality in Disarmament," *Labour Magazine,* vol. XI, no. 6 (October, 1932), 243-6.
24. *New Statesman,* vol. VIII, no. 176 n.s, (July 7, 1934), 4-5.
25. *Daily Herald,* October 16, 1933.
26. *New Statesman,* vol. VI, no. 147 n.s. (December 16, 1933), 800-1.
27. Memo for use at the meeting of the National Executive Committee [1933], "not for publication," author not stated.
28. *PLP Minutes,* April 25, 1934.
29. General Council Memorandum on War and Peace, June 26, 1934, in *Bevin Papers,* Churchill College, Cambridge, 1/4.
30. *LPCR, 1935,* pp. 156-60.
31. *LPCR*, 1934, pp. 152-8, 166.

32. As the *Daily Herald*, October 3. 1934 reported it: "No General Strike against War. Unless Unions Decide So at the Time. Circumstances Will Then Dictate Action: Not Bound in Advance."
33. G. W. Baer, *The Coming of the Italian-Ethiopian War* (Cambridge, Mass., 1967), p. 123.
34. K. Martin, *Editor. A Second Volume of Autobiography, 1931-45* (1968), p. 172.
35. M. Foot, *Aneurin Bevan, a Biography*, vol. I, 1987-1945 (1962), P. 210.
36. H. H. Hall. III, "The Foreign-Policy Making Process in Britain, 1934-1935,a n d the Origins of the Anglo-German Naval Agreement," *Historical Journal,* XIX, 2 (1976), PP. 498-9.
37. ACIQ, No. 458A, July, 1935, "The Anglo-German Naval Agreement," pp. 1-3.
38. 304 HC Deb., 5s.,July 11, 1935, col. 538.
39. F. Hardie, *The Abyssinian Crisis* (1974), pp. 50-4.
40. ACIQ, No 455A, March, 1935, cited in Naylor, pp. 91-2.
41. Labour and Socialist International, "The European Situation" in *Labour Party International Sub-Committee Minutes,* April 25, 1935.
42. ACIQ, NO. 459A, September, 1935.
43. After his resignation, Lansbury wrote a long defence of his position, "A Page of History," *Lansbury Papers,* 28/219. Arthur Ponsonby had already explained his resignation of the leadership of the Labour Party in the House of Lords in a letter to Lansbury, *Lansbury Papers,* 28/208. See A. Thorpe, "George Lansbury 1932-35," in K. Jefferys, ed., *Leading Labour. From Keir Hardie to Tony Blair* (1999), pp. 69-71 and J. Shepherd, *George Lansbury* (2002), pp. 323-30.
44. C. Bryant, *Stafford Cripps. The First Modern Chancellor* (1970, p. 118. In announcing his resignation from the National Executive Committee in a letter of Sept. 15, 1935, he noted that he assumed it was not necessary for him to say that his act would not diminish in the least his eagerness to have the Labour Party gain power, "because I am convinced as ever I was that the sole political party which offers any hope to the British workers is the Labour Party," *Cripps Papers*.
45. Trevelyan to Cripps, Sept. 19, 1935. *Cripps Papers*.
46. See his comments in the House of Commons, March 11and October 22, 1935, cited by Hardie, p. 43.
47. LPCR, 135, pp. 53, 153-80. See also Vigilantes [K. Zilliacus and others], *Abyssinia. The Essential Facts in the Dispute and an Answer to the Question—"Ought We To Support Sanctions?"* (1935).
48. W. Citrine, *Men and Work: An Autobiography* (1964), p. 352.
49. LPCR, 1935, pp. 153-5, 177-80.
50. *Daily Herald,* October 4, 1935.
51. Taylor, *The Trouble Makers,* p. 190.
52. Naylor's phrase.
53. Labour's major newspaper commented on the 'spontaneous burst of public indignation" when the Hoare-Laval proposals became public. *Daily Herald,* December 30, 1935.
54. LPCR, 1936, pp. 32-3. As late as February, 1936, the draft of an Advisory Committee paper, No, 461A, had included a statement that "a policy of inaction should only be adopted if it is considered practically certain that Abyssinia can be left to deal with the menace herself." This hope against hope, in the light of what was already transpiring in Abyssinia, led Arnold Forster to cry out to Noel Baker, "Surely that is monstrous. The League not Abyssinia must defeat Mussolini" and he urged Noel Baker to fight the paper, which indeed was substantially revised. Arnold Forster to Noel Baker, undated, in Noel Baker Papers, 2/33.
55. V. de Bunsen, *Charles Roden Buxton: A Memoir* (1948), pp. 154-7.

Chapter 8

1. The term "Triple Crisis" is Martin Ceadel's in *Semi-Detached Idealists,* p. 326.
2. *PLP Minutes*, May 21, 1935. The *Daily Herald*, October 7, 1936, pleaded for a "sense of proportion" about the size of Labour's disagreement on rearmament in the light of overwhelming agreement on most issues of international policy.
3. *Bevin Papers*, Churchill College, Cambridge, 1/4.
4. *PLP Minutes,* March 4, 1936.
5. Naylor, pp, 151-5, who notes that only three other members of the Parliamentary Labour Party Executive, along with thirty-eight MPs, supported Dalton in abandoning total opposition to the arms program of the government. In the actual vote on the estimates, fifty-seven were opposed and another sixty abstained. See also S. Howe, "Hugh Dalton," in K. Jefferys, ed., *Labour Forces: From Ernest Bevin to Gordon Brown* (2002), pp. 49-50.
6. 309 HC Deb., 5s.,March 6, 1936, cols. 1851-65.
7. Naylor, pp. 155-6.
8. TUC Annual Report, 1936, p. 358.
9. Bullock, *Ernest Bevin*, vol.I, p. 581, quoting *The Fateful Years,* p. 88.
10. *Daily Herald*, March 4, 6, July 29, 1936.
11. *New Statesman*, vol. XI, no. 260 n.s. (Feb. 15, 1936), 216-7 and vol. XI, no. 263, n.s. (March 7, 1936), 332-3.
12. *Daily Herald.* May 15, October 17, 1936; *New Statesman*, vol. 11, no. 259, n . s ., p. 173, vol. 12, no. 292 n.s., pp. 416-7.
13. 307 HC Deb., 5s., December 19, 1935, col. 2062-70.
14. Bryant, *Stafford Cripps,* pp. 121-2; Cripps, *The Struggle for Peace* (1936), pp. 95-6, 146-7.
15. TUC Annual Report, 1936, pp. 181-2.
16. *Daily Herald*, March 8, 11, 1936.
17. Pimlott, *Hugh Dalton*, p. 233; *Dalton Papers, Part I. Diary, File 16,* March 12, 1936.
18. National Executive Committee, August, 1936.
19. Labour Party, "The Demand for Colonial territories and Equality of Economic Opportunity" (1936).
20. C.R. Attlee, "Sanctions Must Stand," *Daily Herald,* May 11, 1936.
21. "Episode Number Three. Oil for Italy: A Study in the Decay of International Trust" in H. Feis, *Seen from E. A. Three International Episodes* (1947), pp. 195-283. A different point of view is in J. C. Robertson, "The Hoare-Laval Plan," in *Journal of Contemporary History*, X (July, 1975), 456-7.
22. B. Moore, "Who Shall Answer for This Crime?" *Daily Herald,* May 4, 1936.
23. TUC Annual Report, 1936, p. 187. See also, "Sanctions Must Go On," *Daily Herald,* May 11, 1936.
24. Still useful are two standard works in English, Dante A. Puzzo, *Spain and the Great Powers* (New York, 1962) and Hugh Thomas, *The Spanish Civil War* (New York, 1961).
25. *Daily Herald,* July 30, August 8, 1936.
26. Naylor, pp. 142-3.
27. Conflicting interpretations of the British Government's role are in David Carlton, "Eden, Blum and the Origins of Non-Intervention," *Journal of Contemporary History*, vol. VI (3), 1971 and Glyn Stone, "Britain, Non-Intervention and the Spanish Civil War," *European Studies Review,* vol. IX, 1979, both cited in Tom Buchanan, *The Spanish Civil War and the British Labour Movement* (Cambridge, 1991), p. 39.

28. Dalton, *The Fateful Years*, p. 94. Ben Pimlott goes perhaps a bit too far in comment-
    ing that Dalton almost came to think of "Spain" and "Communism" as synonymous,
    but he is right in pointing out that Dalton believed the Spanish republicans shared
    responsibility with the Right for the breakdown   of Spanish democracy.
    Pimlott, *Hugh Dalton*, p. 234.
29. Buchanan, *Spanish Civil War*, esp. pp. 221-8. See also the older work by K. W.
    Watkins, *Britain Divided: The Effect of the Spanish Civil War on British Political
    Opinion* 1963), pp. 142-3 where he notes the enormous differences between the
    gradualist leaders of the Labour Party and the trade unions, on the one hand, and the
    "revolutionary" spokesmen of the Labour left. While Watkins exaggerates the differ-
    ences there is no doubt that the left more completely supported the Spanish Repub-
    lic.
30. R. H. Whealey, *Hitler and Spain: The Nazi Role in the Spanish Civil War 1936-1939*
    (Lexington, 1989), p. 136.
31. LPCR, 1936, pp. 28-30. The fact that Moscow had acquiesced in the policy was an
    added spur to Labour's decision. R. Jenkins, *Mr. Attlee: An Interim Biography*
    (1948), pp. 178-9.
32. TUC Annual Report, 1936, pp. pp. 361-86. Buchanan, p. 222 points out that in his
    memoirs Citrine 'simply rewrote his role" to show that he had opposed non-inter-
    vention from the beginning. Cf. Citrine, *Men and Work*, p. 359.
33. Noel Baker to Attlee, September 19, 1936. After the conference Noel Baker wrote
    again to Attlee on November 30, 1936, continuing to disagree with Bevin's argu-
    ments in support of non-intervention and insisting that "the policy of collective
    security demands that munitions should be furnished to the victims of aggression
    and refused to the aggressor. If we think that the Spaniards are in the position of
    being victims of aggression—as we do now—surely we cannot do otherwise than to
    oppose the [non-intervention] bill?." See Noel Baker Papers, 4-656.
34. LPCR, 1936, pp. 169-81.
35. Ibid., pp. 181-4. In his diary even earlier on July 27, 1936 Dalton noted that when
    Labour voted against the arms estimates he would exercise the conscience clause and
    abstain. A lame "get-out" statement had been issued to the press, saying that a vote against the
    estimates didn't mean a vote for unilateral disarmament. He commented: "Hopeless! We shall
    be out for the rest of our lifetimes, which the coming war may shorten or render even more
    unimportant & unhappy than today. Will it come? I have been through deep glooms.
    The Hitler Rearmament races on. Few people in the Labour Party seem to know or
    care anything about it. The general public is preoccupied, or vacant, & utterly
    unaware. The Nazis look like getting away with it everywhere. Perhaps, since
    collective security is off the map since the Abyssinian affair, collective surrender
    will seem better than collective suicide." *Dalton Papers*. Part I. *Diary File # 16.*
36. Ibid.,p. 192. The position was shared by Attlee, the leader of the party. Robert P.
    Shay, Jr., *British Rearmament in the Thirties. Politics and Profits.* (P r i n c e t o n ,
    1977), pp. 217-8.
37. Ibid., p. 258.
38. J. F. Coverdale, *Italian Intervention in the Spanish Civil War* (Princeton, 1975), p.
    389-90.
39. D. W. Pike, *Les Francaise et la Guerre d'Espagne* (Paris, 1975), pp. 369-70.
40. Illustrative leading articles are *Daily Herald*, August 10, 12, 20, 21, 25, 1936.
41. *Daily Herald,* October 22. 1936.
42. Leading articles on "heresy hunts" or the "weakness and timidity" of the National
    Council" along with denunciations of the *Daily Herald* (as a surrogate for the leaders
    of the Labour Party and the trade unions) and critical articles by Bevan, Cripps,

Laski, etc. appeared regularly. See, for example, *Tribune*, February 19, May 21, June 4, July 9, September 17, 1937. The paper was originally called *The Tribune*, but for convenience I have deleted the article throughout.

43. 325 HC Deb., 5s., June 25, 1937, cols. 1552-4, 1567-70.
44. *New Statesman*, vol. XIII, no. 308 n.s. (January 16, 1937), 72-3; no. 424 n.s. (May 8, 1937), 760-1; *Daily Herald,* October 14, December 13, 14, 1937.
45. ACIQ No. 479A, April, 1937.
46. Pimlott, *Hugh Dalton*, pp. 241-2.
47. TUC Annual Report, 1937, pp. 75-6.
48. Ibid., pp. 178-9.
49. Ibid., pp. 402-26.
50. LPCR, 1937,pp. 138, 195-212.
51. Pimlott, *Hugh Dalton*, p. 247. See *Tribune,* October 15, 1937, where the national government is painted as an enemy of democracy and of working-class liberties.
52. 326 HC Deb., 5s., July 15, 1937, col. 1631.
53. 327 HC Deb., 5s., October 11, 1937, cols. 67-76.
54. 328 HC Deb., 5s., November 1, 1937, cols. 576-7.

Chapter 9

1. Minutes of International Sub-Committee of National Executive, December 14, 1937 and unnumbered Advisory Committee memorandum, "Economic Action against Japan," forwarded as a recommendation by the International Sub-Committee.
2. 326 HC Deb., 5s., July 30, 1937, col. 3539; 327 HC Deb., 5s., October 21, 1937, col. 75; 330 HC Deb., 5s., December 21, 1937, col. 1883. Labour's strictures appeared unrealistic to most members of the national government who tended to agree with Sir Robert Craigie, the British Ambassador to Japan, when he advised: "Violent criticism of Japan and hints of economic pressure do infinite harm because they undercut the position of our friends and are dismissed by our enemies, as either bluff or derogatory to Japan's dignity." Craigie's letter of August 22, 1937 is in *Documents on British Foreign Policy 1919-1939,* series 3, vol. 7, p. 36, cited in K. Middlemas, *Diplomacy of Illusion: The British Government andGermany, 1937-1939* (1972, reprinted Aldershot, 1991), p. 286.
3. LPCR, 1937, p. 4.
4. *Daily Herald,* August 18, 1937.
5. Ibid., October 5, December 4, 16, 18, 1937.
6. *Tribune,* February 4, 1938.
7. Ibid., October 15, 1937. The journalist was Edgar Snow, who had spent some considerable time with the Chinese Communists.
8. NEC Minutes, June 23, 1937.
9. 325 HC Deb., 5s., May 6, 1937, col. 1361.
10. *Tribune*, September 24, 1937. Also H. Laski, "Spain, Mr. Eden and Labour," *Tribune,* October 29, 1937.
11. Ibid., June 25, 1937, cols. 167-70.
12. Ibid., 325, June 215, 2937, cols. 1552-4; 326, July 15, 1937, cols. 1582-3, 1590; 328, November 1, 1937, cols. 571-7.
13. *Dalton Papers*. Part I. Diary File #18. September 14, 1937.
14. Middlemas, pp. 132-6.
15. 332 HC Deb., 5s., February 21, 1938, col. 72.
16. Ibid., February 2, 1938, cols. 209-20.
17. Labour Party, "Labour and the Crisis in Foreign Policy" (1938).
18. Ibid., 333 HC Deb., 5s., March 14, 1938, cols. 54-6 and March 21, 1938, col. 1413.

19. TUC Annual Report, 1938, pp. 185-8.
20. In an undated March note to Noel Baker on the Advisory Committee, Buxton added a postscript: "Don't be surprised if I absent myself from the Parliamentary Executive for a while. I haven't the slightest tendency to disloyalty….but I disagree just now on foreign affairs so strongly, and I feel it is hardly fair to act as if I agreed." Noel Baker Papers, 2-4. Similarly, Dalton noted a conversation with Buxton in which the latter said, "I hope you do not regard me as utterly pro-German or being a Nazi agent," to which Dalton reported himself to have replied, "I know that you have always been more pro-German than most of the Party and I think you are less shocked than most of us are by the internal regime in Germany." Buxton replied that he was very shocked by much that was going on and was doing his best to help the refugees from Germany. *Dalton Papers. Part I. Diary File #19,* July 7, 1938.
21. The *Birmingham Post*, March 19, 1938, quoted in C. Cooke, *The Life of Richard Stafford Cripps* (1957), pp. 196-7.
22. K. Martin, "The Inescapable Facts, *New Statesman,* vol. XV, no. 369, n.s. (March 19, 1938), 468-70 and no. 365 (February 19. 1938), 276-7, even before the *Anschluss.*
23. *New Statesman*, vol. XV, no. 363 n.s. (February 5, 1938), 196-7.
24. 335 HC Deb., 5s., May 2, 1938, cols. 546-61.
25. Ibid, col. 645.
26. 336 HC Deb., 5s., May 20, 1938, cols. 782-9.
27. 337 HC Deb., 5s., June 21, 1938, col. 1006.
28. *Daily Herald*, May 13, 1938.
29. *New Statesman,* vol. XVI, no. 386 n.s. (July 16, 1938), 65.
30. W. Mellor, "Spain. 1936-1938," *Tribune*, July 15, 1938.
31. Pimlott, *Hugh Dalton*, pp. 254-5; Naylor, pp. 229-31; Dalton, *The Fateful Years,* p. 166.
32. 335 HC Deb., 5s., May 12, 1938, cols. 1790-1803.
33. ACIQ, No. 490 A, April, 1938.
34. Labour Party, "Labour's Peace Manifesto. A Call to the British People" (1938), which offers as "Labour's Positive Plan for Peace" the calling of the League of Nations Assembly and for special consideration by its European members of the steps to be taken "to bring appeasement in Central Europe and in Spain"; TUC Annual Report, 1938, pp. 208-10.
35. *Tribune,* April 14, 1938.
36. Clarke, pp. 74-5; Naylor, pp. 232-3.
37. D. Blaazer, *The Popular Front and the Progressive Tradition. Socialists, Liberals,and the Quest for Unity, 1884-1939* (Cambridge, 1992), pp. 179-80. By now, Trevelyan had once again changed his mind. Attlee commented to his brother Tom after a visit to Trevelyan at the end of October: "I find CT rather bellicose. He contemplates war with far more equanimity than I can compass. I distrust his judgment." Quoted in K. Harris, *Attlee* (1982), p. 149.
38. "The Labour Party and the Popular Front (Statement by the National Executive Committee of the Labour Party), in NEC Minutes, January 11, 1939.
39. *Daily Herald*, April 14, 1938.
40. Ibid., April 16, 1938.
41. Blaazer, pp. 186-7.
42. *Dalton Papers*. Diary File #19, May 29, 1938; September 19, 1938. It is interesting that Dalton does not reproduce the comments about the meeting with Vansittart in the published version of his autobiography. See also Pimlott, *Hugh Dalton*, p. 255.
43. B. Bond, *British Military Policy between Two World Wars* (Oxford, 1980), p. 338.

44. S. Newton, *Profits of Peace* (1996), pp. 82-3.
45. Labour Party, "Labour and the International Situation" (1938).
46. Noel Baker to Attlee, September 16, 1938, in Noel Baker's *Papers*, 2-4.
47. But Dalton confided to his diary: "I am conscious of the sense of immediate relief at the prospect of six more days of sure life. How weak we democrats are!" *Dalton Papers*, Diary File # 19, September 24, 1938.
48. Naylor, pp. 241-3, citing Dalton's *Fateful Years*, pp. 176-83 and Citrine's *Men and Work*, pp. 361-6. Naylor calls attention to Citrine's complaint about Attlee's lack of leadership in the deliberations of the National Council.
49. *New Statesman*, vol. XVI, no. 395 n.s. (September 17, 1938), 401.
50. *Tribune,* July 29, September 23, October 7, 1938.
51. NEC Minutes, September 29, 1938.
52. 339 HC Deb., 5s., October 3, 1938, cols. 51-66.
53. Ibid., cols. 135-50.
54. Ibid., October 4, 1938, cols. 173-83.
55. Ibid., October 5, 1938, cols, 408-27.
56. Ibid ., October 3, 1938, cols. 90-4.
57. *Tribune*, October 7, 14, November 4, 1938.
58. *New Statesman,* vol. XVI, no. 397 n.s. (October 1, 1938), 479.
59. Ibid., vol. XVII, no. 413, n.s., (January 21, 1939), 76-7.
60. "Labour's Claim to Power. A Supreme National Effort for Peace" (1938).
61. 340 HC Deb., 5s., November 2, 1938, cols. 212-17, 256-8, 31-22.

Chapter 10

1. Newton, *Profits of Peace,* p. 85.
2. Pimlott faults the Labour Party for maintaining a debilitating exclusiveness when it had a chance to lead a broad united opposition against the inadequacies of Chamberlain's foreign policy, but it is at least an open question how broad such an opposition might have been in the face of the caution exhibited by the dissident Tories in the course of the discussions regarding cooperation. Pimlott, *Hugh Dalton*, pp. 202-3, 257-8.
3. "Notes on the memorandum of Sir Stafford Cripps," in NEC Minutes, January 11, 1939, where the memorandum is also reprinted.
4. Ibid., pp. 159-63 and Blaazer, *The Popular Front,* pp. 188-92 are the best accounts of the controversy. See also Clarke, pp. 78-83.
5. "Unity—True or Sham?" (1939).
6. Beatrrice Webb, Diary, January 21, 1939, in N. and J. Mackenzie, eds., *The Diary of Beatrice Webb* (1985), vol. 4, p. 427, cited in Clarke, pp. 81-2.
7. Wilkinson later summed up the view of this group when she wrote, "He forgets that party government is an essential instrument of political liberty in a democracy….Yet by his sheer honesty and selflessness Cripps can always command loyalty. He is a bad leader but a magnificent lieutenant." *Sunday Express*, June 4, 1939, quoted in Bryant, *Stafford Cripps,* p. 182.
8. Ibid., p. 175.
9. LPCR, 1939, pp. 226-30.
10. Foot, *Aneurin Bevan*, vol. 1, p. 637, quoted in Naylor, p. 286.
11. Phillips to Bevin, May 6, 1939 in Bevin *Papers*, 126/57.
12. Bevin to E.C. Waterman, March 21, 1939, Bevin Papers, 126/57.
13. The manifesto is also in Bevin *Papers*, 126/7.
14. The depth of the mistrust appears in a letter from Morgan Phillips, not particularly noted as an extremist, to Bevin: "This man is the tool of international capital, the

enemy of the common people in this and every country of the world….," etc. Phillips to Bevin, May 6, 1939, Bevin *Papers*, 126/57.
15. Bullock, vol. I, p. 637.
16. The conscription debate is in 346 HC Deb., 5s., April 26, 1939, cols. 1151-58 (question time) and April 27, 1939, cols. 1345-1463.
17. *New Statesman,* vol. XVII, no. 425 n.s. (April 15, 1939), 564-5. See also no. 424 (April 8, 1939), 528-9 and no. 432 (June 3, 1939), 848-9.
18. *Tribune,* April 6, May 12, 1939. Taylor, *The Trouble Makers*, pp. 82-282-3, has some interesting comments on Zilliacus.
19. Dalton *Papers*, *Diary* File # 20, June 25, 1939.
20. Ibid., File # 21, July 10, 1939.
21. Ibid., July 11, 1939.
22. 347 HC Deb., 5s., May 10, 1939, col. 455.
23. Ibid., May 19, 1939, cols. 1809-86.
24. ACIQ, No. 502A, March, 1939.
25. LPCR, 1939, p. 240.
26. Naylor, p. 295.
27. Newton, *Profits of Peace*, pp. 111-2.
28. Dalton Papers, Diary File # 20, June 28, 1939.
29. Idem., File # 21, July 4, 5, 11, 1939.
30. *New Statesman*, vol. XVIII, no. 441 n.s. (August 6, 1939), 204.
31. *Tribune*, July 28, 1939.
32. Dalton *Diary*, File # 21, September 18, 1939.
33. TUC Annual Report, 1939, pp. 334-7.
34. *Daily Herald*, August 8, 24, September 18, 30, 1939.
35. *New Statesman*, vol. XVIII, no. 444, n.s (August 26, 1939), 297-8.
36. *Tribune*, August 25, September 1, 8, 1939.

Epilogue

1. B. Pimlott, *The Political Diary of Hugh Dalton 1918-40, 1945-60* (1986), p. 295.
2. Middleton to members of NEC, January 25, 1940 and "Labour and the War" in NEC Papers. Also the pamphlet "Labour, the War and the Peace," February 9, 1940.
3. LPCR, 1941, pp. 137-44; Newton,, Profits *of Peace,* pp. 170-1.
4. Laski, *Will the Peace Last?* (1944), p. 10 and "The Need for a European Revolution" in *Programme for Victory. A Collection of Essays prepared for the Fabian society by Harold J. Laski, Harold Nicolson, Herbert Read, Prof. W.M.Macmillan, Ellen Wilkinson, G.D.H.Cole* (1941), pp. 33-4; M. Foot, *Aneurin Bevan, 1897-1945* (1962), pp. 343-4; Burridge, pp. 106-7; International Sub-Committee in NEC Minutes, April 17, 1942.
5. Dalton *Papers*, *Diary File* # 28, January 5, 1943; Burridge, pp. 116, 168-9; D.Reynolds, W.F.Kimball, and A.O.Chubarian, eds., *Allies at War: The Soviet, American, and British Experience, 1939-1945* (1994), pp. 336-7.
6. TUC Annual Report, 1940, pp. 156-7; Labour Party, "Finland" (1940), pp. 3-17; Burridge, pp. 110-2.
7. J. Schneer, *Labour's Conscience: the Labour Left, 1945-51* (Boston, 1988).

Selected Bibliography

(Place of publication, London, unless otherwise indicated)

Manuscripts and Official Documents

Cambridge, England
Churchill College Archive Centre
        Philip Noel Baker Papers.
        Ernest Bevin Papers.

Coventry, England
University of Warwick, Modern Records Centre
        Ernest Bevin Papers.

Hull, England
University of Hull, Brynmor Jones Library
        Union of Democratic Control Papers.

London, England
London School of Economics, British Library of Political and Economic Sciences
        E. D. Morel Papers.
        Passfield Papers.
        George Lansbury Papers.
        Hugh Dalton Papers.
        Beatrice Webb Manuscript Diary.
Public Record Office
        Cabinet Papers and Memoranda.
        Conclusions of Cabinet Meetings.
        Ramsay MacDonald Papers.
        Records of the Prime Minister's Office.

Manchester, England
Labour Party Archives
        Labour and Socialist International Collection.
        Labour Party National Executive Committee Minutes and Agenda.
        J. S. Middleton Papers
        Reports of Annual Conferences of the Independent Labour Party.

Reports of Annual Conferences of the Labour Party.
Reports of Annual Conferences of the Trades Union Congress.
Minutes and Memoranda of the Labour Party Advisory Committee on International Questions.
Labour Party Pamphlets, Leaflets, and Reports.
Independent Labour Party Pamphlets and National Administrative Committee Minutes.
Trades Union Congress and Labour Party Pamphlets.
Labour Representation Committee Minutes.

Newcastle upon Tyne, England
University of Newcastle, Robinson Library
Charles Philips Trevelyan Papers

Oxford, England
Oxford University, Bodleian Library
Arthur Ponsonby Papers.
Clement Attleee Papers.
Stafford Cripps Papers

Sussex, England
University of Sussex Library
Leonard Woolf Papers

Printed Materials

British Documents on Foreign Affairs, Part II, Series A, C, F.
Cole, Margaret, ed., *Beatrice Webb's Diaries, 1912-24,*1952.
League of Nations, *Verbatim Record,* 1919-1939.
Mackenzie, Norman, ed., *The Letters of Sidney and Beatrice Webb*, 3 vols., 1978.
Parliamentary Debates, House of Commons (1900-1939).
Pimlott, Ben, ed., *The Political Diary of Hugh Dalton, 1918-40,* 1986.

Memoirs and Autobiographies

Angell, Norman, *After All. The Autobiography of Norman Angell,* 1952.
Attlee, Clement, *As It Happened*, 1954.
Brockway, A. Fenner, *Inside the Left.* 1942.
——————, *Socialism over Sixty Years. The Life of Jowett of Bradford,*1946.
Citrine, Walter, *Men and Work. An Autobiography,* 1964.
Clynes, J. R. *Memoirs,* 2 vols., 1937.
Dalton, Hugh, *Call Back Yesterday. Memoirs 1887-1932*, 1953.
——————, *The Fateful Years. Memoirs 1931-1945*, 1957.
Gallacher, William, *The Rolling of the Thunder*, 1947.
Haldane, Richard Burdon, *An Autobiography*, 1929.
Hamilton, Mary Agnes, *Remembering My Good Friends,* 1944.
Hobson, J. A., *Confessions of an Economic Heretic,* 1938.

Martin, Kingsley, *Editor: A Second Volume of Autobiography, 1931-45,* 1968.
Parmoor, Lord, *A retrospect. Looking Back over a Life of More than Sixty Years,* 1936.
Snowden, Philip, *An Autobiography,* 2 vols., 1934.
Swanwick, H. M., *I Have Been Young,* 1935.
Woolf, Leonard, *Beginning Again. An Autobiography of the Years 1911-1918,* 1964.
—————————, *Downhill All the Way. An Autobiography of the Years 1919 to 1939.* New York, 1975.

Contemporary Writings

Angell, Norman, *Human Nature and the Peace Problem,* 1925.
—————————————, *The Peace Treaty and the Economic Chaos of Europe,* 1919.
Arnold Forster, Will, *The Free Seas* (for the National Council for the Prevention of War), 1929.
—————————————, *The Victory of Reason. A Pamphlet on Arbitration,* 1926.
Blatchford, Robert, *What Is This Socialism?,* no date.
Brailsford, H. N., *After the Peace,* 1920.
—————————————, *A League of Nations,* 1917.
—————————————, *The War of Steel and Gold. A Study of the Armed Peace,* 1914.
Cripps, Stafford, *The Struggle for Peace,* 1936.
Dalton, Hugh, *Towards the Peace of Nations,* 1928.
Henderson, Arthur, "War against War," *Labour Magazine,* I (January 1923), 392-3.
MacDonald, J. R., *National Defence. A Study of Militarism,* 1917.
—————————————, *War and the Workers. A Plea for Democratic Control,* no date.
Morel, E. D., *The Horror on the Rhine,* 1920.
Noel Baker, Philip, *Disarmament,* 1926.
—————————————, *Disarmament and the Coolidge Conference,* 1927.
—————————————, *The Geneva Protocol and the Pacific Settlement of International Disputes,* 1925.
—————————————, "The Growth of International Society," *Economica,* 4 (November 1924), 262-77.
—————————————, *The League of Nations at Work,* 1926.
—————————————, "The Obligatory Jurisdiction of the Permanent Court of International Justice," *The British Year Book of International Law,* 1924.
Ponsonby, Arthur, "Disarmament by Example," *Journal of the Royal Institute of International Affairs,* 7, no. 4 (July 1928), 225-40.
Swanwick, H. M., *Builders of Peace: Being Ten Years' History of the Union of Democratic Control,* 1924.
Trevelyan, Charles, *The Union of Democratic Control (an Organizatrion Created to secure the Control over Their Foreign Policy by the British People, and for the Promotion of International Understanding), Founded in November, 1914, Its History and Its Policy,* 3rd and rev. ed., 1921.

Woolf, Leonard, *International Government,* 1916.
Vigilantes [K. Zilliacus and others], *Abyssinia. The Essential Facts in the Dispute and an Answer to the Question—"Ought We To Support Sanctions?,"* 1935.
———————————, *The Dying Peace* [1936].
Why the U.S.S.R. Joined the League, New Fabian Research Bureau, with an Introduction by Hugh Dalton, January,1935.

Periodicals and Newspapers

Bradford Pioneer.
British Citizen and Empire Worker.
Clarion.
Daily Herald (weekly until March 1, 1919).
Foreign Affairs
Forward
Labour
Labour Leader
Labour Magazine
Lansbury's Labour Weekly
New Leader

Secondary Works

Adams, R. J. and Philip P. Poirier, *The Conscription Controversy in Great Britain, 1900-18*, Columbus, Ohio, 1987.
Addison, Paul, *The Road to 1945. British Politics and the Second World War*, 1975.
Ahmann, R., A. M. Birke, and M. Howard, eds., *The Quest for Stability. Problems of West European Security 1918-1957*, 1993.
Baer, George W. *The Coming of the Italian-Ethiopian War*, Cambridge, Mass., 1967.
Bassett, Reginald, *Democracy and Foreign Policy. The Sino-Japanese Dispute, 1931-33*, 1968.
Baylis, John, *Anglo-American Defence Relations 1939-1980*, 1981.
Bellamy, Joyce M. and John Saville, eds., *Dictionary of Labour Biography*, 1972—.
Benn, Caroline, *Keir Hardie*, 1992.
Blaazer, David, *The Popular Front and the Progressive Tradition. Socialists, Liberals, and the Quest for Unity, 1884-1939*, Cambridge, 1992.
Blake, Robert, *The Decline of Power 1915-1964,* New York, 1985.
Bond, Brian, *British Military Policy between Two World Wars*, Oxford, 1980.
Boyce, Robert and Esmonde D. Robertson, eds., *Paths to War. New Essays on the Origins of the Second World War,* New York, 1989.
Brand, Carl F., *British Labour's Rise to Power,* Stanford, 1941.
Brock, Peter and Nigel Young, *Pacifism in the Twentieth Century,* Syracuse, 1999.

Brooke, Stephen, *Labour's War. The Labour Party during the Second World War,* Oxford, 1992.

Brown, K. D. ed., *The First Labour Party 1906-1914,* 1985.

Bryant, Chris, *Stafford Cripps. The First Modern Chancellor*, 1997.

Buchanan, Tom, *The Spanish Civil War and the British Labour Movement,* Cambridge, 1991.

Bullock, Alan, *The Life and Times of Ernest Bevin. Vol. I, Trade Union Leader, 1881-1940,* 1960.

Burridge, T. D., *British Labour and Hitler's War,* 1976.

Campbell, John, *Nye Bevan and the Mirage of British Socialism*, 1987.

Carlton, David, *MacDonald versus Henderson. The Foreign Policy of the Second Labour Government.* New York, 1970.

Carsten, F. L., *War against* War. *British and German Radical Movements in the First World War*, Berkeley, 1982.

Ceadel, Martin, *Pacifism in Britain 1914-1945: The Defining of a Faith*, 1980.
————————, *Semi-Detached Idealists. The British Peace Movement and International Relations 1854-1945,* 2000.

Clarke, Peter, *The Cripps Version. The Life of Sir Stafford Cripps, 1889-1952,* 2002.

Cline, Cathering Ann, *E. D. Morel 1873-1924. The Strategies of Protest*, Belfast, 1980.
————————, *Recruits to Labour. The British Labour Party, 1914-1931*, Syracuse, 1963.

Cole, Margaret, *Makers of the Labour Movement*, 1948.

Cooke, Colin, *The Life of Richard Stafford Cripps*, 1957.

Coverdale, John F., *Italian Intervention in the Spanish Civil War,* Princeton, 1975.

Cross, Colin, *Philip Snowden*, 1966.

Davey, Arthur, *The British Pro-Boers 1877-1902*, Capetown, 1978.

Davies, A. J., *To Build a New Jerusalem. Labour Party from Keir Hardie to Tony Blair*, rev. ed., 1996.

De Bunsen, Victoria, *Charles Roden Buxton. A Memoir*, 1948.

Dowse, Robert E., *Left in the Centre: The Independent Labour Party, 1893-1940*, Evanston, Ill., 1966.

Egerton, George W., *Great Britain and the Creation of the League of Nations: Strategy, Politics, and International Organization, 1914-1919*, Chapel Hill, 1978.

Estorick, Eric, *Stafford Cripps. A Biography*, 1949.

Feis, Herbert, *Seen from E.A. Three International Episodes*, New York, 1947.

Finney, Patrick, ed., *The Origins of the Second World War*, 1997.

Foot, Michael, *Aneurin Bevan. A Biography, Volume One: 1897-1945*, 1962.

Gordon, Michael, *Conflict and Consensus in Labour's Foreign Policy, 1914-1965*, Stanford, 1969.

Graubard, Stephen, *British Labour and the Russian Revolution, 1917-1924*, Cambridge, Mass., 1956.

Gupta, Partha Sarathi, *Imperialism and the British Labour Movement, 1914-1964*, New York, 1975.

Hall, Christopher, *Britain, America and Arms Control, 1921-37*, New York, 1987.

Hardie, Frank, *The Abyssinian Crisis*, Hamden, Conn., 1974.

Harris, Kenneth, *Attlee,* 1982.

Harris, Sally, *Out of Control. British Foreign Policy and the Union of Democratic Control, 1914-1918*, 1996.

Hall, Hines H., III, "The Foreign Policy-Making Process in Britain, 1934-1935, and the Origins of the German Naval Agreement," in *The Historical Journal*, XIX, 2 (1976), pp. 477-99.

Hennessey, Peter, *The Prime Minister. The Office and its Holders since 1945*, New York, 2000.

Hoggart, Simon and David Leigh, *Michael Foot: A Portrait*, 1981.

Howell, David, *British Workers and the Independent Labour Party 1888-1906*, New York, 1981.

——————, *MacDonald's Party. Labour Identities and Crisis 1922-1931*, Oxford, 2002.

Jefferys, Kevin, ed., *Labour Forces. From Ernest Bevin to Gordon Brown*, 2002.

——————, ed., *Leading Labour. From Keir Hardie to Tony Blair*, 1999.

Jenkins, Roy, *Mr. Attlee. An Interim Biography*, 1948.

Jones, Bill, *The Russia Complex. The British Labour Party and the Soviet Union*, Manchester, 1977.

Jones, Peter, *America and the British Labour Party. The 'Special Relationship' at Work*, 1997.

Jones, Raymond A., *Arthur Ponsonby. The Politics of Life*, 1989.

Jordan, W. M., *Great Britain, France and the German Problem*, 1943.

Kent, Bruce, *The Spoils of War. The Politics, Economics, and Diplomacy of Reparations 1918-1932*, Oxford, 1989.

Kramnick, Isaac and Barry Sherman, *Harold Laski. A Life on the Left*, 1993.

Laybourn, Keith, David Jones, Tony Jowitt, eds., *The Centennial History of the Independent Labour Party*, Halifax, 1992.

Laybourn, Keith and Jack Reynolds, *Liberalism and the Rise of Labour 1890-1918*, 1984.

Leffler, Melvyn P., *The Elusve Quest. America's Pursuit of European Stability and French Security, 1919-1933*, Chapel Hill, 1979.

Leventhal, F. M., *Arthur Henderson*, Manchester, 1989.

——————, *The Last Dissenter. H. N. Brailsford and His World*, Oxford, 1985.

Lloyd, Lorna, *Peace Through Law. Britain and the International Court in the 1920s*, Woodbridge, Suffolk, 1997.

Lyman, Richard W., *The First Labour government*, 1957.

Mackintosh, John P., ed., *British Prime Ministers in the Twentieth Century. Volume I. Balfour to Chamberlain*, New York, 1977.

Maisel, Ephraim, *The Foreign Office and Foreign Policy, 1919-1926*, Brighton, 1994.

Marquand, David, *Ramsay MacDonald,* 1977.

Martin, David E. and David Rubinstein, eds., *Ideology and the Labour Movement. Essays Presented to John Saville*, 1979.

Martin, Kingsley, *Harold Laski (1893-1950). A Biographical Memoir,* New York, 1953.

McBriar, A. M., *Fabian Socialism and English Politics 1884-1918*, 1962.

McDougall, W. A., *France's Rhineland Diplomacy, 1914-1924: The Last Bid for a Balance of Power in Europe*, Princeton, 1978.

McKercher, B. J. C., ed., *Anglo-American Relations in the 1920s. The Struggle for Supremacy*, Alberta, Canada, 1990.

——————————————, *Transition of Power. Britain's Loss of Global Pre-eminence to the United States, 1930-1945*, Cambridge, 1999.

McLean, Iain, *Keir Hardie*, 1975.

Miller, Kenneth E., *Socialism and Foreign Policy. Theory and Practice in Britain to 1931*, The Hague, 1967.

Millman, Brock, *Managing Dissent in First World War Britain*, 2000.

Morgan, Austen, *J. Ramsay MacDonald*, 1987.

Morgan, Kenneth O., *Keir Hardie*, 1967.

——————————————, *Labour People. Leaders and Lieutenants, Hardie to Kinnock*, Oxford, 1987.

Morris, A. J. A., *C. P. Trevelyan 1870-1958. Portrait of a Radical*, Belfast, 1977.

——————————————, *Radicalism against War, 1906-1914*, 1972.

——————————————, *The Scaremongers. The Advocacy of War and Rearmament 1986-1914*, 1984.

Naylor, John, *Labour's International Policy. The Labour Party in the 1930's*, Boston, 1969.

Newton, Douglas J., *British Labour, European Socialism and the Struggle for Peace 1889-1914*, Oxford, 1985.

Newton, Scott, *Profits of Peace*, Oxford, 1996.

Northedge, F. S. and Audrey Wells, *Britain and Soviet Communism.The Impact of a Revolution*, 1982.

O'Riordan, Elspeth Y., *Britain and the Ruhr Crisis*, 2001.

Orde, Anne, Great *Britain and International Security 1920-1926*, 1978.

Pearce, Robert, *Attlee*, 1997.

Pelling, Henry, *America and the British Left. From Bright to Bevan*, 1956.

——————————————, *The Origins of the Labour Party 1880-1900*, 1954.

Pike, David Wingate, *Les Francaise et la Guerre d'Espagne*, Paris, 1975.

Pimlott, Ben, *Hugh Dalton,* 1985.

——————————————, *Labour and the Left in the 1930s*, New York, 1977.

Poirier, Philip R., *The Advent of the British Labour Party*, New York, 1958.

Price, Richard, *An Imperial War and the British Working Class. Working-Class Attitudes and Reactions to the Boer War 1899-1902*, 1972.

Reynolds, David, *The Creation of the Anglo-American Alliance1937-41. A Studyin Competitive Co-operation*, Chapel Hill, 1982.

Reynolds, David, Warren F. Kimball, and A. O. Chubarian, eds., *Allies at War. The Soviet, American, and British Experience, 1939-1945*, New York, 1994.

Ridell, Neil, *Labour in Crisis. The Second Labour government 1929-1931*, Manchester, 1999.

Robbins, Keith, *The Abolition of War. The 'Peace Movement' in Britain, 1914-1919*, Cardiff, 1976.

——————————, *Politicians, Diplomacy and War in Modern British Society*, 1994.

Schneer, Jonathan, *Ben Tillett. Portrait of a Labour Leader*, Urbana, Illinois, 1982.

——————————, *George Lansbury*, Manchester, 1990.

——————————, *Labour's Conscience: the Labour Left, 1945-51*, Boston, 1988.

Seyd, Patrick, *The Rise and Fall of the Labour Left*, 1987.

Shay, Robert Paul, Jr., *British Rearmament in the Thirties. Politics and Profits*, Princeton, 1977.

Shepherd, John, *George Lansbury. At the Heart of Old Labour,* Oxford, 2002.

Swartz, Marvin, *The Union of Demcratic Control in British Politics during the First World War*, Oxford, 1971.

Tanner, Duncan, Pat Thane and Nick Tiratsoo, eds., *Labour's First Century*, 2000.

Taylor, A. J. P., *The Trouble Makers. Dissent over Foreign Policy 1792-1939*, 1957.

Taylor, Richard and Nigel Young, *Campaigns for Peace: British Peace Movements in the Twentieth Century*, Manchester, 1987.

Thompson, Laurence, *The Enthusiasts. A Biography of John and Katherine Bruce Glasier*, 1971.

Thorne, Christopher, *The Limits of Foreign Policy. The West, the League and the Far Eastern Crisis of 1931-1933*, 1972.

Tiratsoo, Nick, ed., *The Attlee Years*, 1991.

Tucker, William R., *The Attitude of the British Labour Party towards European and Collective Security Problems, 1920-1939*, Geneva, 1950.

Turner, John, *British Politics and the Great War. Coalition and Conflict 1915-1918*, New Haven, 1992.

Vernon, Betty D., *Ellen Wilkinson 1891-1947*, 1982.

Van Der Slice, Austen, *International Labor, Diplomacy, and Peace, 1914-1919*,Philadelphia, 1941.

Waites, Bernard, *A Class Society at War. England 1914-1918,* Leamington Spa, 1987.

Ward, Paul, *Red Flag and Union Jack. Englishmen, Patriotism and the British Left, 1881-1924*, Woodbridge, Suffolk, 1998.

Watkins, K. W., *Britain Divided. The Effect of the Spanish Civil War on British Political Opinion*, 1963.

Watt, D. Cameron, *Succeeding John Bull. America in Britain's Place 1900-1975*,Cambridge, 1984.

——————————, *Personalities and Policies. Studies in the Foundation of British Foreign Policy in the Twentieth Century,* 1965.

Wedgwood, C. V. *The Last of the Radicals. Josiah Wedgwood, M.P.,* 1951.

Weiler, Peter, *Ernest Bevin,* Manchester, 1993.

Whealey, Robert H., *Hitler and Spain. The Nazi Role in the Spanish Civil War 1936-1939,* Lexington, Ky., 1989.

White, Stephen, *Britain and the Bolshevik Revolution. A Study in the Politics of Diplomacy, 1920-1924,* New York, 1980.

Williams, Andrew J., *Labour and Russia. The Attitude of the Labour Party to the USSR, 1924-34,* Manchester, 1989.

Williams, Francis, *A Pattern of Rulers,* 1965.

Windrich, Elaine, *British Labour's Foreign Policy,* Stanford, 1952.

Winkler, Henry R., "Arthur Henderson," in *The Diplomats 1919-1939,* eds. Gordon Craig and Felix Gilbert, Princeton, 1953.

——————————, "British Labor and the Origins of the Idea of Colonial Trusteeship, 1914-1919," *The Historian,* 13 (Spring 1951), 154-72.

——————————, "The British Labour Party and the Paris Settlement" in *Some Pathways in Twentieth Century History. Essays in Honor of Reginald Charles McGrane,* ed. Daniel Beaver, Detroit, 1969.

——————————, "The Emergence of a Labour Foreign Policy in Great Britain, 1918-1929," *Journal of Modern History,* 28 (September 1956), 247-58.

——————————, *The League of Nations Movement in Great Britain, 1914-1919,* New Brunswick, N.J., 1952.

——————————, *Paths Not Taken. BritishLabour and International Policy in the 1920s,* Chapel Hill, 1994.

Winter, J.M., "Arthrur Henderson, the Russian Revolution, and the Reconstruction of the Labour Party," in *The Historical Journal,* XV, 4 (1972), pp. 753-73.

Wrigley, Chris, *Arthur Henderson,* Cardiff, 1990.

Young, Kenneth, ed., *The Diaries of Sir Robert Bruce Lockhart. Volume One, 1915-1958,* New York, 1974.

Index

Abyssinia, 106, 109, 110; British policy on, 118; conquest of, 113, 114; and League ineffectiveness, 110, 174n54; and pacifism, 107

Adamson, Will, 37

Addison, Christopher, 142-43

Admiralty, and Draft Treaty and Optional Clause, 58, 59

Advisory Committee on International Questions, 41, 62, 68; 82, 164n45; and Anglo-German naval agreement, 105; "appeasement through international justice, " 146; and armed force, 36; Capper resolution, 78; Austen Chamberlain proposals, 71-72; and conference on issues of contention, 112-113; describes Labour Party foreign policy, 146; and deteriorating international situation, 99; and Draft Treaty, 56, 57; and Geneva Protocol, 72, 76; importance of, 28; and Kellogg proposal, 78; and "Labour, the League and Reparations," 53; and the League, 53, 120, 164n42; and "Manifesto to the Peoples of the World," 53; memorandum: "Guarantees to Czechoslovakia: in relation to Spain," 132; mimeographed memoranda, 164n3; and Mussolini and Hitler, 106; and prevention of war, 120; reacts to renewed Japanese aggression, 125-126; reacts to Ruhr crisis, 46, 52-53; and Russian recognition, 40

Albania, 145

Allen, Clifford, 69

America, and reparations, 43; and British troops, 53; and European international relations, 78; and oil supplies to Mussolini, 113

Anderson, W.C., anti-war opinions, 8; domestic and foreign policy, 14; and war, 17; and war credits, 20

Angell, Norman, 42; influence on Labour, 13; and post-war world, 22; and reparations, 166-67n13; treaty revision, 44; and war, 9, 13

Anglo-American relations, 78; MacDonald and, 81, 88; and naval armaments, 88-89; and Far East, 125, 126. *See also* Washington Naval Conference

Anglo-Chinese relations, 94

Anglo-Egyptian relations, 82-83

Anglo-French relations, 89; and arms limitation, 79; *entente*, 41, 45; and Hoare-Laval plan, 108; and naval matters, 45, 89; and Second Labour Government, 83; and security, 120

Anglo-German relations, 90; and German demands, 91; ILP and Labour Party concern about, 5, 13; and National Peace Congress, 4; and naval agreement, 105; and revision of Versailles Treaty, 108; and Second Labour government, 83. *See also* Appeasement

Anglo-Italian agreement, 139-40

Anglo-Japanese relations, 94, 149. *See also* Washington Conference

Anglo-Polish agreement, 149

Anglo-Russian (Tsarist) relations, *entente*, 7, 13; ILP and Labour Party concern about, 5, 7. *See also* Anglo-Soviet relations

Anglo-Soviet relations, 64, 145; failure leads to Nazi-Soviet Pact, 150; provisions, 64-65; regularization, 85-86

Anschluss, 127, 128-29, 131

Appeasement, 85, 90, 129, 146; Chamberlain government and, 145; and democracies, 147; and Labour Party, 141; with military force, 135

Arbitration, 71; compulsory, 87; as a test of aggression, 59-60